Tennessee 30-Hour Course for New Affiliates

1st Edition

PERFORMANCE PROGRAMS COMPANY

Stephen Mettling
David Cusic
Kseniya Korneva

Material in this book is not intended to represent legal advice and should not be so construed. Readers should consult legal counsel for advice regarding points of law

ISBN: 978-1955919173

Tennessee 30-Hour Course for New Affiliates

Table of Contents

Module 7: Property Management

Module 8: Ethics and Etiquette

Module 9: Finance & Closing

Tennessee 30-Hour Course for New Affiliates

Course Overview

The Tennessee 30-Hour Course for New Affiliates (the "TN CNA" Program) has been developed to satisfy Tennessee's 30-hour requirement after completion of the 60-hour prelicense course. The course also fulfills the Real Estate Commission's objective of giving Tennessee real estate licensees a carefully developed reinforcement of key real estate brokerage principles, concepts, and practices necessary to initiate a productive, professional career in real estate.

Beyond an initial review of key principles, the TN CNA Program takes on a further examination of essential skills and practices that will be necessary to meet client and customer transactional requirements within Tennessee's legal framework. Such skills examined include compliance with Tennessee agency and disclosure laws; how to properly represent and disclose property characteristics; and an intensive look at Tennessee transaction contracts: listings; the sales contract; options and contracts for deed. Beyond its agency and contracts topics, the TN CNA further examines the other key subjects required by the Commission: fairing housing; ethics; regulatory compliance; risk reduction; property management; finance; and critical cornerstones of professional practice.

Taken as a whole, the Tennessee 30-Hour Course for New Affiliates program is designed to deepen the new licensee's understanding of how brokerage works in actual practice – and how it is supposed to be undertaken in view of today's standards of professionalism, ethics, and legal compliance.

ABOUT THE AUTHORS

Stephen Mettling. For nearly fifty years, Stephen Mettling has been actively engaged in real estate education. Beginning with Dearborn in 1972, then called Real Estate Education Company, Mr. Mettling managed the company's textbook division and author acquisitions. Subsequently he built up the company's real estate school division which eventually became the country's largest real estate, insurance and securities school network in the country. In 1978, Mr. Mettling founded Performance Programs Company, a custom training program publishing and development company specializing in commercial, industrial, and corporate real estate. Over time, Performance Programs Company narrowed its focus to real estate textbook and exam prep publishing. Currently the Company's texts and prelicense resources are used in hundreds of schools in over 48 states. As of 2022, Mr. Mettling has authored over 100 textbooks, real estate programs and exam prep manuals.

David Cusic, Ph.D. Dr. Cusic has been a training consultant, author, and Performance Programs Company partner for over forty years. As an educator with international real estate training experience, Dr. Cusic has been engaged in vocation-oriented education since 1966. Specializing in real estate training since 1983, he has developed numerous real estate training programs for corporate and institutional clients nationwide. Dr. Cusic is co-author of the Company's flagship title, Principles of Real Estate Practice by Mettling and Cusic, now complemented by over 19 state supplements and 22 exam prep texts.

Kseniya Korneva. Kseniya Korneva is a licensed REALTOR® in Tampa, Florida with a passion for writing and editing. She graduated with a Civil Engineering degree from Clemson University and fell in love with real estate shortly after. Coming from a long line of academics, her love for education runs deep. Kseniya was first introduced to the world of publishing after writing her own ebook in 2019 and realized she wanted to dive deeper. In her free time, she loves to write about personal finance and real estate on her blog (www.TheMoneyMinimalists.com).

Module 1: LISTINGS

I.   The Listing and Selling Process
II. Determining Market Value
III. Advertising
IV. Disclosures

Listing and selling process

1. Characterize the critical phases of acquiring a listing including prospecting strategy; listing presentations; pricing; and marketing the listing to buyers

2. Describe the process of generating offers, presenting offers, and countering offers to obtain an executed agreement.

3. Characterize what is meant by the pre-closing period – what happens, and what the licensee intends to accomplish.

Determining market value

1. Define the essential value concepts underlying residential property value estimation, including the principle of substitution and contribution.

2. Differentiate market value from other forms of value and highlight the key ingredients required to develop a defensible estimate of market value.

3 Summarize the steps involved in generating a comparative market analysis, including selecting and making adjustments and reconciling the adjusted values so derived.

Advertising

1. Cite the most important advertising regulations impacting licensees, including internet, gifts and prizes, and discriminatory advertising practices.

2. Identify the role of advertising as it impacts websites, email, social media, and smartphones in marketing residential properties.

3. Summarize the salient provisions of the Consumer Protection Act

Disclosures

1. Showcase what key aspects of a residential property's condition should be disclosed by the seller in the Residential Property Condition Disclosure report.

2. Describe what properties and transaction types are exempt from this report.

3. Summarize what critical disclosures licensees must perform in a typical residential transaction aside from the seller's property condition report

I. The Listing and Selling Process

Listings are the traditional source of a broker's income. By obtaining a listing, a broker obtains a share of the commission generated whenever a cooperating broker finds a buyer. By contrast, in working with a buyer, it is not so certain that the effort will produce income. In the absence of an exclusive buyer representation agreement, a buyer may move from one agent to another without making any commitment. Agents can spend considerable time with a buyer and earn nothing. Hence the special value of an exclusive listing with a seller: it is likely to generate revenue.

PROSPECTING

Prospecting is any activity designed to generate listing prospects: parties who intend to sell or lease property and who have not yet committed to a broker. Prospecting activities include mailing newsletters and flyers, selling directly and person-to-person, advertising, and selling indirectly via community involvement.

The goal of prospecting is to reach a potential seller or landlord, make that person aware of the agent's and brokerage's services, and obtain permission to discuss the benefits of listing, often in the form of a formal selling presentation.

Prospecting strategies

There are numerous ways to find listings and the most profitable options depend on the market and personality of the listing agent. If an agent is familiar with a particular neighborhood or they have a large network of colleagues, then focusing on marketing to these spheres of influence would be the most profitable way to find clients. This can be done with face-to-face meetings, phone calls, or handwritten cards.

When buyers and sellers are looking for a Realtor, they typically ask their friends first. This is why a referral-based lead generation objective is the most fruitful and sustainable. The leads are already "warm" and comfortable with being approached. Most agents strive to reach this stage of maturity in their business where they do not have to actively market to "cold" leads and can focus on their friends, family and past clientele.

Expireds and FSBOs. If the agent has yet to establish a network or a presence in their local market, then their efforts are better focused on direct outreach to build a database filled with future clients. Some of the more popular methods include cold calling expired listings and For Sale By Owners, or FSBOs.

Expired listings are homes that have had trouble selling with their original real estate agent. These listings are a great target because they are actively looking to sell. When calling expired listings it is important to come from a helpful angle and suggest what could be done differently in order to sell the home. There are paid services out there that offer the phone numbers and addresses of expired listings daily, and some brokerages offer these services to their agents.

Reaching out to FSBOs also requires some preparation and familiarity with common scripts. For Sale By Owners are typically people who are trying to save as much money as possible and believe they can handle everything themselves. These prospects can be found by driving around or by searching online or on social media.

Farming. Besides cold-calling expired listings and FSBOs, agents can also build their network by "farming" a specific neighborhood with mailers and door-knocking, hosting open houses for other agents, purchasing leads through online platforms like Zillow and Realtor.com and utilizing social media such as Facebook and Instagram.

When choosing a neighborhood to "farm", it is important to research the hottest areas. Where are most of the homes selling? Which neighborhoods have the largest turnover rates? The turnover rate can be calculated by adding up all of the sold homes in the last 12 months, and dividing it by the total number of homes. Depending on the market, this rate should be around 7 to 8%. But, before committing to a neighborhood, it is vital to check if there are other agents heavily farming that area or consistently listing homes. If there are a few agents with whom each listing is sold with, then that neighborhood will take longer and more effort to convert. Consider farming neighborhoods that do not have a preference for a given Realtor. One of the ways to find this out is by door-knocking a neighborhood and speaking with some of the current residents.

Once a neighborhood is picked, the agent has to develop a consistent marketing plan in order to see any results. By incorporating regular mailers (postcards, community event calendars, recipes, handwritten letters, market trends), door-knocking, door hangers, and special promotions, the agent will become accepted and trusted by the whole neighborhood. Farming takes consistent effort and time before showing results.

Open houses. An agent does not have to rely on their own listings in order to host an open house. The key to running a successful open house is picking one in a popular neighborhood where the leads are easy to convert. The busiest open houses are ones that have been aggressively pre-marketed for at least one week prior. Pre-marketing an open house can be done through posting on social media, delivering flyers to the neighbors, and door-knocking the surrounding homes with invites to the open house. Open houses are typically held on weekends between the hours of 11-4pm in order to allow for maximum traffic.

When hosting an open house, the goal is to capture the emails and phone numbers of the attendees with a sign-in sheet in order to follow-up with them in the future. The attendees rarely purchase the actual listing, but they are active buyers that literally come knocking on your door.

Open house leads usually take about 3-6 months to convert so it is important to stay on top of following up through phone calls, text messages, and emails.

In the current period, it is very common for agents to also utilize online platforms to build their pipelines. This can be done through social media or by purchasing leads through platforms like Zillow and Realtor.com. These platforms allow buyers to request showings directly through their websites and phone applications. The platform then captures the buyer's information and sends it to local agents who are purchasing leads for that particular zip code. These particular leads have to be responded to almost immediately and converted with a quick phone call or a text message.

LISTING PRESENTATION

The listing presentation is a chance for the listing agent to tour the home and showcase why the seller should list with them. Chances are, the seller will be interviewing multiple agents so it is important to be professional.

Preparations

The agent should come prepared with an estimated net sheet, a detailed marketing plan, and all of the necessary listing paperwork. During the property tour, the agent should ask specific questions about any upgrades the seller may have done, and the age of the major systems (AC, roof, plumbing, and electrical).

Some listing appointments can be casual, for example during a happy hour, whereas others require a top-notch, formal presentation. The key is to adjust to the style of the owner. By mirroring the clients preferences, the agent can quickly adapt and make a better impression.

Optimize the property. During the listing presentation, the agent should discuss how to outshine other active listings. Present the property at its full potential. If possible, the sellers should add a fresh coat of paint and spruce up the landscaping for maximum curb appeal. During the listing presentation it is also vital to highlight the importance of a de-cluttered and clean home. Staging the property and providing professional photography will greatly impact the amount of traffic the listing will have. There are staging companies out there who focus on real estate listings, and there are also staging kits that can be purchased online with minor items to spruce up the showing potential of the home.

LISTING AGREEMENTS

The most common way of creating an agency relationship is by listing agreement. The agreement sets forth the various authorizations and duties, as well as requirements for compensation. A listing agreement establishes an agency for a specified transaction with a stated expiration.

A listing agreement, the document that puts an agent or broker in business, is a legally enforceable real estate agency agreement between a real estate broker and a client, authorizing the broker to perform a stated service for compensation. The unique characteristic of a listing agreement is that it is governed both by agency law and by contract law.

Scope of authority

Customarily, a listing is a special agency, or limited agency, agreement. Special agency limits the scope of the broker's authority to specific activities, generally those which generate customers and catalyze the transaction. A special agency agreement usually does not authorize a broker to obligate the client to a contract as a principal party, unless the agreement expressly grants such authorization, or the client has granted power of attorney to the broker. For example, a listing broker may not tell a buyer that the seller will accept an offer regardless of its terms. Telling the offeror that the offer is accepted would be an even more serious breach of the agreement.

Under agency law, a client is liable for actions the broker performs that are within the scope of authority granted by the listing agreement. A client is not liable for acts of the broker which go beyond the stated or implied scope of authority.

A broker may represent any principal party of a transaction: seller, landlord, buyer, tenant. An owner listing authorizes a broker to represent an owner or landlord.

Types of listing agreement

There are three main types of owner listing agreement:

1.   exclusive right-to-sell (or lease)
2.   exclusive agency
3.   open listing.

Another type of listing, although illegal in Tennessee, is a net listing. The first three forms differ in their statement of conditions under which the broker will be paid. The net listing is a variation on how much the broker will be paid.

Exclusive right-to-sell agreement. A buyer agency or tenant representation agreement authorizes a broker to represent a buyer or tenant. The most commonly used form is an exclusive right-to-represent agreement, the equivalent of an exclusive right-to-sell. However, exclusive agency and open types of agreement may be also used to secure a relationship on this side of a transaction.

The exclusive right-to-sell, also called an exclusive, is the most widely used owner agreement. Under the terms of this listing, a seller contracts exclusively with a single broker to procure a buyer or effect a sale transaction. If a buyer is procured during the listing period, the broker is entitled to a commission, regardless of who is procuring cause. Thus, if anyone--¬the owner, another broker-- sells the property, the owner must pay the listing broker the contracted commission.

The exclusive right-to-lease is a similar contract for a leasing transaction. Under the terms of this listing, the owner or landlord must pay the listing broker a commission if anyone procures a tenant for the named premises.

The exclusive listing gives the listing broker the greatest assurance of receiving compensation for marketing efforts.

In Tennessee all exclusive listings must be in writing to be enforceable.

Exclusive agency. An exclusive agency listing authorizes a single broker to sell the property and earn a commission, but leaves the owner the right to sell the property without the broker's assistance, in which case no commission is owed. Thus, if any party other than the owner is procuring cause in a completed sale of the property, including another broker, the contracted broker has earned the commission.

Open listing. An open listing, or, simply, open, is a non-exclusive authorization to sell or lease a property. The owner may offer such agreements to any number of brokers in the marketplace. With an open listing, the broker who is the first to perform under the terms of the listing is the sole party entitled to a commission. Performance usually consists of being the procuring cause in the finding of a ready, willing, and able customer. If the transaction occurs without a procuring broker, no commissions are payable.

Open listings are rare in residential brokerage but relatively common in commercial brokerage. Residential brokers generally shy away from them because they offer no assurance of compensation for marketing efforts. In addition, open listings are more likely to cause commission disputes. To avoid such disputes, a broker has to register prospects with the owner to provide evidence of procuring cause in case a transaction results.

An open listing may be oral or written.

Net listing. A net listing is one in which an owner sets a minimum acceptable amount to be received from the transaction and allows the broker to have any amount received in excess as a commission, assuming the broker has earned a commission according to the other terms of the agreement. The owner's "net" may or may not account for closing costs.

For example, a seller requires $750,000 for a property. A broker sells the property for $830,000 and receives the difference, $80,000, as commission.

Net listings are generally regarded as unprofessional today, and many states (including Tennessee) have outlawed them. The argument against the net listing is that it creates a conflict of interest for the broker. It is in the broker's interest to encourage the owner to put the lowest possible acceptable price in the listing, regardless of market value. Thus the agent violates fiduciary duty by failing to place the client's interests above those of the agent.

LISTING BENCHMARKS

Once a listing has been procured, it must be fulfilled. To this end, the essential benchmarks in the listing process are pricing, marketing the listing, selling the buyer prospect, obtaining offers, and presenting and finalizing the offer.

Determining a price

It is almost always necessary for an agent seeking a listing to suggest a listing price or price range for the property. It is important to make a careful estimate, because underpricing a property is not in the best interests of the seller, and overpricing it often prevents a transaction altogether. In brief, an agent usually relies on an analysis of comparable properties which have recently sold in the same neighborhood. By making adjustments for the differences between the subject property and the comparables, the agent arrives at a general price range. Agents must be careful to caution sellers that they are not appraisers, and that the suggested price range is not an expert opinion of market value. If a more precise estimate of market value is desired, the seller should hire a licensed appraiser.

Marketing listings

The process of marketing a listed property leads to the desired end of a completed sale contract. During this process, there are critical skills an agent must master during the key phases of marketing plan implementation, selling the buyer prospect, and obtaining an accepted offer.

After the broker formalizes the listing agreement, the agent initiates a marketing plan for the property. An ideal marketing plan is a cohesive combination of promotional and selling activities directed at potential customers. The best combination is one that aims to have maximum impact on the marketplace in relation to the time and money expended.

Professional photography of a home will help garner more attention. Besides photography, professional videos can be filmed, and a Matterport camera can be used in order to share the floorplan with potential buyers.

Once the listing is on the market, the true work begins. Besides "shouting from the rooftops" that a listing is live, there are actual strategies to share a listing with the local market. Broker's opens are open houses geared towards agents only so they can preview the home to see if it is a good fit for their buyers. These are common with luxury listings. Besides broker's opens, cold calling local agents, delivering door hangers to the neighbors, hosting open houses and running social media advertisements will help get more eyes on the listing as well. Real estate is a numbers game, and the sooner a listing is seen by a majority of agents, the faster it will sell.

Selling the buyer prospect

When marketing activities produce prospects, the agent's marketing role becomes more interpersonal. An agent must now:

- qualify prospects' plans, preferences, and financial capabilities
- show properties that meet the customer's needs
- elicit the buyer's reactions to properties
- report material results to the seller or listing agent

At the earliest appropriate time, an agent must make certain disclosures to a prospective customer. An agent is required to disclose the relevant agency relationship, the property's physical condition, and the possible presence of hazardous materials.

Obtaining offers

If a buyer is interested in purchasing a property, an agent obtains the buyer's offer of transaction terms, including price, down payment, desired closing date, and financing requirements. An agent must be extremely careful at this point to abide by statutory obligations to the client, whoever that party may be. Discussions of price are particularly delicate: whether the client is buyer or seller, the agent's duty is to uphold the client's best interests. Thus, it is not acceptable to suggest to a customer what price the client will or will not accept. With pricing and other issues, it is always a good practice to understand what role the client wants the agent to assume in the offering phase of the transaction; in other words, exactly how far the agent may go in developing terms on the client's behalf.

When a buyer or tenant makes an offer, the agent must present it to the seller or landlord at the earliest possible moment. If the terms of the offer are unacceptable, the agent may assist the seller in developing a counteroffer, which the agent would subsequently submit to the customer or customer's agent. The offering and counteroffering process continues until a meeting of the minds results in a sale contract.

Multiple offers. Multiple offer situations are common in seller's markets. If a listing is priced well, in good condition and in a hot area, then it will sell quickly and may result in a bidding war. Multiple offers can be difficult to organize, but one strategy is to call for a "highest and best" offer from all of the agents. This will save time from going back and forth with each agent and ensure that the offers are the strongest option a buyer is willing to make.

Presenting offers. Once all of the new offers are in, organizing the important terms in an Excel sheet is a helpful way to present the offers to the sellers.

The important terms to organize are as follows:

- purchase price
- earnest money deposit
- financing type (cash, conventional, FHA, VA,)
- downpayment amount
- length of inspection period
- closing date
- incentives (are the buyer's asking for any closing cost assistance?)
- miscellaneous additional terms

Once these essential listing benchmarks are achieved, the transaction moves into the pre-closing period where all involved parties satisfy the various terms, conditions and contingencies of the accepted agreement, or sales contract.

PRE-CLOSING ACTIVITIES

Hopefully, the marketing plan, prospect selling and offer presentations generate an executed contract. At this point, between the execution of the sale contract and the closing of the transaction, the property is "under contract" or "contract pending." During this period, buyer and seller have certain things to do to achieve a successful closing. The buyer often needs to arrange financing and dispose of other property;

the seller may need to clear up title encumbrances and make certain property repairs. The sale contract should specify all such required tasks. The time period between contracting and closing is referred to as the contingency period, or pre-closing period.

Broker responsibilities

As dictated by custom and the circumstances of a transaction, an agent has a range of duties and responsibilities during the pre-closing period. An agent's foremost duty following acceptance of an offer is to submit the contract and the earnest money to the managing broker without delay. In Tennessee, earnest money must be deposited promptly after the time of acceptance of a sales contract.

The agent must also complete their due diligence in the listing. This refers to verifying the accuracy of the statements in the listing regarding the property, the owner, and the owner's representations. Especially important facts for a broker to verify are:

- the property condition
- ownership status
- the client's authority to act

Failure to perform a reasonable degree of due diligence may increase an agent's exposure to liability in the event that the property is not as represented or that the client cannot perform as promised.

Other responsibilities are:

- assisting the buyer in obtaining financing
- recommending inspectors, appraisers, attorneys, and title companies
- assisting in communications between principals
- assisting in the exchange of transaction documents

Waiting for the inspection and appraisal results is one of the most stressful times in a real estate transaction. There are so many moving parts and these two reports can completely alter the trajectory of the transaction. An inspection period is the time the buyers have to complete their due diligence and review any inspections that have been ordered for the home. Oftentimes, buyers will request repairs to be completed that are not necessary for insurance purposes so a listing agent's job is to negotiate with the buyers and keep their sellers from completing any unnecessary repairs. A buyer's agents job is to fight for the buyers and negotiate for any repairs they deem necessary.

Not all inspection results are positive, and sometimes a deal has to fall through due to the buyers wanting to move on from the property. In this case, a contract cancellation addendum should be sent to all parties to sign.

The appraisal could also lead to some stress. A third party completes the appraisal by picking comparable properties, and ensuring the safety and condition of the home. Different financing types have different appraisal criteria so it is important to let both the inspector and appraiser know what financing is being used.

If an appraisal comes in below the purchase price with required repairs (i.e. a piece of wood rot was found), then all parties have to come together and work through the issues. Either the buyer will have to come to the closing table with cash to cover the difference or the seller will have to lower the price. Another option is that the seller and buyer split the difference amongst themselves. In regards to any property damage that needs to be fixed for an appraisal, that will have to be negotiated between both parties as well. Once everything is agreed upon and fixed, then a re-appraisal occurs to confirm that the necessary repairs have been made.

The culmination of the pre-closing period -- and all its diligence activities -- is a successful closing where the parties exchange consideration and title, and the transaction is consummated. At this point the sale contract is successfully extinguished.

II. Determining Market Value

CONCEPTS OF VALUE

Basic value determinants

Price is not something of value in itself. It is only a number that *quantifies value*. The economic issue underlying the interplay of supply and demand is, how do trading parties arrive at the value of a good or service as indicated by the price?

Consider consumer demand for air conditioners. Why do air conditioners have value? How do they command the price they do?

The value of something is based on the answers to four questions:

- How much do I desire it?
- How useful is it?
- How scarce is it?
- Am I able to pay for it?

Desire. One determinant of value is how dear the item is to the purchaser. Returning to the air conditioner example, the question becomes "how much do I desire to be cool, dry, and comfortable?" To a person who lives in the tropics, it is safe to say that air conditioning is *more valuable* than a heating system. It is also safe to say the opposite is true for residents of northern Alaska.

Utility. The second determinant of value is the product's *ability to do the job*. Can the air conditioner satisfy my need to stay cool? How cool does it make my house? Does it even work properly? Of course, I won't pay as much if it is old or ineffectual.

Scarcity. The third critical element of value is a product's *availability in relation to demand*. The air conditioner is quite valuable if there are only five units in the entire city and everyone is hot. On the other hand, the value of an air conditioner goes down if there are ten thousand units for sale in a 500-person market.

Purchasing power. A fourth component of value is the *consumer's ability to pay* for the item. If one cannot afford to buy the air conditioner, the value of the air

conditioner is diminished, since it is financially out of reach. If all air conditioners are too expensive, consumers are forced to consider alternatives such as ceiling fans.

In the marketplace, the relative presence or absence of the four elements of value is constantly changing due to innumerable factors. Since price is a reflection of the total of all value factors at any time, changes in the underlying factors of value trigger changes in price.

Valuation principles

A number of economic forces interact in the marketplace to contribute to real estate value. Appraisers must consider these forces in estimating the value of a property. Among the most recognized of these principles are those listed below.

The primary economic principles underlying real estate value are

- supply and demand

- utility
- transferability
- anticipation
- substitution
- contribution
- change
- highest and best use
- conformity
- progression and regression
- assemblage, and subdivision

Supply and demand. The availability of certain properties interacts with the strength of the demand for those properties to establish prices. When demand for properties exceeds supply, a condition of scarcity exists, and real estate values rise. When supply exceeds demand, a condition of surplus exists, and real estate values decline. When supply and demand are generally equivalent, the market is considered to be in balance, and real estate values stabilize.

Utility. The fact that a property has a use in a certain marketplace contributes to the demand for it. Use is not the same as function. For instance, a swampy area may have an ecological function as a wetland, but it may have no economic utility if it cannot be put to some use that people in the marketplace are willing to pay for.

Transferability. How readily or easily title or rights to real estate can be transferred affects the property's value. Property that is encumbered has a value impairment since buyers do not want unmarketable title. Similarly, property that cannot be transferred due to disputes among owners may cause the value to decline, because the investment is wholly illiquid until the disputes are resolved.

Anticipation. The benefits a buyer *expects to derive from a property over a holding period* influence what the buyer is willing to pay for it. For example, if an investor anticipates an annual rental income from a leased property to be one million dollars, this expected sum has a direct bearing on what the investor will pay for the property.

Substitution. According to the principle of substitution, a buyer will *pay no more for a property than the buyer would have to pay for an equally desirable and available substitute property*. For example, if three houses for sale are essentially similar in size, quality and location, a potential buyer is unlikely to choose the one that is priced significantly higher than the other two.

Contribution. The principal of contribution focuses on the degree to which a particular improvement affects market value of the overall property. In essence, the contribution of the improvement is *equal to the change in market value that the addition of the improvement causes*. For example, adding a bathroom to a house may contribute an additional $15,000 to the appraised value. Thus the contribution of the bathroom is $15,000. Note that an improvement's contribution to value has little to do with the improvement's cost. The foregoing bathroom may have cost $5,000 or $20,000. Contribution is what the market recognizes as the change in value, not what an item cost. If continuous improvements are added to a property, it is possible that, at some point, the cost of adding improvements to a property no longer contributes a corresponding increase in the value of the property. When this occurs, the property suffers from *diminishing marginal return,* where the costs to improve exceed contribution.

Change. Market conditions are in a state of flux over time, just as the condition of a property itself changes. These fluctuations and changes will affect the benefits that can arise from the property, and should be reflected in an estimate of the property's value. For example, the construction of a neighborhood shopping center in the vicinity of a certain house may increase the desirability of the house's location, and hence, its value.

Highest and best use. This principle holds that there is, theoretically, a single use for a property that produces the greatest income and return. A property achieves its maximum value when it is put to this use. If the actual use is not the highest and best use, the value of the property is correspondingly less than optimal. Technically, highest and best use must be legally permissible, physically possible, financially feasible, and maximally productive.

For example, a property with an old house on it may not be in its highest and best use if it is surrounded by retail properties. If zoning permits the property to be converted to a retail use, its highest and best use may well be retail rather than residential.

Conformity. This principle holds that a property's maximal value is attained when its form and use are in tune with surrounding properties and uses. For example, a two-bedroom, one-bathroom house surrounded by four-bedroom, three-bathroom homes may derive maximal value from a room addition.

Progression and regression. The value of a property influences, and is influenced by, the values of neighboring properties. If a property is surrounded by properties with higher values, its value will tend to rise (progression); if it is surrounded by properties with lower values, its value will tend to fall (regression).

Assemblage. Assemblage, or the conjoining of adjacent properties, sometimes creates a combined value that is greater than the values of the unassembled properties. The excess value created by assemblage is called **plottage value.**

Subdivision. The division of a single property into smaller properties can also result in a higher total value. For instance, a one-acre suburban site appraised at $50,000 may be subdivided into four quarter-acre lots worth $30,000 each. This principle contributes significantly to the financial feasibility of subdivision development.

DEFINING MARKET VALUE

Market value is an opinion of the price that a willing seller and willing buyer would probably agree on for a property at a given time if:

- the transaction is a cash transaction
- the property is exposed on the open market for a reasonable period
- buyer and seller have full information about market conditions and about potential uses
- there is no abnormal pressure on either party to complete the transaction
- buyer and seller are not related (it is an "arm's length" transaction)
- title is marketable and conveyable by the seller
- the price is a "normal consideration," that is, it does not include hidden influences such as special financing deals, concessions, terms, services, fees, credits, costs, or other types of consideration.

Another way of describing market value is that it is the highest price that a buyer would pay and the lowest price that the seller would accept for the property.

The market price, as opposed to market value, is what a property actually sells for. Market price should theoretically be the same as market value if all the conditions essential for market value were present. Market price, however, may not reflect the analysis of comparables and of investment value that an estimate of market value includes.

Broker's opinion of value (BPO). A broker's opinion of value may resemble an appraisal, but it differs from an appraisal in that it is not necessarily performed by a disinterested third party or licensed professional and it generally uses only a limited form of one of the three appraisal approaches. In addition, the opinion is not subject to regulation, nor does it follow any particular professional standards.

ESTIMATING RESIDENTIAL PROPERTY VALUE: THE SALES COMPARISON APPROACH

The sales comparison approach, also known as the *market data approach*, is used for almost all properties. It also serves as the basis for a broker's opinion of value. It is based on the principle of substitution-- that a buyer will pay no more for the subject property than would be sufficient to purchase a comparable property. It is also reliant on the principle of contribution -- that specific component characteristics of the property each contribute to the value to a property.

The sales comparison approach is widely used because it takes into account the subject property's specific amenities in relation to competing properties. In addition, because of the relative currency of its data, the approach incorporates present market realities.

The sales comparison approach is limited in that every property is unique. As a result, it is difficult to find good comparables, especially for special-purpose properties. In addition, the market must be active; otherwise, sale prices lack currency and reliability.

Steps in the approach

The sales comparison approach consists of comparing sale prices of recently sold properties that are comparable with the subject, and making dollar adjustments to the price of each comparable to account for competitive differences with the subject. After identifying the adjusted value of each comparable, the appraiser weights the reliability of each comparable and the factors underlying how the adjustments were made. The weighting yields a final value range based on the most reliable factors in the analysis.

Steps in the Sales Comparison Approach

1. Identify comparable sales.
2. Compare comparables to the subject and make adjustments to comparables.
3. Weight values indicated by adjusted comparables for the final value estimate of the subject.

Identifying comparables

To qualify as a comparable, a property must:

- resemble the subject in size, shape, design, utility and location
- have sold recently, generally within six months of the appraisal
- have sold in an arm's-length transaction

An appraiser considers three to six comparables, and usually includes at least three in the appraisal report.

Appraisers have specific guidelines within the foregoing criteria for selecting comparables, many of which are set by secondary market organizations such as FNMA. For example, to qualify as a comparable for a mortgage loan appraisal, a property might have to be located within one mile of the subject. Or perhaps the size of the comparable must be within a certain percentage of improved area in relation to the subject.

The time-of-sale criterion is important because transactions that occurred too far in the past will not reflect appreciation or recent changes in market conditions.

An arm's length sale involves objective, disinterested parties who are presumed to have negotiated a market price for the property. If the sale of a house occurred between a father and a daughter, for example, one might assume that the transaction did not reflect market value.

Principal sources of data for generating the sales comparison are tax records, title records, and the local multiple listing service.

Adjusting comparables

The appraiser adjusts the sale prices of the comparables to account for competitive differences with the subject property. Note that the sale prices of the comparables are known, while the value and price of the subject are not. Therefore, adjustments can be made *only to the comparables' prices, not to the subject's.* Adjustments are made to the comparables in the form of a value deduction or a value addition.

Adding or deducting value. If the comparable is *better* than the subject in some characteristic, an amount is *deducted* from the sale price of the comparable. This neutralizes the comparable's competitive advantage in an adjustment category.

For example, a comparable has a swimming pool and the subject does not. To equalize the difference, the appraiser deducts an amount, say $6,000, from the sale price of the comparable. Note that the adjustment reflects the contribution of the swimming pool to market value. The adjustment amount is not the cost of the pool or its depreciated value.

If the comparable is *inferior* to the subject in some characteristic, an amount is *added* to the price of the comparable. This adjustment equalizes the subject's competitive advantage in this area.

Adjustment criteria. The principal factors for comparison and adjustment are *time of sale, location, physical characteristics, and transaction characteristics.*

- **time of sale**

    An adjustment may be made if market conditions, market prices, or financing availability have changed significantly since the date of the comparable's sale. Most often, this adjustment is to account for appreciation.

- **location**

    An adjustment may be made if there are differences between the comparable's location and the subject's, including neighborhood desirability and appearance, zoning restrictions, and general price levels.

- **physical characteristics**

  Adjustments may be made for marketable differences between the comparable's and subject's lot size, square feet of livable area (or other appropriate measure for the property type), number of rooms, layout, age, condition, construction type and quality, landscaping, and special amenities.

- **transaction characteristics**

  An adjustment may be made for such differences as mortgage loan terms, mortgage assumability, and owner financing.

Weighting comparables

Adding and subtracting the appropriate adjustments to the sale price of each comparable results in an adjusted price for the comparables that indicates the value of the subject. The last step in the approach is to perform a weighted analysis of the indicated values of each comparable. The appraiser, in other words, must identify which comparable values are more indicative of the subject and which are less indicative.

An appraiser primarily relies on experience and judgment to weight comparables. There is no formula for selecting a value from within the range of all comparables analyzed. However, there are three quantitative guidelines: the total number of adjustments; the amount of a single adjustment; and the net value change of all adjustments.

As a rule, *the fewer the total number of adjustments, the smaller the adjustment amounts, and the less the total adjustment amount, the more reliable the comparable.*

Number of adjustments. In terms of total adjustments, the comparable with the fewest adjustments tends to be most similar to the subject, hence the best indicator of value. If a comparable requires excessive adjustments, it is increasingly less reliable as an indicator of value. The underlying rationale is that there is a margin of error involved in making any adjustment. Whenever a number of adjustments must be made, the margin of error compounds. By the time six or seven adjustments are made, the margin becomes significant, and the reliability of the final value estimate is greatly reduced.

Single adjustment amounts. The dollar amount of an adjustment represents the variance between the subject and the comparable for a given item. If a large adjustment is called for, the comparable becomes less of an indicator of value. The smaller the adjustment, the better the comparable is as an indicator of value. If an appraisal is performed for mortgage qualification, the appraiser may be restricted from making adjustments in excess of a certain amount, for example, anything in excess of 10-15% of the sale price of the comparable. If such an adjustment would be necessary, the property is no longer considered comparable.

Total net adjustment amount. The third reliability factor in weighting comparables is the total net value change of all adjustments added together. If a comparable's total adjustments alter the indicated value only slightly, the comparable is a good indicator of value. If total adjustments create a large dollar amount between the sale price and the adjusted value, the comparable is a poorer indicator of value. Fannie Mae, for instance, will not accept the use of a comparable where total net adjustments are in excess of 15% of the sale price.

For example, an appraiser is considering a property that sold for $100,000 as a comparable. After all adjustments are made, the indicated value of the comparable is $121,000, a 21% difference in the comparable's sale price. This property, if allowed at all, would be a weak indicator of value.

Broker's comparative market analysis

A broker or associate who is attempting to establish a listing price or range of prices for a property uses a scaled-down version of the appraiser's sales comparison approach called a comparative market analysis, or CMA (also called a competitive market analysis). While the CMA serves a useful purpose in setting general price ranges, brokers and agents need to exercise caution in presenting a CMA as an appraisal, which it is not. Two important distinctions between the two are objectivity and comprehensiveness.

First, the broker is not unbiased: he or she is motivated by the desire to obtain a listing, which can lead one to distort the estimated price. Secondly, the broker's CMA is not comprehensive: the broker does not usually consider the full range of data about market conditions and comparable sales that the appraiser must consider and document. Therefore, the broker's opinion will be less reliable than the appraiser's.

The following exhibit illustrates the sales comparison approach. An appraiser is estimating market value for a certain house. Four comparables are adjusted to find an indicated value for the subject. The grid which follows the property and market data shows the appraiser's adjustments for the differences between the four comparables and the subject.

Sales Comparison Approach Illustration

Data

Subject property:
8 rooms-- 3 bedrooms, two baths, kitchen, living room, family room; 2,000 square feet of gross living area; 2-car attached garage; landscaping is good. Construction is frame with aluminum siding.

Comparable A:
Sold for 1,000,000 within previous month; conventional financing at current rates; located in subject's neighborhood with similar locational advantages; house approximately same age as subject; lot size smaller than subject; view similar to subject; design less appealing than subject's; construction similar to subject; condition similar to subject; 7 rooms-- two bedrooms, one bath; 1,900 square feet of gross living area; 2-car attached garage; landscaping similar to subject.

Comparable B:
Sold for 1,200,000 within previous month; conventional financing at current rates; located in subject's neighborhood with similar locational advantages; house six years newer than subject; lot size smaller than subject; view is better than the subject's; design is more appealing than subject's; construction (brick and frame) better than subject's; better condition than subject; 10 rooms-four bedrooms, three baths; 2,300 square feet of gross living area; 2-car attached garage; landscaping similar to subject.

Comparable C:
Sold for 1,150,000 within previous month; conventional financing at current rates; located in subject's neighborhood with similar locational advantages; house five years older than subject; lot size larger than subject; view similar to subject; design and appeal similar to subject's; construction similar to subject; condition similar to subject; 8 rooms-- three bedrooms, two baths; 2,000 square feet of gross living area; 2-car attached garage; landscaping similar to subject.

Comparable D:
Sold for 1,090,000 within previous month; conventional financing at current rates; located in a neighborhood close to subject's, but more desirable than subject's; house approximately same age as subject; lot size same as subject; view similar to subject; design less appealing than subject's; construction (frame) poorer than subject's; poorer condition than subject; 7 rooms-- two bedrooms, one and one half baths; 1,900 square feet of gross living area; 2-car attached garage; landscaping similar to subject.

Sales Comparison Approach Illustration, cont.

Adjustments

	Subject	A	B	C	D
Sale price		1,000,000	1,200,000	1,150,000	1,090,000
Financing terms		standard	standard	standard	standard
Sale date	NOW	equal	equal	equal	equal
Location		equal	equal	equal	-20,000
Age		equal	-12,000	+10,000	equal
Lot size		+10,000	+10,000	-10,000	equal
Site/view		equal	-10,000	equal	equal
Design/appeal		+10,000	-12,000	equal	+5,000
Construction	good	equal	-30,000	equal	+10,000
Condition	good	equal	-50,000	equal	+20,000
No. of rooms	8				
No. of bedrooms	3	+5,000	-5,000	equal	+5,000
No. of baths	2	+10,000	-15,000	equal	+5,000
Gross living area	2,000	+10,000	-20,000	equal	+10,000
Other space					
Garage	2 car/attd.	equal	equal	equal	equal
Landscaping	good	equal	equal	equal	equal
Net adjustments		+45,000	-144,000	0	+35,000
Indicated value	1,120,000	1,045,000	1,056,000	1,150,000	1,125,000

For comparable A, the appraiser has made additions to the lot value, design, number of bedrooms and baths, and for gross living area. This accounts for the comparable's *deficiencies* in these areas relative to the subject. A total of five adjustments amount to $45,000, or 4.5% of the purchase price.

For comparable B, the appraiser has deducted values for age, site, design, construction quality, condition, bedrooms, baths, and living area. This accounts for the comparable's superior qualities relative to the subject. The only addition is the lot size, since the subject's is larger. A total of nine adjustments amount to $144,000, or 12% of the sale price.

For comparable C, the appraiser has added value for the age and deducted value for the lot size. The two adjustments offset one another for a net adjustment of zero.

For comparable D, one deduction has been made for the comparable's superior location. This is offset by six additions reflecting the various areas where the comparable is inferior to the subject. A total of seven adjustments amount to $35,000, or 3.2% of the sale price.

In view of all adjusted comparables, the appraiser developed a final indication of value of $1,120,000 for the subject. Underlying this conclusion is the fact that Comparable C, since it only has two minor adjustments which offset each other, it is by far the best indicator of value. Comparable D might be the second best indicator, since the net adjustments are very close to the sale price. Comparable A might be the third best indicator, since it has the second fewest number of total adjustments. Comparable B is the least reliable indicator, since there are numerous adjustments, three of which are of a significant amount. In addition, Comparable B is questionable altogether as a comparable, since total adjustments alter the sale price by 12%.

III. Advertising

TENNESSEE ADVERTISING AND MARKETING REQUIREMENTS

Owner and agent advertising requirements

All advertising that promotes the sale or lease of real property, regardless of its nature or the medium used, must conform to the following requirements which are outlined in the rules (Rule 1260-02 - .12).

Advertising defined. Advertising includes traditional print, radio and television advertising, signs, flyers, email signatures, websites, letterheads, video or audio recordings transmitted through internet or broadcast streaming, and social media communications, which specifically includes such internet-based applications or platforms as Facebook, Twitter, Instagram and LinkedIn.

Advertising does not include promotional materials advertising a licensee such as hats, notepads, pens, t-shirts, name tags, business cards, and the sponsorship of charitable and community events.

General advertising requirements. Licensees may not advertise to sell, purchase, rent, lease or exchange real property in any way that that would indicate or give the impression that the licensee is not engaged in the real estate business. Licensee should have a higher level of knowledge of real estate transactions than the general public. The fact that they are licensed must always be obvious.

All advertising must be under the direct supervision of the principal broker, and must include the firm's name and phone number. The firm name must be the same size or larger than the names of licensees or teams featured in the ad, whether by print or other media. The entire firm's name, or dba ("doing business as", or fictitious name) if applicable, must appear as licensed with the Commission.

Any advertising referring to an individual licensee must list the licensee's name as licensed with the Commission. The use of nicknames or shortened versions of a name may not be used unless they have been previously registered with the Commission. If a middle name is used, it must be registered. If a licensee's name is registered including a middle name, but the middle name is not used in advertising, the Commission must be notified of that as well. Any name change may be made on a TREC 1 form available on the Commission's website.

Social media advertising must include required information within one click of the posting.

Signs may not be posted in any location advertising property for sale, purchase, exchange, rent, or lease without the written authorization of the owner of the property or the owner's agent.

Licensees may not advertise property listed by another licensee without the written authorization from the property owner on the listing agreement or other written statement signed by the owner.

False, misleading, or deceptive advertising is prohibited. This includes, in addition to any other deceptive advertising

- advertising that includes only the franchise name without including the firm name
- licensees holding themselves out, as a team, group, or similar entity within a firm, who advertise themselves using terms such as "Real estate," "Real estate brokerage," "Realty," "Company," "Corporation," "LLC," "Corp.," "Inc.," "Associates," or other similar terms that would lead the public to believe that the licensees are offering real estate brokerage services independent of the firm and principal broker

- any webpage containing a link to an unlicensed entity's website in which that entity is engaged or appears to be engaged in activities requiring a licensure

Guarantees, Claims and Offers. Licensees are strictly prohibited from using unsubstantiated selling claims, misleading statement or inferences. Any offer, warranty or guarantee used to induce an individual to enter into an agency relationship or contract must be made in writing and must disclose all pertinent details on the face.

Brokerage franchise advertising regulations

Advertising for Franchise or Cooperative Advertising Groups. Licensees using a franchise trade name or advertising as a member of a cooperative group.

Any licensee using a trade name on business cards, contracts, or other documents related to real estate transaction must clearly and unmistakably indicate on the card or document the licensee's name and firm telephone number as registered with the Commission.

Information required in listing ads

Listing ads must be under the direct supervision of the principal broker and must include the brokerage firm's name and telephone number. The ad must clearly indicate that the licensee is engaged in the real estate business. The exception to these requirements: a licensee who advertises "by owner/agent" on an unlisted property.

"For sale" signs

Licensees may not post "for sale" signs without the written authorization of the owner, either on the listing agreement or in a separate document. "For sale" signs are a form of advertising, and therefore must include the brokerage name, and adhere to all general advertising guidelines. The listing agreement should contain language providing the broker with permission to advertise the property.

Directional signs to a listed property must also include the firm name and firm phone number.

Internet

The listing firm name and telephone number must conspicuously appear on each page of the website. Each page of the website displaying listings from an outside database of available properties must include a statement that some or all of the listings may not belong to the firm whose website is being visited.

The broker must monitor all advertising, including internet ads, to ensure compliance with the rules and any applicable laws. Listing information must be kept current and accurate. This requirement shall apply to "First Generation" advertising as it is placed by the licensee and does not refer to advertising that may be syndicated or aggregated advertising of the original by third parties outside of the licensee's control and ability to monitor (i.e., Trulia, Zillow, etc.).

Gifts and prizes

(Rule 1260-02-.33) A licensee may offer a gift, prize, or other valuable consideration as an inducement to the purchase, listing, or lease of real estate only if the offer is made under the sponsorship and with the approval of the firm with whom the licensee is affiliated. The offer must be in writing and signed by the licensee, with disclosure of all pertinent details, including but not limited to

- accurate specifications of the gift, prize, or other valuable consideration offered
- fair market value (not cost of item)
- the time and place of delivery
- any requirements that must be satisfied by the prospective purchaser or lessor
- accurate specifications of the gift, prize, or other valuable consideration offered
- fair market value
- the time and place of delivery
- any requirements that must be satisfied by the prospective purchaser or lessor

It should be noted that licensees may not give or pay cash, including cash rebates, cash gifts or cash prizes in conjunction with any real estate transaction (TCA 62-13-302 (b)).

Advertisement indicating discrimination

Any advertising that expresses discrimination regarding any protected class is a violation of federal and state law. State laws specify that violations include directly or indirectly publishing, issuing, displaying or mailing material that indicates any goods, services, accommodations, or privileges will be refused, withheld, denied or limited because of race, creed, color, religion, sex or national origin. So, advertising indicating housing is available only to certain individuals is a violation, except senior housing that complies with requirements of law.

Telephone Consumer Protection Act

The TCPA (Telephone Consumer Protection Act) addresses the regulation of unsolicited telemarketing phone calls. Rules include the following:

- telephone solicitors must identify themselves, on whose behalf they are calling, and how they can be contacted
- telemarketers must comply with any do-not-call request made during the solicitation call
- consumers can place their home and wireless phone numbers on a national Do-Not-Call list which prohibits future solicitations from telemarketers.

CAN-SPAM Act

The CAN-SPAM Act (Controlling the Assault of Non-Solicited Pornography and Marketing Act of 2003) supplements the Telephone Consumer Protection Act (TCPA). It

- bans sending unwanted email 'commercial messages' to wireless devices
- requires express prior authorization
- requires giving an 'opt out' choice to terminate the sender's messages

When attending a listing consultation, most sellers will ask for a net sheet with an estimate of their net proceeds after all of the mortgage payoffs, closing costs and commissions. Most title companies and law offices will provide branded ones for agents, or it can be done manually.

Licensees using a franchise trade name or advertising as a member of a cooperative group

Any licensee using a trade name on business cards, contracts, or other documents related to real estate transaction must clearly and unmistakably indicate on the card or document the licensee's name and firm telephone number as registered with the Commission.

Listing ads must be under the direct supervision of the principal broker and must include the brokerage firm's name and telephone number. The ad must clearly indicate that the licensee is engaged in the real estate business. The exception to these requirements: a licensee who advertises "by owner/agent" on an unlisted property.

Licensees may not post "for sale" signs without the written authorization of the owner, either on the listing agreement or in a separate document. "For sale" signs are a form of advertising, and therefore must include the brokerage name, and adhere to all general advertising guidelines. The listing agreement should contain language providing the broker with permission to advertise the property.

Directional signs to a listed property must also include the firm name and firm phone number.

The listing firm name and telephone number must conspicuously appear on each page of the website. Each page of the website displaying listings from an outside database of available properties must include a statement that some or all of the listings may not belong to the firm whose website is being visited.

The broker must monitor all advertising, including internet ads, to ensure compliance with the rules and any applicable laws. Listing information must be kept current and accurate. This requirement shall apply to "First Generation" advertising as it is placed by the licensee and does not refer to advertising that may be syndicated or aggregated advertising of the original by third parties outside of the licensee's control and ability to monitor (i.e., Trulia, Zillow, etc.).

COMMUNICATIONS AND TECHNOLOGY

Multiple listing services (MLS) and websites

The posting and sharing of property listings and data among broker websites, firm websites, and multiple listing services (MLS) is one of the most effective marketing tools available to today's licensees. Broker cooperation assures sellers of maximum exposure for their properties, just as it assures buyers of seeing the widest possible range of listed properties. This system is used for leases, income properties, and residential homes. The MLS contains pertinent information for agents including public record details on the property, commission offered, and open house dates.

To ensure fair use of MLS facilities, the National Association of REALTORS® has developed an Internet Data Exchange (IDX) policy that enables MLS members to display and use MLS data while respecting the rights of property owners and brokers to market their properties however they want. Basically, persons who want to make use of MLS data have to share their own data as well. They can opt out of the sharing policy so that competitors cannot post their properties on competing websites, but then they cannot post competitors' properties on their own sites.

There are a number of websites that provide consumers with the capability to search through listings all over the country and even the world. Of course, it is always wise to recognize that information posted on the internet is not necessarily reliable and that the source of the information should be considered carefully.

In other words, the MLS syndicates with hundreds of websites so the public can get access to current market listings as well. Some of the more popular websites it sends listings to are Zillow, Realtor.com, Redfin, and Trulia. The listings sometimes lag when they are published but usually show up within a day or two.

Most buyers in today's market prefer using the aforementioned websites, but the MLS also has a phone application that agents can share with their clients. Some brokerages have also been investing more of their money into technology and developed their own phone applications that are worth sharing with clients.

Email and texting

Frequent and virtually instantaneous contact between real estate practitioners and consumers is possible via email and texting. As both these forms of communication fall under the category of advertising, practitioners need to carefully observe their state's advertising regulations. In brief, be truthful, direct, and concise. Provide the information required by law, and do not violate prohibitions against unsolicited emails and messages.

Social media

Social media websites allow rapid exchange of information, documents, photos, messages and data with a select group of contacts. They also represent another form of advertising and so are subject to real estate commission advertising regulations in most states.

Another digital form of marketing that is growing popularity is social media. There are many platforms to choose from- LinkedIn, Facebook, Instagram, and TikTok are the most common ones. These platforms allow agents to stay in touch with their database in a subtle way and educate their audience on the real estate market. Constantly engaging with people through these platforms will add another source of lead generation and help grow the transaction pipeline. If possible, having a presence on all platforms is advisable, but most likely the agent will find one they resonate with the most and focus their attention there.

Smartphones

Smartphones facilitate the use, not only of email, texting, and social media, but also of immediate internet access, document review, photo and document sharing, data storage, and video conferencing. They offer, in fact, an almost complete mobile office.

Managing information

The ability to satisfy the needs of clients and customers is largely dependent on a broker's ability to obtain, organize, and manage information. Information is a cornerstone of the broker's perceived value in the marketplace and a major reason why buyers and sellers seek a broker out. Systematic collection and updating of relevant information is therefore a business priority.

Property data

Most brokerages maintain two categories of property data: available properties, and all properties in the market area. In residential brokerage, available property basically consists of the listings in the MLS and for-sale-by-owner properties. Records for all properties in an area are accessible in tax records. Commercial brokerages usually keep track of available and occupied commercial properties in a proprietary database.

Buyer data

Buyer information is usually compiled and maintained, often informally, by each agent in a brokerage. An agency's base of prospects who are looking for property at any given time is valuable for marketing new listings.

Tenant data

In residential and commercial leasing companies, information is compiled and maintained on all tenants in an area, by property type used. Such files contain a tenant's lease expiration, property size, and rent.

Client data

It is important to keep track of both current and former clients. Former clients are likely prospects to become clients again or customers. They are also a source of referrals. Current clients, of course, should be the broker's primary concern.

Market data

Today's clients and customers expect a broker to know the market intimately. It is often the broker with the best market knowledge who dominates business in the market. Knowing a market includes keeping up to date on:

- pricing and appreciation trends
- financing rates and terms
- demographic patterns and trends
- construction trends
- general economic trends

CONSUMER PROTECTION ACT

Unfair or deceptive acts or practices affecting the conduct of any trade or commerce are Class B misdemeanors. These include, among several other deceptive acts,

- disparaging the goods, services or business of another by false or misleading representations
- advertising goods or services with the intent not to sell them as advertised
- causing confusion or misunderstanding with respect to the authority of an affiliate, representative or agent to negotiate the final terms of a consumer transaction

IV: DISCLOSURES

RESIDENTIAL PROPERTY CONDITION DISCLOSURE

Sellers are required to make certain disclosures, on a prescribed form, the Residential Property Condition Disclosure, which can be viewed in TCA 66-5-210. The Act applies to transfers by sale, exchange, installment land sales contract, and lease with an option to buy residential property of one (1) to four (4) dwelling units, whether built on-site or not. It applies even if a real estate licensee is not involved in the transfer.

Transfer of these properties requires the owner to furnish the purchaser one of the following:

- the Residential Property Condition Disclosure form, including any material defects known by the owner

    o the form includes a notice to the purchaser that the information in the disclosure is representation of the owner and not of the real estate licensee, if any

    o the owner is not required to undertake an independent investigation or inspection of the property to make the required disclosures.

- a residential property disclaimer statement indicating the owner makes no representations or warranties regarding condition of the property or its improvements, and that the purchaser will be receiving the property "as is" (with all existing defects, if any), other than specified in the sales contract

    o the disclaimer statement is permitted only if the purchaser waives the disclosure requirement

    o if the purchaser does not waive the disclosure, the Residential Property Condition Disclosure form must be provided

The owner must deliver the written disclosure or disclaimer statement to the purchaser prior to acceptance of a purchase, exchange, or lease with option to buy contract. The disclosure must include all information as shown on the sample form, and may be in the contract, in an addendum to the contract, or may be a separate document.

Failure to provide the disclosure or disclaimer does not permit a purchaser to terminate a purchase contract; however, a purchaser may bring court action as otherwise permitted.

The owner is not liable for an error, omission or inaccuracy if that information was not actually known by the owner or was based on information provided by public agencies or other persons providing information that is required to be disclosed; or, if the owner reasonably believed the information was correct and the owner was not grossly negligent in obtaining the information and transmitting it.

The owner may deliver a report or opinion of a licensed engineer, geologist, surveyor, wood destroying insect control expert, home inspector, or other inspector to satisfy some disclosure requirements.

Not a warranty. The Residential Property Condition Disclosure form is not a warranty by the seller and is not a substitute for inspections by the purchaser or a professional home inspector.

Exclusive use. The disclosure form is provided to potential purchasers for their exclusive use and may not be relied upon by purchasers in subsequent transactions.

If the disclosed information later is discovered to be inaccurate, the inaccuracy does not constitute a violation if, prior to closing, the owner discloses any material changes or certifies to the purchaser at closing that the property condition is substantially unchanged from when the disclosure was provided.

The owner may state that information is unknown or make an approximation of the information if clearly identified as an approximation. This can be stated only if the information is unknown and cannot be used to circumvent disclosure.

The licensee representing the owner must inform the owner of the owner's rights and obligations regarding the disclosure, and must also inform the purchaser if unrepresented by a licensee. A license representing the purchaser must inform the purchaser of his or her rights and obligations regarding the disclosure.

Exempt properties. Certain properties are exempt from providing the disclosure form:

- transfers pursuant to court order

- foreclosures

- probated property

- from one co-owner to another current owner in joint tenancy, tenancy by the entirety, or tenancy in common

- beneficiary of a deed of trust by the trustor or successor in interest in default, by trustor resulting from a foreclosure sale, or by a beneficiary who acquired property at a foreclosure sale under the deed of trust, or acquired property by deed in lieu of foreclosure

- transfers by a fiduciary in administration of a decedent's estate, guardianship, conservatorship or trust

- transfers to a spouse or persons in the lineal line of consanguinity of one (1) or more of the transferors

- transfers between spouses resulting from a decree of divorce or a property settlement stipulation

- transfers due to tax sales

- transfers to or from a governmental entity of public or quasi-public housing authority or agency

- transfers involving initial sale of new construction, if the builder offers a written warranty

- property sold at public auction

- if the owner has not resided on the property at any time within three (3) years prior to the date of transfer

- transfer from a debtor in a chapter 7 or a chapter 13 bankruptcy to a creditor or third party by a deed in lieu of foreclosure or by a quitclaim deed

Remedies for misrepresentation or nondisclosure. The purchaser's remedies for an owner's misrepresentation on a residential property disclosure statement will be either:

- an action for actual damages suffered as a result of defects existing in the property as of the date of execution of the real estate purchase contract, if the owner actually presented to the purchaser the disclosure statement, and the purchaser was not aware of the defect at the earlier of closing or occupancy by the purchaser, in the event of a sale, or occupancy in the event of a lease with the option to purchase

  - any action brought as a result of the disclosure must be commenced within one (1) year of the date the purchaser received the disclosure statement or the date of closing, or occupancy if a lease situation, whichever occurs first.

- termination of the contract prior to closing, based on the liability covered above for errors and omissions in the event of a misrepresentation in a required residential property disclosure statement

  - The buyer may have other remedies or equity legally available against an owner in the event of an owner's intentional or willful misrepresentation of the condition of the property.

Additional required property-related disclosures

In addition to making other required disclosures, the seller must, prior to entering into a contract with a buyer, disclose in the contract or in writing otherwise, including acknowledgement of receipt, the following. Note that these disclosures are required of sellers even if exempted from use of the Residential Property Condition Disclosure form or when using the disclaimer.

- the presence of any known exterior injection well and the results of any known percolation test or soil absorption rate performed on the property that is determined or accepted by the department of environment and conservation

- when known by the seller, whether any single-family residence located on the property has been moved from an existing foundation to another foundation

- the presence of a known sinkhole on the property; this is a subterranean void created by the dissolution of limestone or dolostone strata resulting from groundwater erosion, causing a surface subsidence of soil, sediment, or rock, indicated by the contour lines on the property's recorded plat map

- location in a planned unit development, with a copy of the development's restrictive covenants, homeowner bylaws and master deed upon request

The seller's disclosure contains information regarding the water supply (well or city water) and whether a septic system exists on the property. Licensees should be aware that if a property has access to a public sewage system, the owner may be required to connect to it.

The seller is required to disclose any defect or malfunction in the system. The disclosure form notifies the seller that newly constructed residences on a septic system may not be advertised as having more bedrooms than indicated on the system permit.

Impact fees or adequate facilities taxes (TCA 66-5-211). In transfers involving the first sale of a dwelling, the owner of residential property must furnish the purchaser a statement disclosing the amount of any impact fees or adequate facilities taxes paid to any city or county on any parcel of land subject to transfer by sale, exchange, installment land sales contract, or lease with an option to buy.

Adequate facilities tax is any privilege tax that is a development tax, imposed by a county or city, pursuant to any act of general or local application, when engaging in development. Impact fees are monetary charges imposed by a county or municipal government, to regulate new development on real property. The amount of impact fees is related to the costs resulting from the new development, and the revenues for this fee are to be used in new development.

Environmental issues. The seller must disclose any known lead-based paint and comply with federal regulations pertaining to the disclosure, if the property is built prior to 1978.

If the seller is aware of radon levels that are higher than the EPA's recommended action level of 4.0 pCi/L, this fact should be disclosed. Radon testing is not required in Tennessee, but a buyer or the buyer's transferring employee may require a test. Licensees should never indicate that a radon test is unnecessary. An interactive map of radon in Tennessee is available on the Department of Health website: https://www.tn.gov/health/cedep/environmental/epht/interactive-radon-map.html

If the seller is aware of other environmental issues on the property, those should be disclosed as well.

Homeowner association information (TCA 66-27-502 through -503). When requested by a unit owner, purchaser or a lender to provide information to the owner, purchaser, or their agent, the association must provide the requesting party within ten (10) business days following the date of receipt of the request, certain specific information as required by statute, to the extent applicable. It is the unit owner's responsibility to advise a purchase or lender, when requested, how to contact the association. The association may charge a reasonable fee for providing the information. If the fee remains unpaid, it may be assessed against the unit whose owner, lender or purchaser requested the information.

When construction of a condominium is not yet complete, a declarant, prior to the first sale of any interest in a unit to a third-party purchaser, must when requested and within ten (10) business days following the date of the declarant's receipt of the request, provide the information to the extent applicable and available, to any purchaser or prospective lender to a purchaser. If any of the information is not available within ten (10) business days following the date of the request, it must be provided at least ten (10) business days prior to closing of the sale of the unit.

The information must be provided in writing or by electronic means (by email or posting to a web site and providing a link and access to the web site).

The information to be provided includes contact information of the declarant, master deed of declaration, bylaws, rules and regulations of the association, most recent balance sheet, income statement and approved budget, monthly assessments and any special assessments, insurance coverage and other information as specified in the statutes.

Septic systems (TCA 68-221-409). Prior to constructing, extending or repairing subsurface sewage disposal systems, or removing wastes from the systems, one must secure a permit from the Division of Groundwater Protection of the Tennessee Department of Environment and Conservation. The system must be designed by a registered engineer. Purchasers should be made aware of this requirement, if applicable to the property.

When a licensee is preparing an offer, he or she must include in the offer and make the buyer aware that, for a fee, a septic system inspection letter is available through the Tennessee Department of Environment and Conservation, Division of Grand Water Protection (Rule 1260-02.37).

LICENSEE DISCLOSURES

Commissions, fees, rebates or other valuable consideration. Required disclosures regarding commissions may be made by the licensee to the principal in advance of payment or receipt based on pre-established terms in the brokerage agreement. When a licensee refers a principal to another broker, and the broker receiving the referral knows of the referring licensee's expectation to receive compensation, payment of commission must be disclosed in writing to the principal by the broker working with principal no later than transaction closing. The licensee's principals in a specific transaction include both the client and customer if the customer is working primarily with the broker and is not represented by another broker.

A licensee may give a principal part of a commission received by the licensee that is related to the purchase, sale, lease or exchange of real estate as long as the rebate is disclosed on the closing statement for that transaction. The rebate cannot mislead another licensee, another principal, lender, title company or government agency involved in the transaction regarding the source of funds to complete the transaction. As indicated previously, TCA 62-13-302 (b) prohibits cash rebated, cash gifts, or cash prizes.

The licensee's principals in a specific transaction include both the client and customer if the customer is working primarily with the broker and is not represented by another broker.

No disclosure is required for gifts, products, services, or other things of value given to a principal by a licensee if they are not contingent upon the purchase, sale, lease or exchange of real estate for that transaction. NOTE: The Commission generally frowns on payment in any form by a licensee to any unlicensed entity other than those items in a promotion approved by the broker and including written disclosure of details.

Licensee a transaction principal. When a real estate licensee is a party to the transaction, he or she must disclose that position to the other party to the transaction. It is assumed that a licensee might have a higher level of real estate transaction knowledge than a non-licensee. In order to prohibit a licensee from taking advantage of an individual's possible lack of knowledge, the licensee is required to disclose his or her status as a licensee to the other party. This disclosure should also appear in the sales contract, lease, exchange or property management agreement.

Licensees may not list, sell, buy, exchange, rent, lease or option in their own name or in the name of the firm without first notifying the licensee's broker in writing. Additionally, an agent employed to sell may not be the purchaser of that property, and the agent of the buyer may not be the seller without consent of the principal after full knowledge of all facts. Even with consent, these situations can bring liability. To be an agent of or represent one party while being the other party in the transaction (agency coupled with an interest) is not an ideal situation.

Material facts disclosure

Adverse facts. Real estate licensees are subject to a cause of action for damages or equitable relief for failing to disclose adverse facts of which the licensee has actual knowledge or notice. "Adverse facts" means conditions or occurrences generally recognized by competent licensees as significantly reducing the structural integrity of improvements to real property, or presenting a significant health risk to occupants of the property. Known adverse facts about a property must be disclosed by licensees, but licensees have no obligation to discover or disclose latent defects in a property or to advise on matters outside the scope of their real estate license. (TCA 62-13-405)

Misrepresentation or fraud. A cause of action for damages or equitable remedies may be brought against a real estate licensee for intentionally misrepresenting or defrauding a purchaser (TCA 66-5). The Consumer Protection Act, which allows treble damages, prohibits knowingly advertising a newly constructed residence as having more bedrooms than as permitted (TCA 47-18-104). Also, knowingly advertising a resale property as having more bedrooms than as permitted is considered misrepresentation by the licensee.

Nondisclosure. There is no cause of action against an owner or a real estate licensee for failure to disclose that an occupant of the real property was afflicted with human immunodeficiency virus (HIV) or other disease which has been determined by medical evidence to be highly unlikely to be transmitted through the occupancy of a dwelling place, or that the real property was the site of an act or occurrence which had no effect on the physical structure of the real property, its physical environment or the improvements, or the site of a homicide, felony or suicide. Licensees should note that not only is disclosure not required by Tennessee law, but federal fair housing law prohibits disclosing that an occupant is afflicted with HIV or AIDS.

MODULE 1 SNAPSHOT REVIEW:

LISTINGS

LISTING AND SELLING PROCESS
- primary objective is to obtain exclusive listings

Prospecting
- essential for generating listing leads; all facets of marketing, advertising and direct selling are incorporated
- Prospecting strategies – referral networking; selling expireds and fsbos; farming; open houses

Listing presentations
- tools include net sheet; pricing strategy; marketing plan; optimizing positioning of property

Listing agreements
- establish scope of authority
- may represent seller; buyer; landlord; or tenant via exclusive; exclusive agency; or open listing
- avoid net listings; may be illegal

Listing benchmarks
- pricing – establish price range via comparable analysis
- marketing listings – mix of promotion and selling that addresses market conditions and likely prospects
- selling prospects – qualify buyers' preferences, capabilities; report results to client
- obtaining offers – obtain and present offers to client; assist in negotiations, counteroffers; reach an agreement and an executed sales contract

Pre-closing activities
- assist with financing; clear up contingencies and encumbrances
- manage escrow activities and transaction documents
- validate property condition declarations; complete any repairs required; complete appraisal; assess lender cost estimates

DETERMINING MARKET VALUE

Concepts of value
- **basic value determinants**: desire; utility; scarcity; purchasing power
- **valuation principles –** supply and demand; usefulness; transferability; substitution; contribution
- BPO: broker's opinion of value; uses principle of contribution, substitution to adjust comps

Sales comparison approach
- select comps;
- compare and adjust each comp
- reconcile each adjusted comp to get final estimate
- adjusting comps: if comp is better than subject – subtract value from comp; if comp is worse than subject – add value to comp. Never adjust the subject

ADVERTISING

Owner and agent requirements
- advertising includes all forms of promotions; if selling real property, must conform to rules
- advertising includes most media, e.g., social platforms; websites; streaming

- rules: cannot lend impression advertiser is NOT in the real estate business; licensed status must be clear and obvious
- advertising falls under supervision of principal broker; signs must be authorized by owner
- must use licensed name; no nicknames without registration; must include firm name, phone number
- cannot advertise other licensee's listings without authorization
- cannot engage in false or misleading advertising; cannot discriminate with any protected class
- TCPA: telephone solicitors must ID themselves & how to contact; must comply with do-not-call requests and Do-Not-Call list inclusion requests
- CAN-SPAM Act – cannot send unwanted email to wireless devices; must give opt-out option

Consumer Protection Act

- cannot disparage competing services or businesses with false or misleading statements
- cannot advertise with intent to change terms prior to sale

DISCLOSURES
Residential Property Condition Disclosure

- sellers must complete disclosure on prescribed form (TCA 66-5-210) if transaction is residential 1-4 unit property
- must disclose known defects; not required to do investigations, but seller must provide report unless waived by buyer
- must be delivered prior to acceptance of an offer
- exempt properties: court-related transfers; foreclosures; inheritances; tax sales; new construction

Other seller disclosures

- well-related test results; sinkhole-related issues; PUD covenants; impact fees; environmental issues; radon; lead paint; HOA rules, covenants

Licensee disclosures

- licensee must disclose all sources of compensation to principal if contingent on closing.
- must disclose licensed status if buying or selling real property
- must disclose known adverse material facts, but not obligated to conduct investigations
- cannot misrepresent property features or commit acts of fraud
- licensee not obligated to disclose property stigmas including homicide, AIDS, infectious diseases

MODULE 1 - LISTINGS

QUIZ

Carefully read each question and provide your best answer based on what you learned in this module. Then check your answers against the Answer Key which immediately follows the quiz questions.

1. A new licensee is developing a strategy to generate business in a defined market area in her community. Which of the following strategies would you adopt for optimum results toward your goal of capturing buyers and sellers?

   a. A social media strategy to find new home buyers
   b. A word-of-mouth strategy to neighborhood community groups to generate referrals.
   c. A cold-calling strategy for expired listings
   d. An open house strategy all over town

2. Which two pieces of information are required to be included on a listing advertisement?

   a. The brokerage firm's e-mail and address
   b. The listing agent's telephone number and e-mail address
   c. The brokerage firm's name and telephone number
   d. The listing agent's address and name

3. The cost of constructing a functional equivalent of a subject property is known as _____.

   a. construction cost.
   b. replacement cost.
   c. restitution cost.
   d. reconstruction cost.

4. List three critical economic criteria for defining and setting up a prospecting farm.

   a. An area with numerous expired listings, high-growth, and many open houses
   b. An up-and-coming neighborhood with lots of development, and many restaurants
   c. A high-growth market area with a high turnover rate and one that is not over-saturated with competitors
   d. A low-growth neighborhood with low turnover and numerous listings

5. In an appraisal, loss of value in a property from any cause is referred to as _____.

   a. deterioration.
   b. obsolescence.
   c. depreciation.
   d. deflation.

6. What is another name for a development tax imposed by a city when engaging in development?

   a. Adequate facilities tax
   b. Urban tax
   c. New construction fee
   d. Special assessment fee

7. Which value principle states that there is a use for a property that produces the greatest income and return?

   a. Anticipation principle
   b. Progression principle
   c. Highest and best use principle
   d. Income principle

8. Which of the following properties are exempt from providing a residential property condition disclosure?

   a. For Sale By Owner homes
   b. Foreclosures
   c. Duplexes
   d. Residential sales

9. Which of the following platforms is exempt from advertising requirements?

   a. Websites
   b. Facebook
   c. Radio
   d. None are exempt.

10. To complete the sales comparison approach, the appraiser _____.

    a. averages the adjustments.
    b. weights the comparables.
    c. discards all comparables having a lower value.
    d. identifies the subject's value as that of the nearest comparable.

11. Which statute prohibits knowingly advertising a newly constructed residence as having more bedrooms than permitted?

    a. The Misrepresentation Law
    b. The Fraud in Real Estate Act
    c. The Consumer Protection Act
    d. The Licensee Disclosure Act

12. Which of the following brokerage agreements offers the brokerage firm the fullest protection regarding the payment of compensation in the event that the seller sells to a neighbor?

    a. Exclusive agency
    b. Limited listing agreement
    c. Co-broker agreement
    d. Exclusive right to sell

13. If a seller is aware of radon levels higher than the EPA's recommended level of _____ pCi/L, this fact should be disclosed.

    a. 3.5
    b. 4.0
    c. 2.5
    d. 5.0

14. Which of the following items is not required to be disclosed by a seller?

   a. The condition of the air conditioning system
   b. The presence of a septic tank
   c. That a previous occupant was afflicted with HIV
   d. HOA information

15. The principle of _____ focuses on the degree to which a particular improvement affects market value of the overall property.

   a. highest and best
   b. contribution
   c. change
   d. conformity

16. When requested by a unit owner, a homeowner's association must provide information within _____.

   a. 7 business days.
   b. 15 calendar days.
   c. 10 business days.
   d. 21 calendar days.

17. The seller must disclose any known lead-based paint if the property is built prior to _____.

   a. 1994.
   b. 1978.
   c. 1969.
   d. 1947.

18. As a component of real estate value, the principle of substitution suggests that _____.

   a. if two similar properties are for sale, a buyer will purchase the cheaper of the two.
   b. if one of two adjacent homes is more valuable, the price of the other home will tend to rise.
   c. if too many properties are built in a market, the prices will tend to go down.
   d. people will readily move to another home if it is of equal value.

19. What are two critical considerations to be aware of in pricing a listing?

   a. Stay within 30% of the recent sales prices and try to push it as high as possible
   b. Underprice the listing and provide a hefty commission to buyer's agents
   c. Do not underprice and do not overprice the listing
   d. Overprice the listing and provide a bonus to buyer's agents

20. Net operating income is equal to _____.

   a. gross income minus potential income minus expenses.
   b. effective gross income minus debt service.
   c. potential gross income minus vacancy and credit loss minus expenses.
   d. effective gross income minus vacancy and credit loss.

21. Conditions generally recognized by licensees as significantly reducing the structural integrity of improvements to real property are known as _____.

   a. adverse facts.
   b. misrepresentation disclosures.
   c. non-material disclosures.
   d. personal reports.

22. Which of the following statutes requires giving an 'opt-out' choice to terminate a licensee's e-mails?

   a. CAN-SPAM Act
   b. Marketing Act of 1996
   c. Telephone Protection Act
   d. TCA

23. What supply-demand conditions indicate a scarcity in available properties?

   a. When supply exceeds demand
   b. When real estate values drop
   c. When demand and supply are equivalent
   d. When demand exceeds supply

24. Which of the following marketing tools is the most essential for today's licensees?

   a. IDX
   b. Multiple listing service
   c. TikTok
   d. LinkedIn

25. The income capitalization approach to appraising value is most applicable for which of the following property types?

   a. Single family homes
   b. Apartment buildings
   c. Undeveloped land
   d. Churches

26. If an agent has yet to establish a network in a local market, direct outreach to _____ could be helpful in building a database.

   a. Neighbors
   b. For Sale By Owners
   c. Listing agents
   d. Brokers

27. In transfers involving the first sale of a dwelling, the owner must furnish the purchaser a statement disclosing the amount of _____ paid to the city.

   a. environmental fees
   b. impact fees
   c. hazard assessments
   d. listing fees

28. Prior to repairing subsurface sewage disposal systems, one must secure a permit from _____.

   a. the Environmental Protection Agency.
   b. the Division of Grand Water Protection.
   c. the Septic Tank Division of Tennessee.
   d. the Division of Groundwater Protection of the Tennessee Department of Environment and Conservation.

29. Highest and best use of a property is that use which _____.

   a. is physically and financially feasible, legal, and the most productive.
   b. is legal, feasible, and deemed the most appropriate by zoning authorities.
   c. entails the largest building that zoning ordinances will allow developers to erect.
   d. conforms to other properties in the area.

30. Which statute addresses the regulation of unsolicited telemarketing phone calls?

   a. TCPA
   b. CAN-SPAM Act
   c. PCA
   d. SPEAK Act

MODULE 1 – LISTINGS

ANSWER KEY TO QUIZ

1. **b.** A word-of-mouth strategy to neighborhood community groups to generate referrals.
2. **c.** The brokerage firm's name and telephone number
3. **b.** replacement cost.
4. **c.** A high-growth market area with a high turnover rate and one that is not over-saturated with competitors
5. **c.** depreciation.
6. **a.** Adequate facilities tax
7. **c.** Highest and best use principle
8. **b.** Foreclosures
9. **d.** None are exempt.
10. **b.** weights the comparables.
11. **c.** The Consumer Protection Act
12. **d.** Exclusive right to sell
13. **b.** 4.0
14. **c.** That previous occupant was afflicted with HIV
15. **b.** contribution
16. **c.** 10 business days.
17. **b.** 1978.
18. **a.** if two similar properties are for sale, a buyer will purchase the cheaper of the two.
19. **c.** Do not underprice and do not overprice the listing
20. **c.** potential gross income minus vacancy and credit loss minus expenses.
21. **a.** adverse facts.
22. **a.** CAN-SPAM Act
23. **d.** When demand exceeds supply
24. **b.** Multiple listing service
25. **b.** Apartment buildings
26. **b.** For Sale By Owners
27. **b.** impact fees
28. **d.** the Division of Groundwater Protection of the Tennessee Department of Environment and Conservation.
29. **a.** is physically and financially feasible, legal, and the most productive.
30. **a.** TCPA

MODULE 1: LISTINGS

CHECK YOUR UNDERSTANDING

Instructions:

Carefully read each challenge question, then provide your best answer based on what you learned in this module. Then check your answers against the Answer Key which immediately follows the questions.

1. A new licensee is developing a strategy to generate business in a defined market area in her community. Which of the following strategies would you adopt for optimum results toward your goal of capturing buyers and sellers?

    A. An email campaign to new residents promoting newer properties.
    B. A word-of-mouth strategy to neighborhood community groups to generate referrals.
    C. A direct selling approach in an established neighborhood to generate long-time residents and buyers desiring established neighborhoods.
    D. Develop a farm geography where there is a strong business presence, since employment centers employ the most qualified buyers.

2. List three critical criteria for defining and setting up a prospecting farm.

    1. _____

    2. _____

    3. _____

3. List four specific preparations to complete prior to engaging in a listing presentation.

    1. _____

    2. _____

    3. _____

    4. _____

4. What are the two principal considerations to be aware of in pricing a listing, and how can licensees ultimately defend the listing price they propose?

    Consideration (1): _____

    _____

    Consideration (2): _____

How defend price estimate?   _____

_____

_____

5. If you are the listing broker working on an offer with a customer, what are the two critical guidelines to follow in dealing with the sensitive pricing issue?

Guideline A: _____

Guideline B: _____

6. During the pre-closing process, an important facet of the due diligence the broker must perform is verifying the seller's statements and representations. What are three other broker responsibilities that must be discharged during this phase?

1. _____

2. _____

3. _____

7. There are five overriding thrusts of advertising regulation that comprise the foundations of acceptable residential brokerage practice in Tennessee. Name three of these foundations.

1. _____

2. _____

3. _____

MODULE 1: LISTINGS

CHECK YOUR UNDERSTANDING ANSWER KEY

1. A new licensee is developing a strategy to generate business in a defined market area in her community. Which of the following strategies would you adopt for optimum results toward your goal of capturing buyers and sellers?

   B.   A word-of-mouth strategy to neighborhood community groups to generate referrals.

   Tailor your prospecting and listing efforts to maximize your opportunities to generate referrals. Most agents strive to develop a referral base as this capitalizes on the trust you've generated through past efforts.

2. List three critical criteria for defining and setting up a prospecting farm.

   1. Select a high-growth market area

   2. Select a market area with a high turnover rate

   3. Select a market area that is not over-saturated with competitors and does not have a preference for a given licensee.

3. List four specific preparations to complete prior to engaging in a listing presentation.

   1. A seller's net sheet

   2. A detailed marketing plan

   3. Sample agreements and other documents

   4. A questionnaire for the seller to ascertain data on property condition

4. What are the two principal considerations to be aware of in pricing a listing, and how can licensees ultimately defend the listing price they propose?:

   Consideration (1):   do not underprice as you will short your client

   Consideration (2):   do not overprice as the listing won't sell at all

   How defend price estimate? Perform a comprehensive CMA that can generate seller reliance based on the general validity of the principle of substitution in valuing residential properties. That principle holds that buyers will buy a property if it is priced comparably to other nearby similar homes.

5. If you are the listing broker working on an offer with a customer, what are the two critical professional practice guidelines to follow in moving the transaction to the next phase?

   Guideline A: Do not suggest what price the seller will or will not accept; stick to the listing price!

   **Guideline B: Present the offer to the seller at the earliest opportunity and assist with a
      counteroffer if necessary**

6. During the pre-closing process, an important facet of the due diligence the broker must perform is verifying the seller's statements and representations. What are three other broker responsibilities that must be discharged during this phase?

1. **assisting the buyer in procuring financing**

2. **recommending inspectors, appraisers, title companies**

3. **facilitating communications and document flow between principals**

7. There are five overriding thrusts of advertising regulation that comprise the foundations of acceptable residential brokerage practice in Tennessee. Name three of these foundations.

1. **advertising must not be misleading**

2. **the sponsoring and managing broker are responsible for all ad content**

3. **all advertising must reveal the identity of the brokerage firm; licensee may not use blind ads that conceal their identities**

4. **brokers selling their own property through the brokerage must disclose the brokerage identity**

5. **licensees must include the broker's business identity in any advertising as they may not advertise solely in their own name**

Module 2: AGENCY

I. Tennessee Agency Laws
II. Agency Disclosures
III. Seller and Buyer Listing Agreements

Module 2 Learning Objectives

Tennessee Agency Laws

1. Summarize the types of agency relationships practiced in Tennessee; how they are distinctive, and what duties are entailed in fulfilling one's agency responsibilities.

2. Characterize the key differences between designated agents and facilitators

3. Define subagency and dual agency relationships

Agency Disclosures

1. Identify the key differentiations between verbal and written disclosures

2. Summarize the process of changing one's specific agency status in a given transaction.

3. Describe the parties and timing involved in a licensee's initial, verbal and written agency disclosures.

4. Summarize how licensee commissions are determined and communicated

Seller and Buyer Listing Agreements

1. Identify the key aspects of – and differentiations between -- buyer agency agreements and listing agreements

2. Summarize the various grounds that exist for terminating a listing.

I. Tennessee Agency Laws

CREATION OF RELATIONSHIPS

Agency is how the licensee works with or for the parties in a real estate transaction. Tennessee agency law replaces common law. A licensee may work as an agent of an individual, or serve as a facilitator. These two relationships are covered in detail below.

A Tennessee real estate licensee may provide real estate services to any party in a prospective transaction with or without an agency relationship with any of the parties. Until a licensee enters into a specific, written agreement to establish an agency relationship with one (1) or more parties to a transaction, the licensee is considered a facilitator and not an agent or advocate of any party to the transaction. So, in Tennessee, an agency relationship is never created unintentionally by a licensee's actions or statements, nor does disclosure of agency without a written, signed agreement create an agency agreement. A licensee is a facilitator by default. If there is no signed agency agreement, Tennessee law assumes the licensee's status to be facilitator.

No implied or assumed agency. An agency or subagency relationship is not be assumed, implied or created without a written, bilateral agreement establishing the terms and conditions of that relationship. Again, an important note: a unilateral disclosure of agency does not create an agency agreement; agency can be accomplished only with a bilateral, signed agreement. If a licensee states orally or in writing that he or she represents, or is the agent of, a consumer when a bilateral agency agreement has not been signed, the licensee has clearly misrepresented the facts and violated license law.

Agreements establishing agency. The negotiation and execution of either an exclusive agency listing or an exclusive right to sell listing agreement establishes agency relationship with a prospective seller. Likewise, the execution of an exclusive buyer agency agreement or non-exclusive buyer agency agreement can establish agency with the buyer. Open listings can also establish agency if properly worded.

In either of these listing agreements or buyer agency agreements, the licensee is an agent of one of the party represented, and is also a fiduciary of that party. A fiduciary is someone representing a party in a position of trust. Because the agent represents the party, information provided to the agent is deemed to have been provided to the agent's principal. A fiduciary also protects the interests of the party he or she represents.

It should be noted that a licensee is also a fiduciary and agent of his or her broker, because the license has a written agreement to represent that broker in real estate matters, either as an employee or independent contractor.

Limited agent. If a real estate licensee is engaged as an agent, the licensee serves as a limited agent retained to provide real estate services to a client. The licensee functions as an intermediary in negotiations between the parties to a transaction unless the parties negotiate directly.

A limited agent provides real estate services in which the client's or other party's liability for the actions or statements of an agent, subagent or facilitator is limited to the actions or statements initiated by specific instruction of the client or other party, or those actions or statements of which the client or other party had knowledge. The agent is "limited" because he or she performs only certain real estate activities for the client.

It is important to note that per Tennessee agency law the consumer has limited vicarious liability for the actions, statements or misrepresentations by a licensee (facilitator, subagent, or agent). The client or other party for whom the licensee provides services is not liable for damages for the misrepresentations of the licensee arising out of the licensee's services unless that party knew or had reason to know of the misrepresentation. This does not limit the liability of a licensee's managing broker for the misrepresentations of the licensee (TCA 62-13-407).

GENERAL DUTIES

Real estate licensee engaged as an agent owes all parties to a transaction certain duties, and specifically owes his or her client additional duties.

Licensees must present all written offers and counter-offers in a timely manner.

Real estate licensees are not qualified to provide any legal advice, assist or advise someone on how to terminate a contract, or draft contracts, clauses or riders/addenda.

In the absence of any law to the contrary, the duties to all parties and duties to clients supersede any fiduciary or common law duties.

It is important that licensees clearly understand and differentiate between duties owed to all parties, including the customer who may be represented by another licensee, and those duties owed to the licensee's client. The licensee must always remember which hat he or she is wearing – either serving as an agent, subagent, dual agent or facilitator.

Duty owed to all parties (TCA 62-13-403). A licensee providing real estate services in a real estate transaction owes to all parties to the transaction certain duties. The licensee must

- diligently exercise reasonable skill and care in providing services to all parties to the transaction

- disclose to each party any adverse facts of which the licensee has actual notice or knowledge

- maintain for each party to a transaction the confidentiality of any information obtained by a licensee prior to disclosure to all parties of a written agency or subagency agreement the licensee has entered into to represent either or both parties in a transaction

  - the duty of confidentiality includes any information the party would reasonably expect to be held in confidence, other than information the party has authorized for disclosure and information required to be disclosed

  - this duty survives (extends beyond) the subsequent establishment of an agency relationship and the closing of the transaction

  - this means the agent must keep confidential information after the listing or buyer agency agreement has expired

- provide services to each party with honesty and good faith;

- disclose to each party timely and accurate information regarding market conditions that might affect the transaction only when the information is available through public records and is requested by a party

- timely account for trust fund deposits and all other property received from any party to the transaction

The licensee must NOT

- engage in self-dealing nor act on behalf of licensee's immediate family or on behalf of any individual, organization or business entity in which the licensee has a personal interest without making prior disclosure of the interest and obtaining timely written consent of all parties

- recommend to any party to the transaction the use of services of another individual, organization or business entity in which the licensee has an interest or from whom the licensee may receive a referral fee or other compensation for the referral without timely disclosing to the party who receives the referral the licensee's interest in the referral or the fact that a referral fee may be received; this requirement does not include referrals to other licensees to provide real estate services

A licensee is prohibited from sharing any confidential information that a consumer shares with the licensee prior to the licensee disclosing an agency relationship with the other party.

Duties owed to the client (TCA 62-13-404). A licensee who acts as an agent in a real estate transaction owes to the licensee's client in that transaction the following duties:

- obey all lawful instructions of the client when the instructions are within the scope of the agency agreement between the licensee and client

- be loyal to the interests of the client; a licensee must place the interests of the client before all others in negotiations and other real estate activities, unless the duty would violate duties to a customer or duties to another client in a dual agency

The following duties are also owed to the client by the agent unless specifically and individually waived in writing by the client:

- schedule all property showings on behalf of the client

- receive all offers and counter offers and forward them promptly to the client

- answer any questions that the client may have in negotiating a purchase agreement within the scope of the licensee's expertise

- advise the client as to forms, procedures and steps needed after execution of the agreement for a successful closing of the transaction

Upon waiver of any of these duties, the consumer must be advised in writing by the agent that the consumer may not expect or seek assistance from any other licensees in the transaction for the performance of these duties.

Waiver of some of the agent's duties is a way of "unbundling" brokerage services, and brokers may assign a fee to each of the services. The broker may have a policy permitting or prohibiting the unbundling of services offered by the firm.

DESIGNATED AGENTS AND FACILITATORS

Designated agent. In the absence of designated agency, all licensees in the brokerage company represent clients of the firm. Designated agency creates an agency relationship between the agent and the client only, excluding other licensees in the firm. However, the broker remains the owner of the listing and remains liable for actions of the agent.

A licensee who is entering into a written agreement to represent any party in the buying, selling, exchanging, renting or leasing of real estate may be appointed as the designated agent of that party by the licensee's managing broker. In making this appointment, the broker has excluded all other licensees employed by or affiliated with the managing broker from representing that party. A managing broker providing services in this situation will not be considered a dual agent if any individual licensee appointed as designated agent in a transaction, by either specific appointment or by written company policy, does not represent the interests of any other party to the same transaction.

The use of designated agency does not in any way abolish or diminish the managing broker's contractual rights to any listing or advertising agreement between the firm and a property owner, nor does it lessen the managing broker's responsibilities to ensure that all licensees affiliated with or employed by the broker conduct business in compliance with appropriate laws, rules and regulations.

Imputation of knowledge. There is no imputation of knowledge or information among or between clients, the managing broker and any designated agent or agents in a designated agency situation. As an example, there is no legal assumption that the broker or clients have knowledge of information regarding the transaction of which the designated agent has knowledge.

Facilitator. A facilitator is any licensee who

- assists one or more parties to a transaction who has not entered into a specific written agency agreement representing one or more of the parties, or
- has a specific written agency agreement providing that if the licensee or someone associated with the licensee also represents another party to the same transaction, the licensee will be deemed to be a facilitator and not a dual agent, provided that notice of assumption of facilitator status is provided to the buyer and seller immediately upon the assumption of facilitator status
    - this notice must be confirmed in writing prior to execution of the contract

A facilitator may advise either or both parties to a transaction but cannot be considered a representative or advocate of either party. "Transaction broker" may be used synonymously with, or in lieu of, "facilitator" in any disclosures, forms or agreements used in transactions.

To recap, a facilitator is a non-agent and represents neither party to the transaction. Sometimes "transaction broker" is used synonymously with "facilitator", and either term may be used in disclosures and agreements.

Serving as a facilitator rather than an agent in no way lessens the ability of the licensee to receive a commission. Compensation and agency are not related.

Agent or facilitator, not both. A licensee cannot legally serve as an agent to one party and a facilitator to the other party. A licensee can have only one representation status at a time in any transaction. The seller's agent may assist the buyer by preparing an offer to be presented to the seller, if the licensee ensures that the buyer is informed that the licensee represents the seller and owes duties to the seller, including promoting the best interest of that seller.

SUBAGENCY

Although still legally permitted in Tennessee, subagency is rarely used in today's real estate climate. Subagency is a client relationship between the listing licensee and other licenses who work with the other party to the transaction. The subagent represents the listed party through the listing broker and owes all agency duties to that party.

DUAL AGENCY

Dual agency, that is, one licensee representing both parties to the transaction, is legal in Tennessee, but it is not commonly practiced. Dual agency must be disclosed in writing and consented to by both parties. Dual agency has the potential for added legal liability for the agent and the firm.

If the licensee is a dual agent and one of the clients is a family member, close friend, or long-time client, it becomes very difficult for that agent to act impartially in the transaction.

The managing broker is not considered a dual agent if an individual licensee appointed as designated agent in a transaction does not represent interests of any other party to the transaction. So, if the buyer and seller are each represented by different licensees in the brokerage office, the broker is not a dual agent.

II. Agency Disclosures

VERBAL DISCLOSURE

If a licensee personally assists a prospective buyer or seller in the purchase or sale of real property and that party is not represented by that or any other licensee, the licensee must verbally disclose the licensee's facilitator, agent, subagent or designated agent status in the transaction before providing any real estate services (TCA 62-13-405).

WRITTEN DISCLOSURE

The disclosure of agency status must be confirmed in writing with an unrepresented buyer prior to the preparation of an offer to purchase. A specific form is not required by the Commission.

The disclosure of agency status must be confirmed in writing with an unrepresented seller prior to execution of a listing agreement or presentation of an offer to purchase, whichever comes first.

After delivery of the written disclosure to an unrepresented buyer or seller, the licensee is required to obtain a signed receipt for the disclosure from the party to whom disclosure was made. The receipt must contain a statement acknowledging that the buyer or seller was informed that any complaints alleging any violation of license law must be filed within the applicable statute of limitations set by law, and acknowledgment must include the address and telephone number of the Commission.

Disclosure of agency or facilitator status is not a substitute for a written agreement to establish an agency relationship between the broker and a party to a transaction.

Upon initial contact with any other licensee involved in the same prospective transaction, the licensee must immediately disclose the licensee's role in the transaction, including any agency relationship.

CHANGE OF AGENCY STATUS

If the licensee's role changes, the licensee must immediately notify any other licensees and any parties to the transaction of the change in status. As an example, a listing agent may be contacted by an unrepresented buyer who is interested in the agent's listing. A brokerage company may have a policy requiring the licensees to declare themselves a facilitator in this scenario, in which case the permission may be granted in the listing document. The licensee would then provide written notice back to the seller or buyer previously represented that he or she is now acting as a facilitator and not an agent.

These agency regulations do not apply to real estate transactions involving the transfer or lease of commercial properties, the transfer of property by public auction, the transfer of residential properties of more than four (4) units, or the lease or rental of residential properties.

RECAP OF AGENCY DISCLOSURE

The following chart recaps agency disclosure requirements.

	To whom	When
Initial disclosure	client and unrepresented buyer	before providing any real estate services
	another licensee	initial contact
Written disclosure	unrepresented buyer and receipt obtained	before preparing offer
	unrepresented seller and receipt obtained	listing execution or offer presentation, whichever first
	buyer client	on exclusive buyer agency agreement
	seller client	On exclusive listing
Change of status	Client, unrepresented party, another licensee	immediately

DISCLOSURE OF LICENSEE INTEREST

If a licensee recommends to any party to the transaction the use of services of another individual or service provider in which the licensee has an interest or from whom the licensee may receive a referral fee or other compensation for the referral, the licensee must timely disclose to the party receiving the referral the licensee's interest in the referral or the fact that a referral fee may be received. This disclosure requirement does not apply to referrals to other licensees to provide real estate services. (TCA 62-13-307)

A licensee may not engage in a real estate transaction for himself or herself, act on behalf of licensee's immediate family or act on behalf of another individual, organization or business entity in which the licensee has a personal interest without disclosing the interest and obtaining prior timely written consent of all parties to the transaction.

LICENSEE COMMISSIONS

The main item of performance for the client is payment of compensation, if the agreement calls for it. A broker's compensation is earned and payable when the broker has performed according to the agreement. The amount and structure of the compensation, potential disputes over who has earned compensation, and the client's liability for multiple commissions are other matters that a listing agreement should address.

Negotiated compensation. The amount of a broker's commission is whatever amount the client and broker have agreed to. Compensation may be in the form of a percentage of the sale or lease price, or a flat fee. In practice, commissions vary for different geographical areas, types of property and transaction, and services performed.

Procuring cause. Disputes often arise as to whether an agent is owed a commission. Many such disputes involve open listings where numerous agents are working to find customers for the principal, and none has a clear claim on a commission. In other cases, a client may claim to have found the customer alone and therefore to have no responsibility for paying a commission. There are also situations where cooperating brokers and subagents working under an exclusive listing dispute about which one(s) deserve a share of the listing broker's commission.

The concept that decides such disputes is that the party who was the "procuring cause" in finding the customer is entitled to the commission or commission share. The two principal determinants of procuring cause are:

- being first to find the customer
- being the one who induces the customer to complete the transaction

For example, Broker A and Broker B each have an open listing with a property owner. Broker A shows Joe the property on Monday. Broker B shows Joe the same property on Friday, and then Joe buys the property. Broker A will probably be deemed to be the procuring cause by virtue of having first introduced Joe to the property.

Compensation for buyer brokers. Buyer agency agreements stipulate how the agent will be compensated in the relationship. The compensation may be a client-paid retainer fee or a commission contingent upon a completed transaction or procured seller. It is common practice for the agent to be paid by the customer to the transaction, the seller, as opposed to the fiduciary principal, the buyer or tenant. In addition, the agent may be paid by the buyer in the event that the seller or listing agent refuses to offer any compensation to the buyer broker. This might occur, for example, in the case of a for-sale-by-owner transaction.

In addition to the form of compensation and the parties responsible for paying the agent, the buyer agency agreement defines when the compensation is in fact earned and will be paid. Customarily, the commission is earned when a sales contract is completed by the transacting parties. The agent may be entitled to compensation even if the buyer defaults on the terms of the sales contract. Normally, agents are paid at closing or upon the buyer's default.

III. Seller and Buyer Listing Agreements

Real estate licensee engaged as an agent owes all parties to a transaction certain duties, and specifically owes his or her client additional duties.

Licensees must present all written offers and counter-offers in a timely manner.

Real estate licensees are not qualified to provide any legal advice, assist or advise someone on how to terminate a contract, or draft contracts, clauses or riders/addenda.

In the absence of any law to the contrary, the duties to all parties and duties to clients supersede any fiduciary or common law duties.

It is important that licensees clearly understand and differentiate between duties owed to all parties, including the customer who may be represented by another licensee, and those duties owed to the licensee's client. The licensee must always remember which hat he or she is wearing – either serving as an agent, subagent, dual agent or facilitator.

LISTING AGREEMENT

Listing agreements and buyer agency agreements are contracts, and as such, must have all the legal requirements of any contract.

An agency contract is a valid written contract authorizing a real estate licensee to act as a party's exclusive agent for the purchase, sale or lease of real estate. An agency relationship is the relationship resulting from an agency contract.

As indicated previously, in Tennessee agency can be created only with a written agreement. It cannot be implied or created orally.

Listing and buyer agency agreements are in the name of, and belong to, the broker. They are employment contracts in which the seller or buyer "employs" the broker. Affiliate brokers may not enter into binding contracts with consumers; only the broker may do so. However, affiliate brokers may obtain listings and sell property on behalf of their broker.

A broker may represent any principal party of a transaction: seller, landlord, buyer, tenant. An **owner listing** authorizes a broker to represent an owner or landlord. There are three main types of owner listing agreement: *exclusive right-to-sell* (or lease); *exclusive agency;* and *open listing*. Another type of listing, rarely used today, is a *net listing*. The first three forms differ in their statement of conditions under which the broker will be paid. The net listing is a variation on how much the broker will be paid

Types of listing agreements

Types of Listing

Exclusive Right	$ ➡ Broker	IF customer is procured
Exclusive Agency	$ ➡ Broker	IF customer is procured and client does not procure
Open	$ ➡ Broker	IF broker procures customer
Net	$ ➡ Broker	IF customer is due commission, receives proceeds over seller's minimum
"Multiple Listing"	$ ➡ Broker	Authority to enter listing in multiple listing service

Exclusive right-to-sell listing

The exclusive right-to-sell, also called exclusive authorization-to-sell and, simply, the exclusive, is the most widely used owner agreement. Under the terms of this listing, a seller contracts exclusively with a single broker to procure a buyer or effect a sale transaction. If a buyer is procured during the listing period, the broker is entitled to a commission, *regardless of who is procuring cause*. Thus, if anyone--¬the owner, another broker-- sells the property, the owner must pay the listing broker the contracted commission.

The exclusive right-to-lease is a similar contract for a leasing transaction. Under the terms of this listing, the owner or landlord must pay the listing broker a commission if anyone procures a tenant for the named premises. The exclusive listing gives the listing broker the greatest assurance of receiving compensation for marketing efforts.

Exclusive agency

 An exclusive agency listing authorizes a single broker to sell the property and earn a commission, but leaves the owner the right to sell the property without the broker's assistance, in which case no commission is owed. Thus, if any party other than the owner is procuring cause in a completed sale of the property, including another broker, the contracted broker has earned the commission. This arrangement may also be used in a leasing transaction: if any party other than the owner procures the tenant, the owner must compensate the listing broker.

An exclusive agency listing generally must have an expiration date. Most states allow either an oral or written agreement.

Open listing

An open listing, or, simply, open, is a non-exclusive authorization to sell or lease a property. The owner may offer such agreements to any number of brokers in the marketplace. With an open listing, the broker who is the first to perform under the terms of the listing is the sole party entitled to a commission.

Performance usually consists of being the procuring cause in the finding of a ready, willing, and able customer. If the transaction occurs without a procuring broker, no commissions are payable.

Open listings are rare in residential brokerage. Brokers generally shy away from them because they offer no assurance of compensation for marketing efforts. In addition, open listings cause commission disputes. To avoid such disputes, a broker has to register prospects with the owner to provide evidence of procuring cause in case a transaction results. An open listing may be oral or written.

Net listing

A net listing is one in which an owner sets a minimum acceptable amount to be received from the transaction and allows the broker to have any amount received in excess as a commission, assuming the broker has earned a commission according to the other terms of the agreement. The owner's "net" may or may not account for closing costs.

For example, a seller requires $75,000 for a property. A broker sells the property for $83,000 and receives the difference, $8,000, as commission.

Net listings are generally regarded as unprofessional today, and many states have outlawed them. The argument against the net listing is that it creates a conflict of interest for the broker. It is in the broker's interest to encourage the owner to put the lowest possible acceptable price in the listing, regardless of market value. Thus the agent violates fiduciary duty by failing to place the client's interests above those of the agent.

BUYER AGENCY AGREEMENT

An exclusive buyer representation agreement is an agreement in which a licensee is engaged to represent a buyer in the purchase of a property to the exclusion of all other licensees. In effect, the licensee is "listing" the buyer. As indicated, it must be in writing and signed by the parties. It creates an agency relationship. When entering into the agreement, a licensee must advise and confirm in writing to the buyer

- that the buyer should make all arrangements to view or inspect a property through the licensee and should not directly contact other licensees
- that the buyer should immediately inform any other licensee the buyer may come into contact with (for example, at an open house) that he or she is represented by the licensee
- whether the buyer will owe a commission in the event the buyer purchases a property without the assistance of the licensee through another licensee or directly from an owner

A copy must be provided to the buyer at the time the signature is obtained.

Buyer agents may be paid by the buyer, by the seller, or both. As always, any compensation is paid directly to the broker.

Buyer and tenant agency agreements create a fiduciary relationship with the buyer or tenant just as seller listings create a fiduciary relationship with the seller. Generally, buyer and tenant representation agreements are subject to the same laws and regulations as those applying to owner listings.

Duties of the agent. At the formation of the relationship, the buyer agent has the duty to explain how buyer or tenant agency relationships work. This is culminated by a signed agreement where the principal understands and accepts these circumstances. During the listing term, the buyer or tenant agent's principal duties are to diligently locate a property that meets the principal's requirements. In addition, the agent must comply with his or her state agency-disclosure laws which may differ from those of traditional listing agents. This involves timely disclosures to prospective sellers and their agents, usually upon initial contact

Transaction broker agreement

In terms of agency, a transaction broker is in a non-agency relationship with the seller or buyer. The agent is not bound by fiduciary duties to either party. Nevertheless, transaction brokers enter into binding agreements with buyers and sellers to complete transactions. Such agreements may be exclusive or non-exclusive. Like conventional listings, the transaction brokerage agreement binds the principal to a compensation agreement in the event the broker procures a property or a buyer. Typical agreements affirm the nature of the relationship, contain expiration dates, and describe the terms of the agreement, such as the type of property desired or the price a seller deems acceptable.

Handling offers

Presenting offers. When participating in a transaction, each licensee must always be cognizant of whether he or she is acting as a facilitator or in an agency capacity. If acting as a designated agent, the licensee must keep in mind that no other licensee, even those within his or her firm, represent that client.

All offers must be presented promptly, per license law, until a contract is signed by all parties. Upon obtaining acceptance of an offer or counter offer, the broker or affiliate broker must promptly deliver true executed copies, signed by both parties, to the purchaser and seller.

Brokers and affiliate brokers must verify that all the terms and conditions of the transaction are included in the purchase contract.

If an offer is rejected, the licensee receiving offers must request the seller to note the rejection on the offer and return it to the offeror or the offeror's agent.

If an offer is accepted and signed by all parties, copies must be distributed to each of the parties and to each brokerage firm involved in the transaction. After acceptance, the licensee will follow up on transaction progress, verifying that financing, title work and inspections are in process and by keeping the client informed.

FULFILLMENT AND TERMINATION OF THE LISTING

A listing agreement may terminate in many ways. The only desirable and favorable way is by fulfillment of the contract. Fulfillment results when both parties have performed the actions they have promised to perform

Agent's performance

An agent performs a listing agreement by achieving the result specified in the agreement. When and if the result is achieved, the agent's performance is complete.

Find a customer or effect a transaction. A listing generally specifies the result to be either finding a customer or effecting a completed transaction.

Finding a customer means locating a party who is ready, willing, and able to transact under the client's terms. Effecting a completed transaction means finding a customer who is not only ready, willing, and able, but one who makes an acceptable offer.

A ready, willing, and able customer is one who is:

- amenable to the terms of the transaction (ready and willing)
- financially capable of paying the price and legally capable of completing the transaction (able)

Specific responsibilities. A listing agreement authorizes a broker to undertake actions relevant to achieving the performance objective. Authorized activities usually include the following:

- show or seek property
- locate buyer, seller, tenant, or landlord
- communicate the client's transaction terms
- promote features and advantages of the terms to customers
- assist in negotiating a meeting of the minds between parties

Due diligence. Due diligence in the listing context refers to verifying the accuracy of the statements in the listing regarding the property, the owner, and the owner's representations. Especially important facts for a broker or agent to verify are:

- the property condition
- ownership status
- the client's authority to act

Failure to perform a reasonable degree of due diligence may increase an agent's exposure to liability in the event that the property is not as represented or that the client cannot perform as promised.

Delegation of responsibilities. In the normal course of business, a listing broker delegates marketing responsibilities to affiliates. An affiliate may not, however, seek compensation directly from a client. Only the broker can obtain and disburse the compensation.

Causes for termination

A listing may terminate on grounds of:

- performance: all parties perform; the intended outcome
- infeasibility: it is not possible to perform under the terms of the agreement
- mutual agreement: both parties agree to cancel the listing
- revocation: either party cancels the listing, with or without the right
- abandonment: the broker does not attempt to perform
- breach: the terms of the listing are violated
- lapse of time: the listing expires
- invalidity of contract: the listing does not meet the criteria for validity
- incapacitation or death of either party
- involuntary title transfer: condemnation, bankruptcy, foreclosure
- destruction of the property

Listing expiration. In most states, open listings do not require a stated expiration date. Rather, they expire after a "reasonable" period of time as locally defined.

The other types of listing generally must specify a termination date and may not have an automatic renewal mechanism. Courts in many states construe any listing that has no expiration as an open listing.

MODULE 2 SNAPSHOT REVIEW:

AGENCY

TENNESSEE AGENCY LAWS

Creation of relationships
- licensees may work with or without an agency relationship; creation of agency requires a written agency agreement
- real estate agents are limited agents to provide specific services
- licensees have general duties to all parties, additional duties to clients; client may waive specific duties

General duties
- to all parties: reasonable care and skill; disclosure of known adverse facts; confidentiality; honesty and good faith; market non-proprietary information on request; accounting; no self-dealing; disclosure of interest in referral; receive and present all written offers and counter-offers promptly
- to a client, the above, plus: obey lawful instructions; loyalty; show properties; answer negotiating questions; advise on forms and procedures

Designated agents and facilitators
- designated agent is only company representative of client; broker has contractual right to listings and buyer agency agreements
- facilitator assists one or more parties who do not have agency agreements; may advise but is not a representative or advocate of the parties
- in a single transaction, licensee is facilitator or agent, but not both

Subagency
- legal, but seldom used; subagent represents listing party through the listing broker

Dual agency
- dual agent represents both parties to the transaction; has potential for added liability; ust have written consent of both parties to act as dual agent

AGENCY DISCLOSURES

Verbal disclosure
- initial disclosure prior to providing service to any party; disclosure to other licensee at initial contact

Written disclosure
- written confirmation to unrepresented buyer prior to offer preparation, to unrepresented seller prior to execution of listing or presentation of offer, whichever is first
- written confirmation to buyer client with exclusive buyer agency agreement; written confirmation to seller client with exclusive listing agreement

Change of status
- change of licensee status given to all parties and other licensee immediately

DISCLOSURE OF LICENSEE INTEREST

- licensee must disclose to referred party any interest in service provider referred to client, or referral fee received by licensee other than from other licensees for real estate services
- licensee must disclose when engaging in real estate transaction for self, for entity in which licensee has an interest, or for immediate family members

LICENSEE COMMISSIONS
- commission earned upon performance of agreement's provisions
- negotiated commission: rate of compensation is negotiated between licensee and principal
- procuring cause: determines who gets paid; defined by being first to find customer and induce such party to transact

SELLER AND BUYER LISTING AGREEMENTS
- agreements trigger transaction duties for the licensee
- licensee must present all offers
- licensees must not give legal advice or interpret meaning of contract provisions

LISTING AGREEMENT
- listings are contracts that must meet contract validity tests; listings create agency relationships
- TN agency only created by written agreement; cannot be implied or oral.
- listings belong to the broker; affiliate brokers and salespersons cannot enter into listing agreement.
- **Seller listings** – exclusives; exclusive agency ; open listing
- **Buyer agency agreements** - exclusive buyer agency agreement creates agency relationship with buyer, excluding all other licensees; because agency and payment of commission are not related, buyer's agent may be paid by buyer or seller through broker
- **Transaction broker agreement** – non-agency agreement with seller or buyer; licensee not bound to fiduciary duties; agreement identifies duties, terms, effective period
- Handling offers – must present promptly; licensees must verify completeness of terms; if accepted, licensee must distribute copies to all parties

FULFILLMENT AND TERMINATION
- Licensee must perform to the terms of the listing; find customer who is ready willing and able
- Specific duties: showings; locate customer; communicate terms; promote property; negotiate meeting of the minds

Termination causes
- performance; infeasibility; mutual agreement; revocation; abandonment; breach; expiration; invalidity of contract; death or incapacitation of either party; bankruptcy; destruction of property

MODULE 2 - AGENCY

QUIZ

Carefully read each question and provide your best answer based on what you learned in this module. Then check your answers against the Answer Key which immediately follows the quiz questions.

1. If a licensee is engaged as an agent, the licensee serves as a _____.

   a. limited agent.
   b. dual agent.
   c. single agent.
   d. double agent.

2. Which concept decides which party is owed a commission if there are numerous agents working with a customer?

   a. First come first serve
   b. Procuring cause
   c. Entitlement process
   d. Transaction origination

3. When one licensee represents both parties to the transaction, the licensee is considered a _____.

   a. subagent.
   b. double agent.
   c. single agent.
   d. dual agent.

4. Which type of transactions do agency disclosure regulations NOT apply to?

   a. Purchase of a previously-occupied residential property
   b. Lease of a residential home
   c. Sale of a commercial property
   d. Lease of a condominium

5. The three main types of owner listing agreements are exclusive right-to-sell; exclusive agency; and _____.

   a. open listing.
   b. net listing.
   c. broker listing.
   d. gross listing.

6. A licensee must _____.

   a. disclose to each party any adverse facts.
   b. act on behalf of the licensee's immediate family without making a prior disclosure.
   c. recommend a vendor to a buyer, even if the licensee has a personal interest in the vendor.
   d. share the consumer's confidential information with the other party.

7. A seller requires $275,000 for a property. A broker sells the property for $283,000 and receives the difference, $8,000, as commission. What type of listing agreement allows this?

    a. Open listing
    b. Net listing
    c. Right-to-sell agreement
    d. Exclusive agency agreement

8. The most widely used listing agreement is called the _____.

    a. exclusive right-to-sell listing agreement.
    b. net listing agreement.
    c. selling agreement.
    d. authorization-to-buy agreement.

9. A licensee may work as an agent of an individual or serve as a(n) _____.

    a. facilitator.
    b. assumed agent.
    c. limited agent.
    d. general licensee.

10. What is a common instance where compensation for buyer brokers is paid by the buyer?

    a. In a regular listing
    b. In a foreclosure transaction
    c. In the case of a for-sale-by-owner transaction
    d. In a short-sale deal

11. When must a licensee disclose his or her agent status to a prospective buyer?

    a. The licensee must verbally disclose his or her status before providing any real estate services.
    b. The licensee has 5 days to provide the disclosure.
    c. The licensee must provide a written disclosure when the buyer goes under contract.
    d. The licensee has until closing day to provide a written disclosure.

12. An agent is not bound by fiduciary duties to either party in a(n) _____.

    a. buyer agency agreement.
    b. exclusive buyer brokerage agreement.
    c. right-to-buy agreement.
    d. transaction broker agreement.

13. What is the name of an agency relationship between the agent and the client only (excluding all other licensees at the firm)?

    a. Exclusive agency
    b. Designated agency
    c. Private listing agreement
    d. Dual agency

14. Which listing type authorizes a single broker to sell the property and earn a commission, but leaves the owner the right to sell the property without the broker's assistance?

    a. Right-to-sell listing
    b. Exclusive agency
    c. Net listing
    d. Open listing

15. What is the main item of performance for the client in a transaction?

    a. Executing the closing day paperwork
    b. Writing the contract
    c. Signing of the listing agreement
    d. Payment of compensation

16. What is the name of the client relationship between the listing licensee and other licensees who work with the other party to the transaction?

    a. Dual agency
    b. Listing agency
    c. Subagency
    d. Managing agency

17. Which listing agreement allows an owner to set a minimum acceptable amount to be received from the transaction and allows the broker to have any amount received in excess as a commission?

    a. Net listing
    b. Gross commission
    c. Excess listing
    d. Exclusive listing

18. Agency can only be accomplished with a _____.

    a. unilateral, verbal agreement.
    b. bilateral, signed agreement.
    c. unilateral, signed agreement.
    d. bilateral, verbal agreement.

19. How long does a licensee have to notify other licensees if his or her role changes?

    a. The licensee has 5 days to notify the other licensees.
    b. The licensee has until the closing day to notify all parties.
    c. The licensee has 30 days to notify the other licensees in the transaction.
    d. The licensee must notify all parties immediately

20. A _____ may advise either or both parties to a transaction but cannot be considered a representative of either party.

    a. dual agent
    b. listing agent
    c. double agent
    d. facilitator

MODULE 2 – AGENCY

ANSWER KEY TO QUIZ

1. a. limited agent.
2. b. Procuring cause
3. d. dual agent.
4. c. Sale of a commercial property
5. a. open listing.
6. a. disclose to each party any adverse facts.
7. b. Net listing
8. a. exclusive right-to-sell listing agreement.
9. a. facilitator.
10. c. In the case of a for-sale-by-owner transaction
11. a. The licensee must verbally disclose his or her status before providing any real estate services.
12. d. transaction broker agreement.
13. b. Designated agency
14. b. Exclusive agency
15. d. Payment of compensation
16. c. Subagency
17. a. Net listing
18. b. bilateral, signed agreement.
19. d. The licensee must notify all parties immediately.
20. d. facilitator

MODULE 2: AGENCY

CHECK YOUR UNDERSTANDING

Instructions:

Carefully read each challenge question, then provide your best answer based on what you learned in this module. Then check your answers against the Answer Key which immediately follows the questions.

1. A facilitator is any licensee who assists one or more parties to a transaction and has not entered into a specific agency agreement representing one of the parties. True or False?

2. List three services a real estate licensee is not qualified to provide to clients.

   1. _____

   2. _____

   3. _____

3. If a licensee personally assists a prospective buyer in the purchase of real property, the licensee must provide a written disclosure of his or her status in the transaction. True or False?

4. List four transaction types where agency disclosure regulations do not apply.

   1. _____

   2. _____

   3. _____

   4. _____

5. In a dispute where numerous agents are helping a customer, the concept that decides which agent is owed commission is called _____.

   A. procuring cause.
   B. negotiated compensation.
   C. commission mediation.
   D. compensation arbitration.

6. List the three most common types of listing agreements.

   1. _____

   2. _____

   3. _____

MODULE 2: AGENCY

CHECK YOUR UNDERSTANDING ANSWER KEY

1. A facilitator is any licensee who assists one or more parties to a transaction and has not entered into a specific agency agreement representing one of the parties.

   True

2. List three services a licensee is not qualified to provide to clients.

   1. Drafting contracts

   2. Writing addenda

   3. Legal advice

3. If a licensee personally assists a prospective buyer in the purchase of real property, the licensee must provide a written disclosure of his or her status in the transaction.

   False

4. List four transaction types where agency disclosure regulations do not apply.

   1. Commercial lease

   2. Public auction

   3. Transfer of residential property with four or more units

   4. Rental of residential properties

5. In a dispute where numerous agents are helping a customer, the concept that decides which agent is owed commission is called _____.

   A. **procuring cause.**

6. List the three most common types of listing agreements.

   1. Exclusive agency

   2. Open listing

   3. Exclusive right-to-sell listing

Module 3: CONTRACTS

I.   Contract Law
II. Contracts for Sale
III. Option-to-Buy Contracts
IV. Contracts for Deed

Module 3 Learning Objectives

Contract Law

1. Identify the characteristics that make contracts valid and enforceable as well as void versus voidable.
2. Define the differences between offers and contracts and the key factors involved in accepting versus countering an offer.
3. Distinguish between oral v written contracts; express v implied contracts; bilateral v unilateral contracts and an executory v executed contract
4. Describe the criteria for legally terminating a contract

Contracts for Sale

1. Describe how an earnest money escrow and a contingency affect the fulfillment of the sale contract.

2. Highlight the salient characteristics of Tennessee contract law as they relate to offering and acceptance

3. Characterize the salient provisions of a Tennessee sale contract.

Option-to-Buy Contracts

1. Differentiate between offeror and offeree

2. Summarize the criteria that must be present to constitute a valid option

Contracts for Deed

1. Identify the essential purposes and operating mechanics of a contract for deed.

2. Describe the rights and obligations of the vendee and vendor in a contract for deed

3. Summarize the principal risks involved in entering into a contract for deed transaction

I. Contract Law

Real estate contracts are the legal agreements that underlie the transfer and financing of real estate, as well as the real estate brokerage business. Sale and lease contracts and option agreements are used to transfer real estate interests from one party to another. Mortgage contracts and promissory agreements are part of financing real estate. Listing and representation contracts establish client relationships and provide for compensation.

In order to work with real estate contracts, it is imperative first to grasp basic concepts that apply to all contracts in general. These concepts provide a foundation for understanding the specifics of particular types of real estate contract.

CONTRACT VALIDITY AND ENFORCEABILITY

A contract is an agreement between two or more parties who, in a "meeting of the minds," have pledged to perform or refrain from performing some act. A *valid* contract is one that is *legally enforceable* by virtue of meeting certain requirements of contract law. If a contract does not meet the requirements, it is not valid and the parties to it cannot resort to a court of law to enforce its provisions.

Note that a contract is not a legal form or a prescribed set of words in a document, but rather the intangible agreement that was made in "the meeting of the minds" of the parties to the contract.

Real estate contracts are the legal agreements that underlie the transfer and financing of real estate, as well as the real estate brokerage business. Sale and lease contracts and option agreements are used to transfer real estate interests from one party to another. Mortgage contracts and promissory agreements are part of financing real estate. Listing and representation contracts establish client relationships and provide for compensation.

In order to work with real estate contracts, it is imperative first to grasp basic concepts that apply to all contracts in general. These concepts provide a foundation for understanding the specifics of particular types of real estate contract.

A contract is an agreement between two or more parties who, in a "meeting of the minds," have pledged to perform or refrain from performing some act. A valid contract is one that is legally enforceable by virtue of meeting certain requirements of contract law.

If a contract does not meet the requirements, it is not valid and the parties to it cannot resort to a court of law to enforce its provisions.

Note that a contract is not a legal form or a prescribed set of words in a document, but rather the intangible agreement that was made in "the meeting of the minds" of the parties to the contract.

Legal status of contract

In terms of validity and enforceability, a court may construe the legal status of a contract in one of four ways:

- valid
- valid but unenforceable
- void
- voidable

Valid. A valid contract is one which meets the legal requirements for validity. These requirements are explained in the next section.

A valid contract that is in writing is enforceable within a statutory time period. A valid contract that is made orally is also generally enforceable within a statutory period, with the exceptions noted below.

Valid but unenforceable. State laws declare that some contracts are enforceable only if they are in writing. These laws apply in particular to the transfer of interests in real estate. Thus, while an oral contract may meet the tests for validity, if it falls under the laws requiring a written contract, the parties will not have legal recourse to enforce performance. An oral long-term lease and an oral real estate sales contract are examples of contracts that may be valid but not enforceable.

Note that such contracts, if valid, remain so even though not enforceable. This means that if the parties fully execute and perform the contract, the outcome may not be altered.

Void. A void contract is an agreement that does not meet the tests for validity, and therefore is no contract at all. If a contract is void, neither party can enforce it.

For example, a contract that does not include consideration is void. Likewise, a contract to extort money from a business is void. Void contracts and instruments are also described as "null and void."

Voidable. A voidable contract is one which initially appears to be valid, but is subject to rescission by a party to the contract who is deemed to have acted under some kind of disability. Only the party who claims the disability may rescind the legal effect of the contract.

For example, a party who was the victim of duress, coercion, or fraud in creation of a contract, and can prove it, may disaffirm the contract. However, the disaffirmation must occur within a legal time frame for the act of rescission to be valid. Similarly, if the party who has cause to disaffirm the contract elects instead to perform it, the contract is no longer voidable but valid.

A voidable contract differs from a void contract in that the latter does not require an act of disaffirmation to render it unenforceable.

Criteria for validity

A contract is valid only if it meets all of the following criteria.

Exhibit 3.1 Contract Validity Requirements

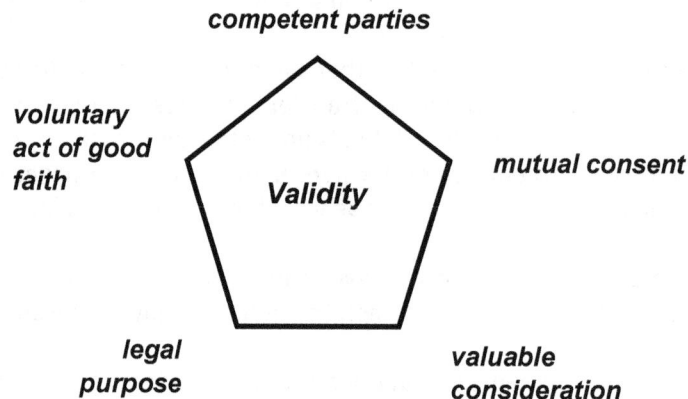

competent parties

voluntary
act of good
faith

Validity

mutual consent

legal
purpose

valuable
consideration

Competent parties. The parties to a contract must have the capacity to contract, and there must be at least two such parties. Thus, the owner of a tenancy for life cannot deed his interest to himself in the form of a fee simple, as this would involve only one party. Capacity to contract is determined by three factors:

- legal age
- mental competency
- legitimate authority

Depending on state law, a contract involving a minor as a party may be either void or voidable. If the law allows a minor to contract, the contract will generally be voidable and the minor can disaffirm the contract.

To be mentally competent, a party must have sufficient understanding of the import and consequences of a contract. Competency in this context is separate and distinct from sanity. Incompetent parties, or parties of "unsound mind," may not enter into enforceable contracts. The incompetency of a party may be ruled by a court of law or by other means. In some areas, convicted felons may be deemed incompetent, depending on the nature of the crime.

During the period of one's incompetency, a court may appoint a guardian who may act on the incompetent party's behalf with court approval.

If the contracting party is representing another person or business entity, the representative must have the *legal authority* to contract. If representing another person, the party must have a bona fide power of attorney. If the contracting party is representing a corporation, the person must have the appropriate power and approval to act, such as would be conferred in a duly executed resolution of the Board of Directors. If the contracting entity is a general partnership, any partner may validly contract for the partnership. In a limited partnership, only general partners may be parties to a contract.

Mutual consent. Mutual consent, also known as *offer and acceptance* and *meeting of the minds,* requires that a contract involve a clear and definite offer and an intentional, unqualified acceptance of the offer. In effect, the parties must agree to the terms without equivocation. A court may nullify a contract where the acceptance of terms by either party was partial, accidental, or vague.

Valuable consideration. A contract must contain a two-way exchange of valuable consideration as compensation for performance by the other party. The exchange of considerations must be two-way. The contract is not valid or enforceable if just one party provides consideration.

Valuable consideration can be something of tangible value, such as money or something a party promises to do or not do. For example, a home builder may promise to build a house for a party as consideration for receiving money from the home buyer. Or, a landowner may agree not to sell a property as consideration for a developer's option money. Also, valuable consideration can be something intangible that a party must give up, such as a homeowner's occupancy of the house in exchange for rent. In effect, consideration is the price one party must pay to obtain performance from the other party.

Valuable consideration may be contrasted with good consideration, or "love and affection," which does not qualify as consideration in a valid contract. Good consideration is something of questionable value, such as a child's love for her mother. Good consideration disqualifies a contract because, while one's love or affection is certainly valuable to the other party, it is not something that is specifically offered in exchange for something else. Good consideration can, however, serve as a nominal consideration in transferring a real property interest as a gift.

In some cases, what is promised as valuable consideration must also be deemed to be *sufficient* consideration. Grossly insufficient consideration, such as $50,000 for a $2 million property, may invalidate a contract on the grounds that the agreement is a gift rather than a contract. In other cases where there is an extreme imbalance in the considerations exchanged, a contract may be invalidated as a violation of good faith bargaining.

Exhibit 3.2 Consideration

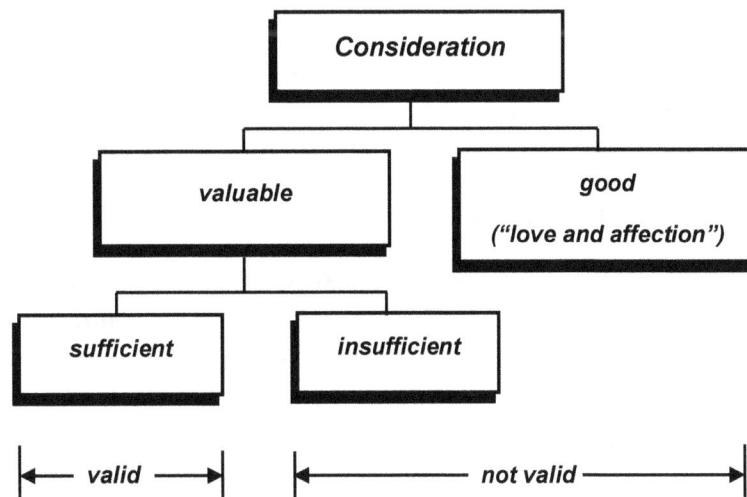

Legal purpose. The content, promise, or intent of a contract must be lawful. A contract that proposes an illegal act is void.

Voluntary, good faith act. The parties must create the contract in good faith as a free and voluntary act. A contract is thus voidable if one party acted under duress, coercion, fraud, or misrepresentation.

For example, if a property seller induces a buyer to purchase a house based on

assurances that the roof is new, the buyer may rescind the agreement if the roof turns out to be twenty years old and leaky.

Validity of a conveyance contract

In addition to satisfying the foregoing requirements, a contract that conveys an interest in real estate must:

- be in writing
- contain a legal description of the property
- be signed by one or more of the parties

A lease contract that has a term of one year or less is an exception. Such leases do not have to be in writing to be enforceable.

Enforcement limitations

Certain contracts that fail to meet the validity requirements are voidable if a damaged party takes appropriate action. The enforcement of voidable contracts, however, is limited by **statutes of limitation.** Certain other contracts which are valid may not be enforceable due to the **statute of frauds**.

Statute of limitations. The statute of limitations restricts the time period for which an injured party in a contract has the right to rescind or disaffirm the contract. A party to a voidable contract must act within the statutory period.

Statute of frauds. The statute of frauds requires that certain contracts *must be in writing* to be enforceable. Real estate contracts that convey an interest in real property fall in this category, with the exception that a lease of one year's duration or less may be oral. All other contracts to buy, sell, exchange, or lease interests in real property must be in writing to be enforceable. In addition, *listing agreements* in most states must be in writing.

The statute of frauds concerns the enforceability of a contract, not its validity. Once the parties to a valid oral contract have executed and performed it, even if the contract was unenforceable, a party cannot use the Statute of Frauds to rescind the contract.

For example, a broker and a seller have an oral agreement. Following the terms of the agreement, the broker finds a buyer, and the seller pays the commission. They have now executed the contract, and the seller cannot later force the broker to return the commission based on the statute of frauds.

Electronic contracting

Contracting electronically through email and fax greatly facilitates the completion of transactions. Clients, lenders, title agents, inspectors, brokers, and other participants in a transaction can quickly share documentation and information. Electronic contracting is made possible by the Uniform Electronic Transactions Act (UETA) and the Electronic Signatures in Global and National Commerce Act (E-Sign), which are federal laws. UETA, which has been accepted in most states, provides that electronic records and signatures are legal and must be accepted. E-Sign makes contracts, records, and signatures legally enforceable, regardless of medium, even where UETA is not accepted.

OFFERS VERSUS CONTRACTS

The mutual consent required for a valid contract is reached through the process of offer and acceptance: The **offeror** proposes contract terms in an **offer** to the **offeree**. If the offeree accepts all terms without amendment, the offer becomes a contract. The exact point at which the offer becomes a contract is when the offeree gives the offeror notice of the acceptance.

CONTRACT DRAFTING

Offer and acceptance

Offer, Counteroffer and Acceptance

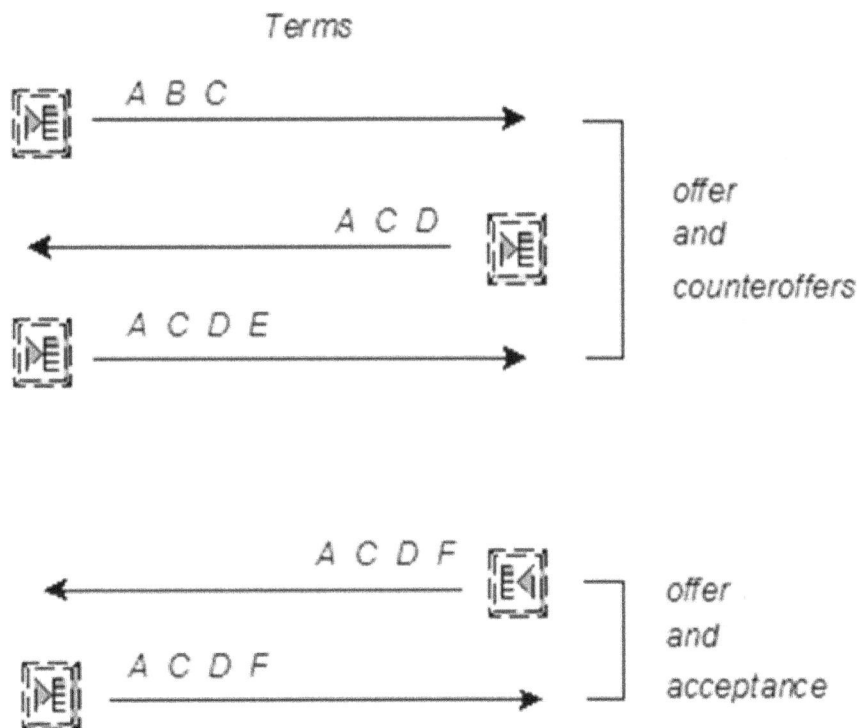

Offer. An offer expresses the offeror's intention to enter into a contract with an offeree to perform the terms of the agreement in exchange for the offeree's performance. In a real estate sale or lease contract, the offer must clearly contain all intended terms of the contract in writing and be communicated to the offeree.

If an offer contains an expiration date and the phrase "time is of the essence," the offer expires at exactly the time specified. In the absence of a stated time period, the offeree has a "reasonable" time to accept an offer.

Acceptance. An offer gives the offeree the power of accepting. For an acceptance to be valid, the offeree must manifestly and unequivocally accept all terms of the offer without change, and so indicate by signing the offer, preferably with a date of signing. The acceptance must then be communicated to the offeror. If the communication of acceptance is by mail, the offer is considered to be communicated as soon as it is placed in the mail.

Counteroffer. By changing any of the terms of an offer, the offeree creates a counteroffer, and the original offer is void. At this point, the offeree becomes the offeror, and the new offeree gains the right of acceptance. If accepted, the counteroffer becomes a valid contract provided all other requirements are met.

For example, a seller changes the expiration date of a buyer's offer by one day, signs the offer and returns it to the buyer. The single amendment extinguishes the buyer's offer, and the buyer is no longer bound by any agreement. The seller's amended offer is a counteroffer which now gives the buyer the right of acceptance. If the buyer accepts the counteroffer, the counteroffer becomes a binding contract

Offer termination. Any of the following actions or circumstances can terminate an offer:

- acceptance: the offeree accepts the offer, converting it to a contract
- rejection: the offeree rejects the offer
- revocation: the offeror withdraws the offer before acceptance
- lapse of time: the offer expires
- counteroffer: the offeree changes the offer
- death or insanity of either party

Assignment of a contract

A real estate contract that is not a personal contract for services can be assigned to another party unless the terms of the agreement specifically prohibit assignment.

Listing agreements, for example, are not assignable, since they are personal service agreements between agent and principal. Sales contracts, however, are assignable, because they involve the purchase of real property rather than a personal service.

Contract preparation

State laws define the extent to which real estate brokers and agents may legally prepare real estate contracts. Such laws, referred to as "broker-lawyer accords," also define what types of contracts brokers and agents may prepare. In some states, brokers and agents may not draft contracts, but they may use standard promulgated forms and complete the blanks in the form.

As a rule, a broker or agent who completes real estate contracts is engaging in the unauthorized practice of law unless the broker is a party to the agreement, such as a in a listing agreement or sales contract. Brokers and agents may not complete leases, mortgages, contracts for deed, or promissory notes to which they are not a party.

Agents must be fully aware of what they are legally allowed to do and not do in preparing and interpreting contracts for clients. In addition to practicing law without a license, agents expose themselves to lawsuits from clients who relied on a contract as being legally acceptable.

CLASSIFICATION OF CONTRACTS

Oral vs. written. A contract may be in writing or it may be an oral, or **parol**, contract. Certain oral contracts are valid and enforceable, others are not enforceable, even if valid. For example, most states require listing agreements, sales contracts, and leases exceeding one year to be in writing to be enforceable.

Express vs. implied. An **express contract** is one in which all the terms and covenants of the agreement have been manifestly stated and agreed to by all parties, whether verbally or in writing.

An **implied contract** is an unstated or unintentional agreement that may be deemed to exist when the *actions of any of the parties* suggest the existence of an agreement.

A common example of an implied contract is an implied agency agreement. In implied agency, an agent who does not have a contract with a buyer performs acts on the buyer's behalf, such as negotiating a price that is less than the listing price. In so doing, the agent has possibly created an implied contract with the buyer, albeit unintended. If the buyer compensates the agent for the negotiating efforts, the existence of an implied agency agreement becomes even less disputable.

Bilateral vs. unilateral. A **bilateral contract** is one in which both parties promise to perform their respective parts of an agreement in exchange for performance by the other party.

An example of a bilateral contract is an exclusive listing: the broker promises to exercise due diligence in the efforts to sell a property, and the seller promises to compensate the broker when and if the property sells.

In a **unilateral contract**, only one party promises to do something, provided the other party does something. The latter party is not obligated to perform any act, but the promising party must fulfill the promise if the other party chooses to perform.

An option is an example of a unilateral contract: in an option-to-buy, the party offering the option (optionor) promises to sell a property if the optionee decides to exercise the option. While the potential buyer does not have to buy, the owner must sell if the option is exercised.

Executed vs. executory. An **executed contract** is one that has been fully performed and fulfilled: neither party bears any further obligation. A completed and expired lease contract is an executed contract: the landlord may re-possess the premises and the tenant has no further obligation to pay rent.

An **executory contract** is one in which performance is yet to be completed. A sales contract prior to closing is executory: while the parties have agreed to buy and sell, the buyer has yet to pay the seller and the seller has yet to deed the property to the buyer.

CONTRACT TERMINATION

Termination of a contract, also called cancellation and discharge, may occur for any of the following causes: performance; infeasibility; mutual agreement; rescission; revocation; abandonment; lapse of time; or invalidity.

Forms of contract termination

Performance. A contract terminates when fully performed by the parties. It may also terminate for:

- partial performance, if the parties agree
- sufficient performance, if a court determines a party has sufficiently performed the contract, even though not to the full extent of every provision

Infeasibility. An otherwise valid contract can be canceled if it is not possible to perform. Certain personal services contracts, for example, depend on the unique capabilities of one person which cannot be substituted by someone else. If such a person dies or is sufficiently disabled, the contract is cancelable.

Mutual agreement. Parties to a contract can agree to terminate, or renounce, the contract. If the parties wish to create a new contract to replace the cancelled contract, they must comply with the validity requirements for the new contract. Such substitution is called novation.

Cooling-period rescission. Rescission is the act of nullifying a contract where parties to certain contracts are allowed a statutory amount of time after entering into a contract, or "cooling period", to rescind the contract without cause. No reason need be stated for the cancellation, and the cancelling party incurs no liability for performance.

For example, consider the unsuspecting buyer of a lot in a new resort development. Such buyers are often the targets of hard-sell tactics which lead to a completed sales contract and a deposit. The statutory cooling period gives the buyer an opportunity to reconsider the investment in the absence of the persistent salesperson.

Revocation. Revocation is cancellation of the contract by one party without the consent of the other. For example, a seller may revoke a listing to take the property off the market. While all parties have the power to revoke, they may not have a defensible right. In the absence of justifiable grounds, a revocation may not relieve the revoking party of contract obligations.

Abandonment. Abandonment occurs when parties fail to perform contract obligations. This situation may allow the parties to cancel the contract.

Lapse of time. If a contract contains an expiration provision and date, the contract automatically expires on the deadline.

Invalidity of contract. If a contract is void, it terminates without the need for disaffirmation. A voidable contract can be cancelled by operation of law or by rescission.

Breach of contract and remedies

A breach of contract is a failure to perform according to the terms of the agreement. Also called default, a breach of contract gives the damaged party the right to take legal action.

The damaged party may elect the following legal remedies:

- rescission
- forfeiture
- suit for damages
- suit for specific performance

Rescission. A damaged party may rescind the contract. This cancels the contract and returns the parties to their pre-contract condition, including the refunding of any monies already transferred.

Forfeiture. A forfeiture requires the breaching party to give up something, according to the terms of the contract. For example, a buyer who defaults on a sales contract may have to forfeit the earnest money deposit.

Suit for damages. A damaged party may sue for money damages in civil court. The suit must be initiated within the time period allowed by the statute of limitations. When a contract states the total amount due to a damaged party in the event of a breach, the compensation is known as liquidated damages. If the contract does not specify the amount, the damaged party may sue in court for unliquidated damages.

Suit for specific performance. A suit for specific performance is an attempt to force the defaulting party to comply with the terms of the contract. Specific performance suits occur when it is difficult to identify damages because of the unique circumstances of the real property in question. The most common instance is a defaulted sale or lease contract where the buyer or seller wants the court to compel the defaulting party to go through with the transaction, even when the defaulter would prefer to pay a damage award.

II. Contracts for Sale

LEGAL CHARACTERISTICS

Overview

A real estate sale contract is a binding and enforceable agreement wherein a buyer, the vendee, agrees to buy an identified parcel of real estate, and a seller, the vendor, agrees to sell it under certain terms and conditions. It is the document that is at the center of the transaction.

The conventional transfer of real estate ownership takes place in three stages. First, there is the negotiating period where buyers and sellers exchange offers in an effort to agree to all transfer terms that will appear in the sale contract. Second, when both parties have accepted all terms, the offer becomes a binding sale contract and the transaction enters the pre-closing stage, during which each party makes arrangements to complete the sale according to the sale contract's terms. Third is the closing of the transaction, when the seller deeds title to the buyer, the buyer pays the purchase price, and all necessary documents are completed. At this stage, the sale contract has served its purpose and terminates.

Other names for the sale contract are *agreement of sale, contract for purchase, contract of purchase and sale, and earnest money contract.*

Executory contract. A sale contract is executory: the signatories have yet to perform their respective obligations and promises. Upon closing, the sale contract is fully performed and no longer exists as a binding agreement.

Signatures. All owners of the property should sign the sale contract. If the sellers are married, both spouses should sign to ensure that both spouses release homestead, dower, and curtesy rights to the buyer at closing. Failure to do so does not invalidate the contract but can lead to encumbered title and legal disputes.

Contract enforceability

To be enforceable, a sale contract must:
- be validly created (mutual consent, consideration, legal purpose, competent parties, voluntary act)
- be in writing
- identify the principal parties
- clearly identify the property, preferably by legal description
- contain a purchase price
- be signed by the principal parties

Written vs. oral form. A contract for the sale of real estate is enforceable only if it is in writing. A buyer or seller cannot sue to force the other to comply with an oral contract for sale, even if the contract is valid.

Assignment. Either party to a sale transaction can assign the sale contract to another party, subject to the provisions and conditions contained in the agreement.

Who may complete. A broker or agent may assist the buyer and seller in completing an offer to purchase, provided the broker represents the client faithfully and does not charge a separate fee for the assistance. It is advisable, and legally required in most states, for a broker to use a standard contract form promulgated by state agencies or real estate boards, as such forms contain generally accepted language. This relieves the broker of the dangers of creating new contract language, which can be construed as a practice of law for which the broker is not licensed.

Contract creation

Offer and acceptance. A contract of sale is created by full and unequivocal acceptance of an offer. Offer and acceptance may come from either buyer or seller. The offeree must accept the offer without making any changes whatsoever. A change terminates the offer and creates a new offer, or counteroffer. An offeror may revoke an offer for any reason prior to communication of acceptance by the offeree.

Equitable title. A sale contract gives the buyer an interest in the property that is called equitable title, or ownership in equity. If the seller defaults and the buyer can show good faith performance, the buyer can sue for specific performance, that is, to compel the seller to transfer legal title upon payment of the contract price.

Earnest money escrow

The buyer's earnest money deposit fulfills the consideration requirements for a valid sale contract. In addition, it provides potential compensation for damages to the seller if the buyer fails to perform. The amount of the deposit varies according to local custom. It should be noted that the earnest money deposit is not the only form of consideration that satisfies the requirement.

The sale contract provides the escrow instructions for handling and disbursing escrow funds. The earnest money is placed in a third party trust account or escrow. A licensed escrow agent employed by a title company, financial institution, or brokerage company usually manages the escrow. An individual broker may also serve as the escrow agent.

The escrow holder acts as an impartial fiduciary for buyer and seller. If the buyer performs under the sale contract, the deposit is applied to the purchase price.
Strict rules govern the handling of earnest money deposits, particularly if a broker is the escrow agent. For example, state laws direct the broker when to deposit the funds, how to account for them, and how to keep them separate from the broker's own funds.

Contract contingencies

A sale contract often contains contingencies. A contingency is a condition that must be met before the contract is enforceable.

Financing contingency. The most common contingency concerns financing. A buyer makes an offer contingent upon securing financing for the property under certain terms on or before a certain date. If unable to secure the specified loan commitment by the deadline, the buyer may cancel the contract and recover the deposit. An appropriate and timely loan commitment eliminates the contingency, and the buyer must proceed with the purchase.

It is possible for both buyers and sellers to abuse contingencies in order to leave themselves a convenient way to cancel without defaulting. To avoid problems, the statement of a contingency should:

- be explicit and clear
- have an expiration date
- expressly require diligence in the effort to fulfill the requirement

A contingency that is too broad, vague, or excessive in duration may invalidate the entire contract on the grounds of insufficiency of mutual agreement.

Default

A sale contract is bilateral, since both parties promise to perform. As a result, either party may default by failing to perform. Note that a party's failure to meet a contingency does not constitute default, but rather entitles the parties to cancel the contract.

Buyer default. If a buyer fails to perform under the terms of a sale contract, the breach entitles the seller to legal recourse for damages. In most cases, the contract itself stipulates the seller's remedies. The usual remedy is forfeiture of the buyer's deposit as **liquidated damages**, provided the deposit is not grossly in excess of the seller's actual damages. It is also customary to provide for the seller and broker to share the liquidated damages. The broker may not, however, receive liquidated damages in excess of what the commission would have been on the full listing price.

If the contract does not provide for liquidated damages, the seller may sue for damages, cancellation, or specific performance.

Seller default. If a seller defaults, the buyer may sue for specific performance, damages, or cancellation.

TENEESSEE OFFERS TO PURCHASE

Contracting procedures

When dealing with offers to purchase property, licensees must

- prepare all offers in writing when received and promptly present them to the seller
- quickly deliver true, executed copies of a written acceptance of an offer to all parties as soon as obtained
- ensure that all of the terms and conditions of the transaction are included in the offer
- ensure that changes or modifications made during negotiation are in writing and initialed and dated by both parties before continuing with the transaction

Unauthorized practice of law. Licensees may complete sales contracts by filling in form blanks as directed by the client or customer. However, licensees are considered to be practicing law without a license if they create contract provisions using their own wording. Caution is therefore well-advised when completing the written sales contract form.

What contract form to use. Licensees are strongly advised to restrict usage of contract forms to those adopted by the firm or those promulgated by the state or by the local board of Realtors®. The benefit of using forms is that the form's language is typically accepted practice which insulates the licensee from exposure to creating problematic contracts or practicing law without a license.

Rejected offers without a counter. If an offer is rejected without a counter, the licensee must sign the Commission-**promulgated Real Estate Offer Rejection Form** which affirms presentation of the offer. The licensee must provide this form to the offeror, whether the licensee is the agent of the buyer or the seller or is acting as a transaction broker.

Electronic communication of offers.   A licensee may communicate an offer and/or counteroffer by fax or other secure electronic means including the Internet. The signatures, initials, and handwritten or typewritten modifications on those electronic documents are considered as valid and binding on the parties as the signatures, initials, and other modifications on the original hard-copy documents would be.

Buyer/seller acknowledgements. The bottom of each page of the agreement has spaces for all buyers and sellers to initial that they "have read this page."

Tennessee sales contract provisions and considerations

Parties, consideration, and property. One or more clauses will identify the parties, the property, and the basic consideration, which is the sale of the property in return for a purchase price.

There must be at least two parties to a sale contract: one cannot convey property to oneself. All parties must be identified, be of legal age, and have the capacity to contract.

The property clause contains the legal identification of the property. This provision also identifies fixtures and personal property included in the sale. Unless expressly excluded, items commonly construed as fixtures are included in the sale. Similarly, items commonly considered personal property are not included unless expressly included.

Price and terms. This clause states the final price and details how the purchase will occur. Of particular interest to the seller is the buyer's down payment, since the greater the buyer's equity, the more likely the buyer will be able to secure financing. In addition, a large deposit represents a buyer's commitment to complete the sale.

If seller financing is involved, this provision sets forth the terms of the arrangement: the amount and type of loan, the rate and term, and how the loan will be paid off. It is important for all parties to verify that the buyer's earnest money deposit, down payment, loan proceeds, and other promised funds together equal the purchase price stated in the contract.

Earnest money deposit. These provisions specify how the buyer will pay the earnest money. It may allow the buyer to pay it in installments or all at once. The former option enables a buyer to hold on to the property briefly while obtaining the additional deposit funds. For example, a buyer who wants to buy a house makes an initial deposit of $200, to be followed in twenty-four hours with an additional $2,000. The sale contract includes the seller's acknowledgment of receipt of the deposit.

Closing and possession dates. This provision states when title will transfer, as well as when the buyer will take physical possession. Customarily, possession occurs on the date when the deed is recorded, unless the buyer has agreed to other arrangements.

The closing clause generally describes what must take place at closing to avoid default. A seller must provide clear and marketable title. A buyer must produce purchase funds. Failure to complete any pre-closing requirements stated in the sale contract is default and grounds for the aggrieved party to seek recourse.

Time is of the essence. This provision introduces the requirement that certain deadlines must be met or else the party who fails to act in a timely manner is in default. This in turn enables the other party to opt out of the contract.

Conveyed interest; type of deed. One or more provisions in the contract will state what type of deed the seller will use to convey the property, and what conditions the deed will be subject to. Among common "subject to" conditions are easements, association memberships, encumbrances, mortgages, liens, and special assessments. Typically, the seller conveys a fee simple interest by means of a general warranty deed.

Title evidence. The seller covenants to produce the best possible evidence of property ownership. This is commonly in the form of title insurance. Also implied here is that the seller is conveying marketable title, meaning free and clear of clouds, liens and other encumbrances on title.

Damage and destruction. This provision stipulates the obligations of the parties in case the property is damaged or destroyed during the pre-closing period. Here, the parties may negotiate alternatives including whose obligation it is to repair, and the buyer's obligation to buy if repairs are made. Finally, the clause may provide the option for either party to cancel.

Repair procedure. The Tennessee agreement has a very detailed set of paragraphs dealing with an agreed upon repair procedure. The contract states that the parties agree to the procedure outlined, unless a Due Diligence Addendum is agreed upon and attached to the contract.

Appraised value. This paragraph is the place to indicate by a checkmark whether or not the contract is contingent upon the lender's appraisal.

Default. Here, the contract specifies what constitutes default and what remedies are available for the damaged party. These are basically threefold: specific performance, liquidated damages, or a lawsuit. Specific performance is typically a buyer's remedy for a defaulting seller. Here, the court orders the defaulting party to comply with the terms of the agreement. Liquidated damages is basically the buyer's forfeiture of the deposit in the event the buyer defaults on a given term. Thirdly, either party can file a lawsuit for damages which can vary depending on the case.

Covenants and conditions disclosure. The sales contract should disclose or make reference to the existence of any restrictions imposed on the property by prior owners or by any homeowners association.

C.L.U.E. Report. The CLUE report (Comprehensive Loss Underwriting Exchange) is a claims history database used by insurance companies in underwriting or rating insurance policies. A CLUE Home Seller's Disclosure Report shows a five-year insurance loss history for a specific property. Among other things, it describes the types of any losses and the amounts paid. Many home buyers now require sellers to provide a CLUE Report as a contingency appended to the purchase offer.

Mediation. This provision explains mediation as an alternative dispute resolution system and explains that participants voluntarily decide the settlement terms with the help of a mediator. The provision further states that any dispute relating to the contract will be submitted to mediation.

Transaction information. Although not technically a provision, most Tennessee purchase contracts include a page that contains transactional information, including

- escrow agent name, contact information, and signature
- licensee and brokerage information for both the listing and selling sides
- type of agency representation each broker is providing

a note about designated agency which states that the broker-in-charge and all associated licensees, except the designated agents, are dual agents.

STATUTE OF FRAUDS

In Tennessee, contracts are not required to be in writing to be valid. However, certain contracts, including real estate contracts, must be in writing to be enforceable in court (TCA 29-2-101; 47-2-201). As covered in the national portion, the Statute of Frauds requires that certain documents be in writing and signed by the parties to be enforceable. Among Tennessee contracts affecting real estate that must be writing to be enforceable are

- sale of goods if the price is five hundred dollars ($500) or more
- contracts by executor or administrator regarding promise to answer debt or damages of the decedent's estate
- contracts for marriage
- contracts for the loan of money
- contracts for the sale of real estate
- exclusive right to sell and exclusive agency contracts
- exclusive right to represent a buyer
- contracts that include a co-signor.
- contracts that cannot be completed within one year, including leases for more than one year.
- employment contract between broker and affiliates.
- contracts that cannot be completed within one year, including leases for more than one year. note: leases for a year or less do not have to be written and signed to be enforceable.

III. Option-to-buy Contracts

OVERVIEW

An option-to-buy is an enforceable contract in which a potential seller, the **optionor**, grants a potential buyer, the **optionee**, the right to purchase a property before a stated time for a stated price and terms. In exchange for the right of option, the optionee pays the optionor valuable consideration.

For example, a buyer wants to purchase a property for $150,000, but needs to sell a boat to raise the down payment. The boat will take two or three months to sell. To accommodate the buyer, the seller offers the buyer an option to purchase the property at any time before midnight on the day that is ninety days from the date of signing the option. The buyer pays the seller $1,000 for the option. If buyer exercises the option, the seller will apply the $1,000 toward the earnest money deposit and subsequent down payment. If the optionee lets the option expire, the seller keeps the $1,000. Both parties agree to the arrangement by completing a sale contract as an addendum to the option, then executing the option agreement itself.

An option-to-buy places the optionee under no obligation to purchase the property. However, the seller must perform under the terms of the contract if the buyer exercises the option. An option is thus a unilateral agreement. Exercise of the option creates a bilateral sale contract where both parties are bound to perform. An unused option terminates at the expiration date.

An optionee can use an option to prevent the sale of a property to another party while seeking to raise funds for the purchase. A renter with a lease option-to-buy can accumulate down payment funds while paying rent to the landlord. For example, an owner may lease a condominium to a tenant with an option to buy. If the tenant takes the option, the landlord agrees to apply $100 of the monthly rent paid prior to the option date toward the purchase price. The tenant pays the landlord the nominal sum of $200 for the option.

Options can also facilitate commercial property acquisition. The option period gives a buyer time to investigate zoning, space planning, building permits, environmental impacts, and other feasibility issues prior to the purchase without losing the property to another party in the meantime.

CONTRACT REQUIREMENTS

To be valid and enforceable, an option-to-buy must:

- include actual, non-refundable consideration

  The option must require the optionee to pay a specific consideration that is separate from the purchase price. The consideration cannot be refunded if the option is not exercised. If the option is exercised, the consideration may be applied to the purchase price. If the option is a lease option, portions of the rent may qualify as separate consideration.

- include price and terms of the sale

The price and terms of the potential transaction must be clearly expressed and cannot change over the option period. It is customary practice for the parties to complete and attach a sale contract to the option as satisfaction of this requirement.

- have an expiration date

  The option must automatically expire at the end of a specific period.

- be in writing

  Since a potential transfer of real estate is involved, most state statutes of fraud require an option to be in writing.

- include a legal description

- meet general contract validity requirements

  The basics include competent parties, the optionor's promise to perform, and the optionor's signature. Note that it is not necessary for the optionee to sign the option.

Legal issues

Equitable interest. The optionee enjoys an equitable interest in the property because the option creates the right to obtain legal title. However, the option does not in itself convey an interest in real property, only a right to do something governed by contract law.

Recording. An option should be recorded, because the equitable interest it creates can affect the marketability of title.

Assignment. An option-to-buy is assignable unless the contract expressly prohibits assignment.

Right of first refusal

A right of first refusal granted by a seller to a buyer gives the buyer a "right" to buy the seller's property should he or she desire to do so within an agreed upon time parameter and for a given price. In effect a right of first refusal gives a person an option that may or may not be exercised by the option holder.

In practice the right of first refusal is an informal and not necessarily enforceable agreement between an owner and a buyer. Generally there are too many unspecified details in the agreement to make it "leak proof" enough to enforce. Key issues such as price, timing, duration of the agreement, etc. make these agreements untenable at best in a court of law.

IV. Contracts for Deed

ESSENTIAL PURPOSES AND FEATURES

A contract for deed is also called a *land contract*, an *installment sale*, a *conditional sales contract*, and an *agreement for deed*. It is a bilateral agreement between a seller, the **vendor**, and a buyer, the **vendee**, in which the vendor defers receipt of some or all of the purchase price of a property over a specified period of time. During the period, *the vendor retains legal title* and the vendee acquires equitable title. The vendee takes possession of the property, makes stipulated payments of principal and interest to the vendor, and otherwise fulfills obligations as the contract requires. At the end of the period, the buyer pays the vendor the full purchase price and the vendor deeds legal title to the vendee.

Like an option, a contract for deed offers a means for a marginally qualified buyer to acquire property. In essence, the seller acts as lender, allowing the buyer to take possession and pay off the purchase price over time. A buyer may thus avoid conventional down payment and income requirements imposed by institutional lenders. During the contract period, the buyer can work to raise the necessary cash to complete the purchase or to qualify for a conventional mortgage.

A contract for deed serves two primary purposes for a seller. First, it facilitates a sale that might otherwise be impossible. Second, it may give the seller certain tax benefits. Since the seller is not liable for capital gains tax until the purchase price is received, the installment sale lowers the seller's tax liability in the year of the sale.

RIGHTS AND OBLIGATIONS OF THE PARTIES

Vendor's rights and obligations. During the contract period, the seller may:

- mortgage the property
- sell or assign whatever interests he or she owns in the property to another party
- incur judgment liens against the property

The vendor, however, is bound to the obligations imposed by the contract for deed. In particular, the vendor may not breach the obligation to convey legal title to the vendee upon receipt of the total purchase price. In addition, the vendor remains liable for underlying mortgage loans.

Vendee's rights and obligations. During the contract period, the buyer may occupy, use, enjoy, and profit from the property, subject to the provisions of the written agreement. The vendee must make periodic payments of principal and interest and maintain the property. In addition, a vendee may have to pay property taxes and hazard insurance.

Legal form

Like other conveyance contracts, a contract for deed instrument identifies:

- the principal parties
- the property's legal description
- consideration: specifically what the parties promise to do
- the terms of the sale

- obligations for property maintenance
- default and remedies
- signatures and acknowledgment

The contract specifies the vendee's payments, payment deadlines, when the balance of the purchase price is due, and how the property may be used.

Default and recourse

Seller default. If the seller defaults, such as by failing to deliver the deed, the buyer may sue for specific performance, or for cancellation of the agreement and damages.

Buyer default. States differ in the remedies they prescribe for the seller in case of buyer default. Some states consider the default a breach of contract that may be remedied by cancellation, retention of monies received, and eviction. Others provide foreclosure proceedings as a remedy.

MANAGING RISKS WITH CFD'S

Most real estate markets do not have standardized language or uniform provisions for the contract for deed transaction in any form sanctioned by associations and agencies. Therefore, this kind of conveyance presents certain pitfalls and dangers for buyer and seller.

In some states, a breach of the contract for deed is remedied under *local contract law* rather than foreclosure law. Therefore, the buyer may not have the protections of a redemption period or other buyer-protection laws which accompany formal foreclosure proceedings. The vendor might sue the vendee for breach of contract for the slightest infraction of the contract terms.

A second danger for the vendee is that the vendor has the power and the right to encumber the property in ways that may not be desirable for the buyer. For example, the seller could place a home equity loan on the property, then fail to make periodic payments. The bank could then foreclose on the vendor, thus jeopardizing the vendee's eventual purchase.

For the seller, the principal danger is that the buyer acquires possession in exchange for a minimal down payment. A buyer might damage or even vacate the property, leaving the seller to make repairs and retake possession. Further, since the contract is recorded, the seller must also bear the time and expense of clearing the title.

To minimize risk, principal parties in a contract for deed should observe the following guidelines:

- use an attorney to draft the agreement
- adopt the standard forms, if available
- become familiar with how the contract will be enforced
- utilize professional escrow and title services
- record the transaction properly
- be prepared for the possible effect on existing financing

MODULE 3 SNAPSHOT REVIEW:

CONTRACTS

CONTRACT LAW

Contract validity

- **contract**: mutual promises based on "meeting of the minds" to do or refrain from doing something; potentially enforceable if created validly
- **legal status of contract** – valid; void; voidable; valid yet unenforceable
- **criteria for validity** - competent parties; mutual consent; valuable consideration; legal purpose; voluntary, good faith act
- **validity of conveyance contract** - must be in writing; contain a legal description; be signed by one or more parties
- **enforcement limitations** - statute of frauds: must be written to be enforceable; statute of limitations: must act within time frame
- **electronic contracting** - electronic records and signatures are legal; must be accepted; enforceable regardless of medium

CONTRACT DRAFTING

Offer and acceptance

- valid offer and valid acceptance creates contract; offer becomes contract on communication of acceptance by offeree to offeror
- **Counteroffer** - any offer in response to an offer or any altered original offer; nullifies original offer
- **Revocation of an offer** - offeror may revoke offer prior to communication of acceptance by offeree
- **Termination of an offer** - acceptance; rejection; revocation; expiration; counteroffer; death or insanity
- **Assignment of a contract** - assignable unless expressly prohibited or a personal service
- **Contract preparation** - restricted unless licensed as attorney or a party to the contract

CLASSIFICATIONS OF CONTRACTS

- oral or written; express or implied; unilateral or bilateral; executed or executory

CONTRACT TERMINATION

- Forms of contract termination - performance; infeasibility; mutual agreement; cooling-period rescission; revocation; abandonment; lapse of time; invalidity of contract; breach of contract
- Breach of contract - default without cause; legal remedies: rescission; forfeiture; suit for damages; specific performance

CONTRACTS FOR SALE

Legal characteristics

- vendor = seller; vendee = buyer
- 3 stages of conveyance: negotiate offers; accept all terms and create contract; closing
- executory: sale contract parties have yet to perform; upon performance, contract goes away
- signatures: all parties must sign contract
- **contract enforceability** -- must be valid; in writing; parties identified; price identified; signed
- **assignment:** contracts are assignable
- offer completion: licensees may assist principals in completing offer; should use a standard form

Contract creation

- **offer and acceptance** – must be complete and unequivocal without any changes. If changed, offer expires and new offer is created; offeror can revoke any offer prior to its acceptance
- **equitable title** – buyer's interest once an offer is accepted; if seller defaults, buyer can compel seller to sell

Earnest money escrow

- fulfills consideration requirement; contract provides instructions for handling and disbursing trust funds; must comply with strict depositing and disbursing rules; must keep separate from operating funds

Contract contingencies - must be explicit; have expiration date; require diligence to complete

Default

- if buyer defaults; seller can take deposit as liquidated damages; if seller defaults, buyer can sue for specific performance

TENNESSEE OFFERS TO PURCHASE

Contracting guidelines

- put all offers in writing; promptly present to seller; deliver copies of executed documents in timely manner to all parties
- ensure all terms included in offer; make sure changes are initialized by all principals
- avoid creating contract provisions, which constitutes practice of law; use Realtors® contract forms
- if offer is rejected without counter: must sign the "**Real Estate Offer Rejection**" form and give to the offeror

Tennessee contract provisions

- parties; price and terms; deposit; closing, possession dates; time of the essence; conveyed interest; type of deed; damage and destruction; repairs; default; title evidence; closing costs; damage and destruction; default

- secondary provisions: inspections, owner's association disclosure; survey; environmental hazard disclosure; other provisions; addenda

THE OPTION-TO-BUY CONTRACT

- optionor gives option to optionee; unilateral contract: seller must perform; buyer need not; if option exercised, option becomes bilateral sale contract

Contract requirements

- must include: non-refundable consideration for the option right; price and terms of the sale; option period expiration date; legal description; must be in writing and meet contract validity requirements

Common clause provisions -- special provisions: how to exercise option; terms of option money forfeiture; how option money will be applied to purchase price

Legal aspects -- creates equitable interest; is assignable; should be recorded

CONTRACT FOR DEED

- purchase price is paid over time in installments; seller retains title; buyer takes possession; at end of period, buyer pays balance of price, gets legal title

Interests and rights

- seller may encumber or assign interest; remains liable for underlying mortgage
- buyer may use, possess, profit; must make periodic payments, maintain the property, and purchase at end of term

Default and recourse

- if seller defaults, buyer may sue for cancellation and damages or specific performance; seller's default remedies vary by area; may sue for specific performance or damages, or may need to foreclose

MODULE 3 - CONTRACTS

QUIZ

Carefully read each question and provide your best answer based on what you learned in this module. Then check your answers against the Answer Key which immediately follows the quiz questions.

1. A void contract is an agreement that does not meet the tests for _____.

   a. validity.
   b. enforcement.
   c. considerability.
   d. competency.

2. Which principle requires that certain contracts must be in writing to be enforceable?

   a. Statute of limitations
   b. Written Contract Act
   c. Statute of frauds
   d. Law of Execution

3. A signed sales contract prior to closing is _____.

   a. infeasible.
   b. executory.
   c. performed.
   d. obligatory.

4. How much is a typical earnest money deposit?

   a. $1,000
   b. 3% of the purchase price
   c. $6,000
   d. It varies according to local custom.

5. Which principle requires that a contract involves a clear and definite offer and an intentional acceptance of the offer?

   a. Valuable consideration
   b. Mutual consent
   c. Exclusive acceptance
   d. Validity

6. Which type of contract grants a buyer the right to purchase a property before a stated time for a stated price and terms?

   a. Rent-to-own contract
   b. Option-to-buy contract
   c. Purchase-lease contract
   d. Seller-financed contract

7. The cancellation of the contract by one party without the consent of the other is also called _____.

    a. revocation.
    b. invalidity.
    c. cooling-period.
    d. an option.

8. A sale contract gives the buyer an interest in the property that is called _____.

    a. equitable title.
    b. contracted deed.
    c. promissory note.
    d. transferrable equity.

9. Which types of contracts are assignable in real estate?

    a. Exclusive listing agreements
    b. Sales contracts
    c. Buyer-broker agreements
    d. No real estate contract is assignable

10. Which principle restricts the time period for which an injured party in a contract has the right to rescind the contract?

    a. Frauds principle
    b. Enforcement limitation
    c. Time is the essence
    d. Statute of limitations

11. By changing any of the terms of an offer, the offeree creates a(n) _____, and the original offer is void.

    a. executory contract
    b. implied offer
    c. accepted offer
    d. counteroffer

12. Which of the following is a responsibility of the vendee?

    a. Mortgage the property
    b. Assign interest to another party
    c. Make the agreed upon periodic payments
    d. Incur judgment liens against property

13. Which type of contract has been fully performed and fulfilled?

    a. Executed
    b. Unilateral
    c. Optional
    d. Closed

14. What payments is a typical buyer/borrower required to make during the loan period?

    a. Property taxes only
    b. Principal, interest, taxes and hazard insurance
    c. Home insurance and principal
    d. Market value rent and interest

15. Which type of contract has all of the terms and covenants of the agreement manifestly stated and agreed to by all parties?

    a. Oral contract
    b. Unilateral contract
    c. Express contract
    d. Bilateral contract

16. What is the most common remedy for a buyer default?

    a. Lawsuit for specific performance
    b. Jail time
    c. Forfeiture of buyer's deposit as liquidated damages
    d. A fine paid to the multiple listing service

17. The act of nullifying a contract where parties to certain contracts are allowed a statutory amount of time after entering a contract is also called _____.

    a. mutual agreement.
    b. cooling-period rescission.
    c. cancellation.
    d. avoidance.

18. During a contract for deed, the _____ retains legal title while the other party acquires equitable title.

    a. vendor
    b. buyer
    c. vendee
    d. listing agent

19. The competence of a party is determined by his or her legal age, mental competency and
    _____.

    a. job status.
    b. religious background.
    c. legitimate authority.
    d. citizenship status.

20. In which type of contract do both parties promise to perform their respective parts of an agreement in exchange for performance by the other party?

    a. Bilateral contract
    b. Express contract
    c. Implied contract
    d. Written contract

21. The optionee enjoys a(n) _____ the property because the option creates the right to obtain legal title.

    a. equitable interest in
    b. recorded deed on
    c. warrantable deed for
    d. enforced interest in

22. A _____ requires the breaching party to give up something, according to the terms of the contract.

    a. suit for specific performance
    b. rescission
    c. forfeiture
    d. relinquishment

23. What is the most common contract contingency?

    a. Financing contingency
    b. Appraisal contingency
    c. Lead-based paint contingency
    d. Property disclosure contingency

24. The principle of _____ states an otherwise valid contract can be canceled if it is not possible to perform.

    a. mutual agreement
    b. lapse of time
    c. infeasibility
    d. performance

25. If an offer is rejected without a counter, the licensee must _____.

   a. send notice to the local MLS.
   b. sign the Real Estate Offer Rejection Form.
   c. have the buyer sign the Contract Rejection Form.
   d. Nothing is required of the licensee.

MODULE 3 – CONTRACTS

ANSWER KEY TO QUIZ

1. a. validity.
2. c. Statute of frauds
3. b. executory.
4. d. It varies according to local custom.
5. b. Mutual consent
6. b. Option-to-buy contract
7. a. revocation.
8. a. equitable title.
9. b. Sales contracts
10. d. Statute of limitations
11. d. counteroffer
12. c. Make the agreed upon periodic payments
13. a. Executed
14. b. Principal, interest, taxes and hazard insurance
15. c. Express contract
16. c. Forfeiture of a buyer's deposit as liquidated damages
17. b. cooling-period rescission.
18. a. vendor
19. c. legitimate authority.
20. a. Bilateral contract
21. a. equitable interest in
22. c. forfeiture
23. a. Financing contingency
24. c. infeasibility
25. b. sign the Real Estate Offer Rejection Form.

MODULE 3: CONTRACTS

CHECK YOUR UNDERSTANDING

Instructions:

Carefully read each challenge question, then provide your best answer based on what you learned in this module. Then check your answers against the Answer Key which immediately follows the questions.

1. A valid contract is one that is legally enforceable by virtue of meeting certain requirements of contract law. True or false?

2. List three critical criteria for contract validity.

    1. _____

    2. _____

    3. _____

3. To minimize risks of a pitfall in a transaction, principal parties in a contract should _____.

    A. use an attorney to draft the agreement.
    B. use their broker to write the contract.
    C. ask the local association's leader to review the agreement.
    D. have the team leader draft the contract.

4. By changing any of the terms of an offer, the offeree creates a valid contract. True or false?

5. In an option-to-buy contract, the optionee enjoys a(n) _____ in the property.

    A. optional interest
    B. right of first refusal
    C. rightful deed
    D. equitable interest

6. The C.L.U.E. report is a claims history database used by insurance companies in underwriting insurance policies. True or false?

7. Which type of contract only has one party that promises to do something?

    A. Implied
    B. Unilateral
    C. Written
    D. Bilateral

8. List three common contract provisions.

   1. _____

   2. _____

   3. _____

MODULE 3: CONTRACTS

CHECK YOUR UNDERSTANDING ANSWER KEY

1. A valid contract is one that is legally enforceable by virtue of meeting certain requirements of contract law.

    True

2. List three critical criteria for contract validity.

    1. Competent parties

    2. Mutual consent

    3. Legal purpose

3. To minimize risks of a pitfall in a transaction, principal parties in a contract should _____.

    A. **use an attorney to draft the agreement.**

4. By changing any of the terms of an offer, the offeree creates a valid contract.

    False

5. In an option-to-buy contract, the optionee enjoys a(n) _____ in the property.

    D. **equitable interest**

6. The C.L.U.E. report is a claims history database used by insurance companies in underwriting insurance policies.

    True

7. Which type of contract only has one party that promises to do something?

    B. **Unilateral**

8. List three common contract provisions.

    1. Price and terms

    2. Closing and possession dates

    3. Earnest money deposit

MODULE 3: CONTRACTS

CASE STUDY EXERCISE: Offers and Acceptance

Situational data:

Agent John showed Broker Eric's listing to buyer clients, Adam and Eve. The list price in the MLS was $210,000. John contacted Eric to inquire about any offers on the property. Eric told John he had no offers. John then prepared an offer to submit to Eric.

Eric did have an offer for $185,000 cash from Jill and Jack. The seller accepted the offer, not knowing that John's clients submitted a bid for $205,000 with FHA financing and a 5% down payment.

Once John had submitted the offer, he asked Eric for written confirmation that the offer was presented to the seller. Eric never presented the offer, nor were Adam and Eve advised that there was another offer.

When asked, Eric stated that the seller had rejected the offer for a cash deal. Eric decided not to present the offer to the seller because it involved financing and would take longer to close. Eric wanted it to close before the end of the month to win an office selling contest.

Analysis Questions:

1. How would you have handled the offers if you were Eric?

   _____

   _____

2. What Articles of the Code of Ethics do you feel were violated?

   _____

   _____

3. What specific Standards of Practices do you feel were violated?

   _____

   _____

CASE DEBRIEF:

1. Eric should have presented both offers. He then should have explained the pros and cons of each offer. The final decision is up to the sellers on whom they want to buy their house.

2. In this situation, the Professional Standards board determined that Eric violated Articles 1 and 3 of the NAR Code of Ethics.

3. The Standards of Practices violated are:

   SP 1.6 – Submit all offers and counteroffers objectively and as quickly as possible.

   SP 1.7 – The listing brokers must continue to submit offers they receive up to closing.

   SP 1.15 – When asked by the cooperating broker, the listing broker should disclose that he has other offers.

   SP 3.6 – The Realtor® should reveal the existence of accepted offers.

Module 4: FAIR HOUSING & ANTITRUST

I. Fair Housing Laws
II. ADA
III. TN Fair Housing and Human Rights
IV. TN Antitrust Laws

Module 4 Learning Objectives

Fair Housing Laws

1. Summarize the overriding purposes of the Fair Housing Laws.
2. Define the Civil Rights Acts and list the predominant forms of illegal discrimination.
3. Identify violations and the general enforcement process of Fair Housing Laws
4. Characterize the salient provisions and purposes of fair financing laws including TILA, Reg Z, ECOA and RESPA

ADA

1. Describe the components, requirements, and penalties associated with the Americans with Disabilities Act

2. Differentiate between the five titles to the ADA (Titles I – V)

Tennessee Fair Housing and Human Rights

1. Define the central provisions and exemptions to the Tennessee Human Rights Law
2. Describe the prohibited activities in Tennessee Fair Housing and Human Rights laws
3. Identify the penalties for violating Tennessee Fair Housing and human rights laws

Tennessee Antitrust Laws

1. Define the central purpose of Tennessee Antitrust Laws

I. Fair Housing Laws

PURPOSE OF FAIR HOUSING LAWS

Federal and state governments have enacted laws prohibiting discrimination in the national housing market. The aim of these **fair housing laws,** or **equal opportunity housing laws,** is to give all people in the country an equal opportunity to live wherever they wish, provided they can afford to do so, without impediments of discrimination in the purchase, sale, rental, or financing of property.

CIVIL RIGHTS ACTS

Civil Rights Act of 1866. The original fair housing statute, the Civil Rights Act of 1866, prohibits discrimination in housing *based on race.* The prohibition relates to selling, renting, inheriting, and conveying real estate.

Executive Order 11063. While the Civil Rights Act of 1866 prohibited discrimination, it was only marginally enforced. In 1962, the President issued Executive Order 11063 to *prevent discrimination in residential properties financed by FHA and VA loans.* The order facilitated enforcement of fair housing where federal funding was involved.

Title VIII (Fair Housing Act). Title VIII of the Civil Rights Act of 1968, known today as the Fair Housing Act, prohibits discrimination in housing *based on race, color, religion, or national origin.* The Office of Fair Housing and Equal

Opportunity (FHEO) administers and enforces Title VIII under the supervision

of the Department of Housing and Urban Development (HUD).

FORMS OF ILLEGAL DISCRIMINATION

The Fair Housing Act specifically prohibits such activities in residential brokerage and financing as the following.

Discriminatory misrepresentation. An agent may not conceal available properties, represent that they are not for sale or rent, or change the sale terms for the purpose of discriminating. For example, an agent may not inform a minority buyer that the seller has recently decided not to carry back second mortgage financing when in fact the owner has made no such decision.

Discriminatory advertising. An agent may not advertise residential properties in such a way as to restrict their availability to any prospective buyer or tenant.

Providing unequal services. An agent may not alter the nature or quality of brokerage services to any party based on race, color, sex, national origin, or religion. For example, if it is customary for an agent to show a customer the latest MLS publication, the agent may not refuse to show it to any party. Similarly, if it is customary to show qualified buyers prospective properties immediately, an agent may not alter that practice for purposes of discrimination.

Steering. Steering is the practice of directly or indirectly channeling customers toward or away from homes and neighborhoods. Broadly interpreted, steering occurs if an agent describes an area in a subjective way for the purpose of encouraging or discouraging a buyer about the suitability of the area.

For example, an agent tells Buyer A that a neighborhood is extremely attractive, and that desirable families are moving in every week. The next day, the agent tells Buyer B that the same neighborhood is deteriorating, and that values are starting to fall. The agent has blatantly steered Buyer B *away* from the area and Buyer A *into* it.

Blockbusting. Blockbusting is the practice of inducing owners in an area to sell or rent to avoid an impending change in the ethnic or social makeup of the neighborhood that will cause values to go down.

For example, Agent Smith tells neighborhood owners that several minority families are moving in, and that they will be bringing their relatives next year. Smith informs homeowners that, in anticipation of a value decline, several families have already made plans to move.

Restricting MLS participation. It is discriminatory to restrict participation in any multiple listing service based on one's race, religion, national origin, color, or sex.

Redlining. Redlining is the residential financing practice of refusing to make loans on properties in a certain neighborhood regardless of a mortgagor's qualifications. In effect, the lender draws a red line around an area on the map and denies all financing to applicants within the encircled area.

Title VIII exemptions

The Fair Housing Act allows for exemptions under a few specific circumstances. These are:

- a privately owned single-family home where no broker is used and no discriminatory advertising is used, with certain additional conditions
- rental of an apartment in a 1-4 unit building where the owner is also an occupant, provided the advertising is not discriminatory
- facilities owned by private clubs and leased non-commercially to members
- facilities owned by religious organizations and leased non-commercially to members, provided membership requirements are not discriminatory

Jones v. Mayer

In 1968, the Supreme Court ruled in *Jones v. Mayer* that all discrimination in selling or renting residential property based on race is prohibited under the provisions of the Civil Rights Act of 1866. Thus, while the Federal Fair Housing Act exempts certain kinds of discrimination, anyone who feels victimized by discrimination *based on race* may seek legal recourse under the 1866 law.

Equal opportunity in housing poster

In 1972, HUD instituted a requirement that brokers display a standard HUD poster. The poster affirms the broker's compliance with fair housing laws in selling, renting, advertising, and financing residential properties. Failure to display the poster may be construed as discrimination.

Fair housing amendments of 1988

Amendments to federal fair housing laws prohibit discrimination based on sex and discrimination against handicapped persons and families with children.

Exemptions. Federal fair housing laws do not prohibit age and family status discrimination under the following circumstances:

- in government-designated retirement housing
- in a retirement community if all residents are 62 years of age or older
- in a retirement community if 80 % of the dwellings have one person who is 55 years of age or older, provided there are amenities for elderly residents
- in residential dwellings of four units or less, and single family houses if sold or rented by owners who have no more than three houses

DISCRIMINATION BY THE CLIENT

Fair housing laws apply to home sellers as well as to agents, with the exception of the exemptions previously cited. If an agent goes along with a client's discriminatory act, the agent is equally liable for violation of fair housing laws. It is thus imperative to avoid complicity with client discrimination. Further, an agent should withdraw from any relationship where client discrimination occurs.

Examples of potential client discrimination are:

- refusing a full-price offer from a party
- removing the property from the market to sidestep a potential purchase by a party
- accepting an offer from one party that is lower than one from another party

VIOLATIONS AND ENFORCEMENT

Persons who feel they have been discriminated against under federal fair housing laws may file a complaint with the Office of Fair Housing and Equal Opportunity (FHEO) within HUD, or they may file suit in a federal or state court.

Filing an FHEO complaint. Complaints alleging fair housing violations must be filed with the Office of Fair Housing and Equal Opportunity within one year of the violation. HUD then initiates an investigation in conjunction with federal or local enforcement authorities.

If HUD decides that the complaint merits further action, it will attempt to resolve the matter out of court. If efforts to resolve the problem fail, the aggrieved party may file suit in state or federal court.

Filing suit. In addition to or instead of filing a complaint with HUD, a party may file suit in state or federal court within two years of the alleged violation.

Penalties. If discrimination is confirmed in court, the respondent may be enjoined to cease practicing his or her business. For example, a discriminating home builder may be restrained from selling available properties to buyers. Also, the plaintiff may be compensated for damages including humiliation, suffering, and pain. In addition, the injured party may seek equitable relief, including forcing the guilty party to complete a denied action such as selling or renting the property. Finally, the courts may impose civil penalties for first-time or repeat offenders.

FAIR FINANCING LAWS

TILA & Regulation Z.

The Consumer Credit Protection Act, enacted in 1969 and since amended by the Truth-in-Lending Simplification and Reform Act, is implemented by the Federal Reserve's **Regulation Z**. Regulation Z applies to all loans secured by a residence. It does not apply to commercial loans or to agricultural loans over $25,000. Its provisions cover *the disclosure of costs, the right to rescind the credit transaction, advertising credit offers, and penalties for non-compliance with the act.*

The Dodd-Frank Wall Street Reform and Consumer Protection Act of 2010 (Dodd-Frank Act) established the Consumer Financial Protection Bureau (CFPB.) to protect consumers by carrying out federal consumer financial laws. The CFPB consolidates most Federal consumer financial protection authority in one place, including enforcement of RESPA, ECOA, and Truth in Lending.

Disclosure of costs. Under Regulation Z, a lender must disclose all finance charges as well as the true Annualized Percentage Rate (APR) in advance of closing. A lender does not have to show the total interest payable over the loan term or include in finance charges such settlement costs as fees for appraisal, title, credit report, survey, or legal work. Disclosure must be distinctly presented in writing.

Rescission. A borrower has a limited right to cancel the credit transaction, usually within three days of completion of the transaction. The right of rescission does not apply to "residential mortgage transactions," that is, to mortgage loans used to finance the purchase or construction of the borrower's primary residence.

However, state law may require a rescission period and notice on these transactions as well.

Advertising. Any type of advertising to offer credit is subject to requirements of full disclosure if it includes:

- a down payment percentage or amount
- an installment payment amount
- a specific amount for a finance charge
- a specific number of payments
- a specific repayment period
- a statement that there is no charge for credit

If any of these items appears in the advertising, the lender must disclose the down payment amount or percentage, repayment terms, the APR, and whether the rate can be increased after consummation of the loan.

Noncompliance. Willful violation of Regulation Z is punishable by imprisonment of up to a year and/or a fine of up to $5,000. Other violations may be punished by requiring payment of court costs, attorneys' fees, damages, and a fine of up to $1,000.

Parallel anti-discrimination and consumer protection laws have been enacted in the mortgage financing field to promote equal opportunity in housing.

Home Mortgage Disclosure Act. This statute requires lenders involved with federally guaranteed or insured loans to exercise impartiality and nondiscrimination in the geographical distribution of their loan portfolio. In other words, the act is designed to prohibit redlining. It is enforced in part by requiring lenders to report to authorities where they have placed their loans.

ECOA

ECOA prohibits discrimination in extending credit based on race, color, religion, national origin, sex, marital status, age, or dependency upon public assistance. A creditor may not make any statements to discourage an applicant on the basis of such discrimination or ask any questions of an applicant concerning these discriminatory items. A real estate licensee who assists a seller in qualifying a potential buyer may fall within the reach of this prohibition. A lender must also inform a rejected applicant in writing of reasons for denial within 30 days. A creditor who fails to comply is liable for punitive and actual damages.

RESPA

RESPA is a federal law which aims to *standardize settlement practices and ensure that buyers understand settlement costs*. RESPA applies to purchases of residential real estate (one- to four-family homes) to be financed by "federally related" first mortgage loans. Federally related loans include:

- VA- and FHA-backed loans
- other government-backed or -assisted loans
- loans that are intended to be sold to FNMA, FHLMC, GNMA, or other government-controlled secondary market institutions
- loans made by lenders who originate more than one million dollars per year in residential loans.

In addition to imposing settlement procedures, RESPA provisions prohibit lenders from paying kickbacks and unearned fees to parties who may have helped the lender obtain the borrower's business. This would include, for example, a fee paid to a real estate agent for referring a borrower to the lender.

To assist in informing and educating borrowers, RESPA requires that lenders provide a loan applicant with a **loan information booklet** and a **loan estimate**. The booklet, produced by the Consumer Financial Protection Bureau, explains RESPA provisions, general settlement costs, and the required **Closing Disclosure** form. The lender must provide the estimate of closing costs within three days following the borrower's application.

Disclosures. The Consumer Financial Protection Bureau (CFPB) requires lenders to use two specific forms to disclose settlement costs to the buyer. A lender must provide a Loan Estimate (H-24) within three days of receiving the loan application and allow the buyer to see the Closing Disclosure (H-25) three days before loan consummation. A lender must also provide a buyer with a copy of the information booklet, "Your Home Loan Toolkit," concerning mortgage loan, closing costs and closing procedures. The disclosures specify:

- settlement charges
- title charges
- recording and transfer fees
- reserve deposits required
- tax and insurance escrow deposits required
- any other fees or charges
- total closing costs

The disclosure forms vary, depending on loan type. The costs in the Closing Disclosure must match those in the Loan Estimate within certain standards.

II. ADA

COMPONENTS, REQUIREMENTS, PENALTIES

Purpose. The ADA, which became law in 1990, is a civil rights law that prohibits discrimination against individuals with disabilities in all areas of public life, including employment, education, transportation, and facilities that are open to the general public. The purpose of the law is to make sure that people with disabilities have the same rights and opportunities as everyone else.

The Americans with Disabilities Act Amendments Act (ADAAA) became effective on January 1, 2009. Among other things, the ADAAA clarified that a disability is "a physical or mental impairment that substantially limits one or more major life activities." This definition applies to all titles of the ADA and covers private employers with 15 or more employees, state and local governments, employment agencies, labor unions, agents of the employer, joint management labor committees, and private entities considered places of public accommodation. Examples of the latter include hotels, restaurants, retail stores, doctor's offices, golf courses, private schools, day care centers, health clubs, sports stadiums, and movie theaters.

Components. The law consists of five parts.

- Title I (Employment) concerns equal employment opportunity. It is enforced by the U.S. Equal Employment Opportunity Commission.

- Title II (State and Local government) concerns nondiscrimination in state and local government services. It is enforced by the U.S. Department of Justice.

- Title III (Public Accommodations) concerns nondiscrimination in public accommodations and commercial facilities. It is enforced by the U.S. Department of Justice.

- Title IV (Telecommunications) concerns accommodations in telecommunications and public service messaging. It is enforced by the Federal Communications Commission.

- Title V (Miscellaneous) concerns a variety of general situations including how the ADA affects other laws, insurance providers, and lawyers.

Real estate practitioners are most likely to encounter Titles I and III and should acquire familiarity with these. In advising clients, licensees are well-advised to seek qualified legal counsel.

Requirements. The act requires landlords in certain circumstances to modify housing and facilities so that disabled persons can access them without hindrance.

The ADA also requires that disabled employees and members of the public be provided access that is equivalent to that provided to those who are not disabled.

- Employers with at least fifteen employees must follow nondiscriminatory employment and hiring practices.

- Reasonable accommodations must be made to enable disabled employees to perform essential functions of their jobs.

- Modifications to the physical components of a building may be necessary to provide the required access to tenants and their customers, such as widening doorways, changing door hardware, changing how doors open, installing ramps, lowering wall-mounted telephones and keypads, supplying Braille signage, and providing auditory signals.

- Existing barriers must be removed when the removal is "readily achievable," that is, when cost is not prohibitive. New construction and remodeling must meet a higher standard.

- If a building or facility does not meet requirements, the landlord must determine whether restructuring or retrofitting or some other kind of accommodation is most practical.

Penalties. Violations of ADA requirements can result in citations, business license restrictions, fines, and injunctions requiring remediation of the offending conditions. Business owners may also be held liable for personal injury damages to an injured plaintiff.

III. TN Fair Housing and Human Rights

TENNESSEE HUMAN RIGHTS LAW

Tennessee law (TCA 4-21) includes age as a category regarding equal treatment in public accommodations and employment, an important note for brokerage firms. Violating any federal, state or municipal law that prohibits discrimination in the sale or rental of real estate because of race, creed, color, religion, sex, national origin, familial status or disability can result in disciplinary action, in prosecution and/or a lawsuit.

Definitions. Tennessee law defines discriminatory practices as direct or indirect acts or practices that exclude, restrict, make distinction, segregate, place limitations, refusal or denial, or differentiation or preference in the treatment of a person because of race, creed, color, religion, sex, age or national origin.

Per Tennessee fair housing law, "family" includes single individuals, and "national origin" includes national origin of ancestors (ancestry).

Exemptions. A private club is exempted if the club's policies are determined by members and its facilities and services are available only to it members and bona fide guests.

Tennessee law (TCA 4-21-602) provides additional exemptions:

- the rental of housing accommodations in a building containing accommodations for no more than two (2) families living independently of each other, if the owner or a member of the owner's family lives in one of the units; although federal law specifies four (4) units, Tennessee's law is more restrictive

- rental of a room or rooming unit in a housing accommodation by an individual if he or she, or his or her family member, resides there; or regarding sex, rooms or units where tenants would be required to share a common bath

- a religious organization or association, a nonprofit organization or institution operated, supervised or controlled by or in conjunction with a religious group that limits rental, sale or occupancy of dwellings it owns or operates for other than commercial purposes to persons of that religion, or gives preference of persons of that religion, unless membership is restricted based on any other protected class

- regarding sex, the rental of housing accommodations of single-sex dormitory properties, including dormitories operated by higher educational institutions

- regarding family status, exemptions for housing for older persons include dwellings

    o intended for, and at least ninety percent (90%) occupied by, at least one person who is fifty-five (55) or older per unit

    o providing significant services and facilities that are specifically designed to meet physical or social needs of persons (fifty-five) 55 or older and

    ○   publishing and adhering to policies and procedures that demonstrate an intent by the owner or manger to provide housing for persons fifty-five (55) and older

    ○   intended and occupied solely by persons 62 years of age or older

The law does not prohibit conduct against someone who has been convicted of illegal manufacture or distribution of a controlled substance.

Licensees should be cognizant of the fact that federal law prohibits discrimination based on race under any circumstances (no exemptions based on race).

Complaints. Employment complaints may be filed with the Tennessee Human Rights Commission within one hundred eighty (180) days of the alleged discrimination. The aggrieved has the option of filing housing discrimination complaints

- with the Tennessee Human Rights Commission within one hundred eighty (180) days, or

- with HUD within three hundred sixty-five (365) days

Human Rights Commission access to records. The Human Rights Commission has authority to require access to pertinent brokerage records to investigate a complaint regarding discrimination.

PROHIBITED ACTIVITIES

Advertisement indicating discrimination (TCA 4-21-502 and federal fair housing laws). Any advertising that expresses discrimination regarding any protected class is a violation of federal and state law. State laws specify that violations include directly or indirectly publishing, issuing, displaying or mailing material that indicates any goods, services, accommodations, or privileges will be refused, withheld, denied or limited because of race, creed, color, religion, sex or national origin. So, advertising indicating housing is available only to certain individuals is a violation, except senior housing that complies with requirements of law.

Blockbusting (TCA 4-21-603). Licensees are prohibited from representing that a change has occurred or may occur in the composition of a neighborhood with respect to race, color, creed, religion, sex, disability, familial status or national origin of the owners or occupants. Violations also include indicating that change will or may result in the lowering of property values, an increase in criminal or antisocial behavior, or a decline in the quality of schools.

Restrictive covenants and conditions (TCA 4-21-604). Restrictive covenants may not in any way discriminate based on any of the protected classes, and honoring any discriminatory covenant is a violation.

Agency no defense in proceeding (TCA 4-21-605). A violation cannot be defended because it was requested or sought by someone who is not a licensee. Licensees must not discriminate, or be involved in a transaction in which the licensee is aware that a party is planning to discriminate.

Restricting access in residential real estate-related transactions (TCA 4-21-606). It is a fair housing violation for any person or entity whose business includes engaging in residential real estate-related transactions to discriminate against any person in making available the transaction, or in the terms and conditions of the transaction, based on any of the protected classes. This includes

- the selling, brokering, or appraising of residential real estate

- making or purchasing of loans or providing financial assistance

- purchasing, constructing, improving, repairing, or maintaining a dwelling

- when the security is residential real estate

Malicious harassment (TCA 4-21-701, -702). There is a civil cause of action for malicious harassment. A person may be liable to the victim of malicious harassment for both special and general damages, including, but not limited to, emotional distress, reasonable attorney's fees and costs, and punitive damages. This does not preclude victims from seeking other criminal or civil remedies.

PENALTIES

In cases involving discriminatory housing practices only, the guilty party may be required to pay a civil penalty

- up to ten thousand dollars ($10,000) for the first occurrence by the individual

- up to twenty-five thousand dollars ($25,000) for the second occurrence of discrimination

- up to fifty thousand dollars ($50,000) if the respondent has committed two (2) or more unlawful discriminatory housing practices during the seven-year period ending on the date of the filing of the complaint

If the discriminatory housing practice stated in the complaint is committed by a person who has been previously found guilty of committing unlawful discriminatory housing acts, the civil penalties may be imposed without regard to the period of time that any subsequent discriminatory housing practice occurred.

The Human Rights Commission may publish, or cause to be published, the names of persons who have been found guilty of a discriminatory practice.

IV. TN Antitrust Laws

TENNESSEE ANTITRUST LAWS

Tennessee anti-trust laws (TCA 47-25-101 – 47-25-109) closely parallel federal laws. While federal laws address unfair practices affecting interstate trade, Tennessee reinforces some of those laws and provides for enforcement by the Tennessee attorney general within the state.

The state's anti-trust laws address price-fixing and other unfair trade practices that are intended to restrict or destroy competition. Underpricing a product with the intent of destroying or harming competition, and any agreement, contract, or trust designed to advance, reduce, or control the price or the cost to the producer or the consumer of a product or article are also prohibited.

Individuals who participate in practices considered destructive to full and free competition or a conspiracy against trade commit a Class E felony. Any violation conviction by a corporation can result in a fine of up to one million dollars ($1,000,000). Additionally, a violation can result in a lawsuit.

Consumers benefit from competition; when competition is destroyed or harmed, consumers pay a higher price for goods or services. Anti-trust laws are designed to ensure that free competition is not hampered.

MODULE 4: SNAPSHOT REVIEW:

FAIR HOUSING AND ANTITRUST

FAIR HOUSING LAWS

Purpose of fair housing laws

- enacted to create equal opportunity and access to housing and housing finance
- state laws generally reflect federal fair housing laws; federal laws do not pre-empt local zoning laws but prohibit them from discriminating

Civil Rights Acts

- Civil Rights Act of 1866 -- no discrimination in selling or leasing housing based on race
- Executive Order 11063 -- no race discrimination involving FHA- or VA-backed loans
- Civil Rights Act of 1968 -- Title VIII (Fair Housing Act): no housing discrimination based on race, color, religion, national origin
- certain exceptions permitted

Forms of illegal discrimination

- discriminatory misrepresentation, advertising, and financing; unequal services; steering; blockbusting; restricting access to market; redlining

ADA

- no discrimination against those with disabilities; applies to employment, education, transportation, public facilities; equivalent access
- Titles I (employment) and III (public accommodation) most common for real estate agents

TN FAIR HOUSING AND HUMAN RIGHTS

- protected classes: race, creed, color, religion, sex, national origin, family status, disability, ad in some cases, age; family" includes single individuals, "national origin" includes ancestry; certain exemptions apply
- Tennessee Human Rights Commission oversees fair housing; housing discrimination; complaints may be filed with the Commission within 180 days or with HUD within 365 days
- prohibited activities - ads must contain no discrimination; per federal law, no discrimination based on race
- penalties -- penalties range from $10,000 for first offense to up to $50,000 for subsequent offenses

TN ANTITRUST LAWS

- Tennessee laws closely parallel federal laws and provide for enforcement by Tennessee attorney general; addresses price-fixing and unfair trade practices destructive to free competition; violations are Class E felony; corporation may be fined up to $1 million

MODULE 4 – FAIR HOUSING AND ANTI-TRUST

QUIZ

Carefully read each question and provide your best answer based on what you learned in this module. Then check your answers against the Answer Key which immediately follows the quiz questions.

1. What was the name of the original fair housing statute?

   a. Civil Rights Act of 1866
   b. Executive Order 1106
   c. Fair Housing Law of 1986
   d. Title VIII

2. Employers with at least _____ employees must follow nondiscriminatory employment and hiring practices.

   a. 2
   b. 5
   c. 10
   d. 15

3. Which residential financing practice refuses to make loans on properties in a certain neighborhood regardless of a mortgagor's qualifications?

   a. Disqualifying
   b. Redlining
   c. Misguiding
   d. Steering

4. Which statute addresses unfair practices affecting interstate trade in Tennessee?

   a. Trading laws of Tennessee
   b. Inter-state trading laws
   c. Tennessee anti-trust law
   d. Price-fixing laws

5. The federal law which aims to standardize settlement practices is called _____.

   a. ETA
   b. ECOA
   c. CD
   d. RESPA

6. Which Tennessee statute includes age as a category regarding equal treatment in public accommodations?

   a. Tennessee Fair Housing Law
   b. Tennessee Human Rights Law
   c. Tennessee Blockbusting Law
   d. Civil Rights Act of Tennessee

7. The practice of directly or indirectly channeling customers toward certain neighborhoods is called
_____.

   a. guiding.
   b. leading.
   c. pushing.
   d. steering.

8. Which law prohibits discrimination against individuals with disabilities in all areas of public life?

   a. Americans with Disabilities Act
   b. Title IV
   c. Civil Rights Act of 1898
   d. Fair Housing Law of 1974

9. The ADAAA became effective on _____ and clarified that a disability is defined as a physical or mental impairment that substantially limits one or more major life activities.

   a. 1990
   b. 2009
   c. 1970
   d. 1984

10. Regulation Z applies to which of the following?

    a. Primary residence
    b. Commercial loan
    c. Agricultural loan of $50,000
    d. Warehouse loan

11. Individuals who participate in practices considered destructive to free competition commit a
_____.

    a. misdemeanor.
    b. Class B felony.
    c. minor misdemeanor.
    d. Class E felony.

12. Which statute is known today as the Fair Housing Act?

    a. Civil Rights Act of 1866
    b. Executive Order 1205
    c. Title VIII of the Civil Rights Act of 1968
    d. Title IV

13. Tennessee's anti-trust laws address _____ and other unfair trade practices.

    a. price-fixing
    b. racism
    c. discrimination
    d. blockbusting

14. Which government entity enforces the telecommunications portion of the ADA?

   a. Department of Justice
   b. FCC
   c. Department of Communications
   d. FTC

15. Which Supreme Court case ruled that all discrimination in selling residential property based on race is prohibited?

   a. Fair Housing v. Maryland
   b. Swift v. Johnson
   c. Jones v. Mayer
   d. Marbury v. Madison

16. Which government authority can require access to pertinent brokerage records to investigate complaints regarding discrimination?

   a. Human Rights Commission
   b. Civil Rights Authority
   c. Fair Housing Group
   d. Prohibition Authority

17. Which statute prohibits discrimination in extending credit based on race, color, religion, national origin, and marital status?

   a. RESPA
   b. ECOA
   c. TILA
   d. Title IV

18. Which section of the ADA law concerns equal employment opportunity?

   a. Title I
   b. Marbury vs. Madison
   c. Section XX
   d. The ADA does not focus on equal employment opportunities.

19. Which practice consists of inducing owners in an area to sell to avoid an impending change in the social makeup of the neighborhood?

   a. Avoidance
   b. Blockbusting
   c. Redlining
   d. Outlining

20. The right of _____ allows a borrower to cancel the credit transaction within three days of completion of the transaction.

    a. disclosure
    b. cancellation
    c. rescission
    d. consumer protection

MODULE 4 – FAIR HOUSING AND ANTI-TRUST

ANSWER KEY TO QUIZ

1. a. Civil Rights Act of 1866
2. d. 15
3. b. Redlining
4. c. Tennessee anti-trust law
5. d. RESPA
6. b. Tennessee Human Rights Law
7. d. steering.
8. a. Americans with Disabilities Act
9. b. 2009
10. a. Primary residence
11. d. Class E felony.
12. c. Title VIII of the Civil Rights Act of 1968
13. a. price-fixing
14. b. FCC
15. c. Jones v. Mayer
16. a. Human Rights Commission
17. b. ECOA
18. a. Title I
19. b. Blockbusting
20. c. rescission

MODULE 4 – FAIR HOUSING AND ANTI-TRUST

CHECK YOUR UNDERSTANDING

Instructions:

Carefully read each challenge question, then provide your best answer based on what you learned in this module. Then check your answers against the Answer Key which immediately follows the questions.

1. List three examples of exemptions for housing for older persons.

   1. _____

   2. _____

   3. _____

2. The Civil Rights Act of 1866 prohibits discrimination in housing based on race. True or false?

3. List three forms of illegal discrimination.

   1. _____

   2. _____

   3. _____

4. Who has the authority to require access to pertinent brokerage records to investigate a complaint regarding discrimination?

   A. The National Association of Realtors
   B. The Human Rights Commission
   C. The Department of Real Estate
   D. The Fraud Department of Real Estate

5. The state's anti-trust laws address price-fixing and other unfair trade practices. True or false?

6. The _____ clarified that a disability is a physical or mental impairment that substantially limits one or more major life activities.

    A. ADA
    B. The Civil Rights Act of 1989
    C. ADAAAA
    D. The Disability Act of 1955

7. List three items Tennessee anti-trust laws address.

    1. _____

    2. _____

    3. _____

8. The ADA civil rights law consists of three parts. True or false?

MODULE 4 – FAIR HOUSING AND ANTI-TRUST

CHECK YOUR UNDERSTANDING ANSWER KEY

1. List three examples of exemptions for housing for older persons.

   1. Dwellings that are 90% occupied by at least one person who is fifty-five or older

   2. Dwellings occupied solely by 62 years of age or older

   3. Dwellings providing significant services that are specifically designed to meet social needs of persons 55 or older

2. The Civil Rights Act of 1866 prohibits discrimination in housing based on race.

   True

3. List three forms of illegal discrimination.

   1. Steering

   2. Blockbusting

   3. Redlining

4. Who has the authority to require access to pertinent brokerage records to investigate a complaint regarding discrimination?

   B. The Human Rights Commission

5. The state's anti-trust laws address price-fixing and other unfair trade practices.

   True

6. The _____ clarified that a disability is a physical or mental impairment that substantially limits one or more major life activities.

   C. ADAAA

7. List three items Tennessee anti-trust laws address.

   1. Price-fixing

   2. Unfair trade practices

   3. Underpricing a product with the intent of destroying the competition

8. The ADA civil rights law consists of three parts. True or false?

   False

MODULE 4 – FAIR HOUSING AND ANTI-TRUST

CASE STUDY EXERCISE: Fair Housing Applications

Situational data:

Mallory has been getting many calls on her current listing with questions about the home, neighborhood, etc. She was used to answering these common questions, but last Wednesday, she got a voicemail from a man named Chase who asked about the neighborhood's demographics. He wanted to know what races lived in the area and whether it was a predominantly white neighborhood. His top priority was living in a suburb that has a high white population.

He also let it be known that he is an all-cash buyer and would submit proof of funds to her as soon as he got home.

Analysis Questions:

How should Mallory approach the situation? What should she say to Chase?

_____

_____

_____

_____

_____

_____

Case Study Debrief Observations:

Federal and state governments have enacted laws prohibiting discrimination in the national housing market. The aim of these fair housing laws, or equal opportunity housing laws, is to give all people in the country an equal opportunity to live wherever they wish, provided they can afford to do so, without impediments of discrimination in the purchase, sale, rental, or financing of the property. One of the protected classes under the Fair Housing Act is race. Since it is a protected class, Mallory cannot risk answering Chase's questions.

So what should she do? One way to tackle this situation is to urge Chase to complete his due diligence by running online searches on the local neighborhood's demographics. There are lots of market data available online, and Chase can discover the answers for himself without putting Mallory's license at risk.

Module 5: RISK REDUCTION

I. Risk Management Strategies and Procedures
II. Primary Risk Areas in Brokerage

Module 5 Learning Objectives

Risk Management Strategies and Procedures

1. Identify the key differences between the risk management strategies of avoidance, reduction, transference, and retention

2. Describe the various risk management procedures including education, disclosure, documentation, recordkeeping and insurance

3. Identify the components of a documented paper trail that minimizes occupational risk.

Primary Risk Areas in Brokerage

1. Identify the primary risk areas in everyday brokerage practice, including agency, property disclosures, listing and selling, contracting, fair housing, misrepresentation, recommending providers, financing and closing, and trust fund handling

I. Risk Management Strategies and Procedures

RISK MANAGEMENT STRATEGIES

Not all of these strategies are always possible or available, but a real estate firm or licensee who fails to make a conscious effort to employ one or more of them increases the likelihood of loss from the many potential risks that are always present in the real estate business. The four principal risk management strategies are avoidance, risk reduction, transference and retention.

Avoidance

Avoidance includes refraining from an activity that carries risk. One can avoid the risks of being in an automobile accident by not riding in automobiles. Avoiding risks also means missing the opportunity to benefit from the avoided activity. By avoiding automobile travel, one is confined to modes of transportation, such as buses and walking, that do not offer the same high degree of personal freedom and efficiency. Complete avoidance of risk in real estate practice is almost impossible. A broker, for instance, may believe that hiring only experienced affiliates eliminates the risk that affiliates will commit license law violations. However, even experienced practitioners may not know the law, and, sometimes, people break the law deliberately. The risk may be reduced, but it remains.

Reduction

Reduction involves taking steps to reduce the probability or the severity of a potential loss. However, this strategy may result in reducing risk in one area only to increase it in another. A familiar example is a sprinkler system that dispenses water to reduce the risk of fire but at the same time increases the risk of water damage.

In real estate practice, one risk reduction tactic is to share responsibility for making a decision. The agent provides the consumer with expertise, and perhaps some advice, but lets the consumer decide how much to offer. In this way, the agent gets some relief from the risks inherent in the buyer's decision to purchase

Transference

Transference means passing the risk to another party, by contract or other means. An insurance policy is the common example, but sometimes the wording of a sales or personal services contract can transfer risk without resorting to insurance.

In the real estate business, transference is typically and most successfully accomplished by means of an errors and omissions (E&O) insurance policy, either on the individuals in a firm or on the firm itself. State law may require such insurance.

Retention

Retention of risk means entering into an activity in spite of known risks and taking full responsibility for the consequences. This is, in effect, self-insurance, the only strategy left when risk cannot be reduced or transferred and one has decided not to avoid it because of the desirability of the potential benefits.

RISK MANAGEMENT PROCEDURES

Education

Education is the first line of defense against risk. When agents are familiar with the forms provided by the office, how and when to complete them and where to send them, the likelihood of errors is reduced. Likewise, agents need to be able to identify and understand common contract elements, complete contract forms developed by attorneys, and evaluate offers received from co-op agents on their listings without committing a license violation or breach of law.

In most states, brokers have a legal obligation to provide training to affiliated licensees. Licensees also have the obligation to seek out appropriate education and training outside the brokerage to ensure that they know how to comply with the law. In addition, licensees must satisfy legal requirements for continuing education, while those who care about personal excellence will seek further education and training to enhance their professional skills.

Disclosure

By ensuring that all parties have the information they are entitled to, proper disclosure reduces the risk that clients and customers will accuse a licensee of misleading or inducing them to make a decision with incomplete information. Further, laws in every state require disclosures of one kind or another.

Disclosure may be made in writing or verbally and may or may not require written acknowledgment from the receiving party.

Required disclosures usually include:

- agency relationships
- property condition
- duties and obligations
- personal interest in the transaction
- personal interest in referrals

Documentation & recordkeeping

Documentation provides evidence of compliance with laws and regulations. It proves what clients and customers and licensees said and did in a transaction. Some documentation is required by law.

The components of a thoroughly documented paper trail include:

- Policy and procedure manuals
- Standard forms
- Communication records
- Transaction records
- Contracts
- Accounting
- Other important documents

Policy manual. A written and uniformly enforced company policy lets everyone in the firm know what to expect before problems arise. The policy manual should cover the company's rules in such areas as floor duty privileges, assignment of relocation properties to agents, referrals between agents within the company, and requirements for continuing education, sales meeting participation, and property tours.

Procedures manual. A company procedures manual should spell out how to handle every aspect of the company's business that agents and brokers need to know—from handling consumers' funds and documents, conducting consumer transactions, dealing with MLS-related matters, and placing signage, to all procedures prescribed by state or federal law, especially license, banking and fair housing laws. Adherence to a procedures manual reduces the risk that an individual will inadvertently commit an unlawful act. Whenever changes are made to the policy or procedures manual, each agent should sign the revised manual as evidence that the agent has examined it.

Standard forms. Standard forms save time and protect against the unauthorized practice of law. Since they are most often prepared by lawyers familiar with the market area, they can address contingencies that are common in the area in a manner that reflects the real estate laws of the state. On the other hand, a licensee often needs to adapt a standardized form for a client by assisting with filling in blanks, modifying terms, and attaching addenda. The licensee must always remain aware of the limitations the state has placed on such activities.

Here are a few of the standard forms a brokerage should provide for its agents and affiliates:

- buyer and seller representation agreements, exclusive and nonexclusive
- agreement to show property
- purchase and sale agreement
- agency disclosure form
- property condition disclosure, disclaimer, and exemption form
- lease agreement
- personal interest disclosure form
- referral for service disclosure form
- lead-based paint disclosure form
- special disclosure forms (mold, radon, subsurface sewage system, impact fees/adequate facilities taxes, etc.)
- referral agreement
- independent contractor agreement
- closing checklist

Communication records. Some communications with transaction parties are good and necessary for business. Others are required by law, such as certain disclosures. A transaction checklist is a good tool for managing risk associated with the failure to make required communications to all principals and for keeping track of required communications from co-op agents.

Retaining evidence that information has been communicated is a necessary procedure. Electronic communications should be archived on suitable electronic media. Copies of mailed or faxed communications should be maintained in the transaction folder.

It is always difficult to document telephone or face-to-face conversations, especially with the constant use of cell phones from a variety of locations. It is a good practice to make brief notes at the time and then write them up later for mailing or faxing to the other party. Be sure, however, that you can produce these notes on demand, lest you be accused later of withholding documentation that has been promised.

Maintaining a good record of communications is useful for resolving disagreements where parties dispute what has been said because it allows the agent to produce a dated document that resolves the issue definitively.

Transaction records. State laws require licensees to document transactions. Firms are required to keep written records of all real estate transactions for a number of years (usually three to five) after closing or termination. Required records typically include:

- listing agreements
- offers
- contracts
- closing statements
- agency agreements
- disclosure documents
- correspondence and other communication records
- notes and any other relevant information

Accounting. In addition to other accounting records, there is the requirement to maintain written accounting of escrow funds. For each transaction, property, and principal, escrow records will include:

- depositor
- date of deposit
- date of withdrawal
- payee
- other information deemed pertinent by the real estate commission

Other documents. Additional documents may be required by law or regulation, or should be kept simply as protection in case of disputes and lawsuits. These would include copies of advertising materials, materials used in training agents, records of compliance with continuing education requirements, safety manuals, and anything else that shows how the firm conducts its business and safeguards its staff as well as the rights of consumers.

Insurance

Many forms of insurance are available for property owners and managers. Some of these types are also used to manage certain risks of brokers and licensees.

General Liability. General liability insurance provides coverage for risks incurred by a property owner when the public or a licensee enters the owned property (**public liability**). The insurer pays the covered claim and legal fees, costs, and expenses, including medical expenses, resulting from owner negligence or other causes. This type of insurance does not cover **professional liability,** for which an Errors & Omissions policy is necessary.

Errors and Omissions. Professional liability is of two general types:

1. Unprofessional conduct – a claim that one has failed to carry out fiduciary duties and provide an acceptable standard of care

2. Breach of contract – a claim that one has failed to perform services under the terms of a contract in a timely manner

The primary method for transferring the professional liability risks of brokers, managers, and licensees is Errors & Omissions (E&O) insurance. A standard E&O policy provides coverage for "damages resulting from any negligent act, error or omission arising out of Professional Services." A standard policy does NOT cover:

- violations of law
- fraudulent, dishonest, criminal or malicious acts
- mishandling of escrow moneys, earnest money deposits, or security deposits
- antitrust violations
- sexual harassment
- Fair Housing violations
- agent-owned properties
- environmental violations
- failure to detect or disclose environmental conditions, including mold
- acts committed prior to licensure or after termination of active status
- activities as an appraiser if licensing other than a real estate license is required E&O insurance, in short, covers "mistakes" but not crimes.

Fire and hazard. The risks of property damage caused by fire, wind, hail, smoke, civil disturbance, and other such causes are covered by fire and hazard insurance.

Flood. The risks of property damage caused by floods, heavy rains, snow, drainage failures, and failed public infrastructures such as dams and levies are covered by a specialized flood policy. Regular hazard policies do not include flood coverage.

Other insurance. Other common types of insurance coverage for income and commercial properties include:

- **casualty**—coverage for specific risks, such as theft, vandalism, burglary, illness and accident, machinery damage

- **workers' compensation**—hospital and medical coverage for employees injured in the course of employment, mandated by state laws

- **contents and personal property**—coverage for building contents and personal property when they are not actually on the building premises

- **consequential loss, use, and occupancy**—coverage for the business losses resulting from a disaster, such as loss of rent and other revenue, when the property cannot be used for business

- **surety bond**—coverage against losses resulting from criminal or negligent acts of an employee

II. Primary Risk Areas in Brokerage

AGENCY

The risks of agency will occur in one of two areas:

- the requirement to inform and disclose
- the requirement to carry out an agency duty.

Most states require agency relationships to be in writing and to be disclosed to all parties to a transaction. State law may spell out agency duties, or the duties may be a part of general agency law. In states that do not use agency, there is still the obligation to explain and disclose the nature of the relationship.

Disclosure requirements. A licensee may be acting in a transaction as facilitator, agent, subagent, designated agent, single agent, dual agent, non-agent or in some capacity. Regardless of status, the licensee must follow state disclosure requirements. These are, typically, to:

- disclose status *verbally* to other licensees on initial contact
- disclose status *verbally* to buyer and seller before providing real estate services
- confirm the disclosure *in writing* before signing a listing agreement or presenting a purchase offer (to an unrepresented seller) or before preparing a purchase offer (to an unrepresented buyer)
- get a *signed receipt* indicating the written disclosure has been made

Carrying out the duties of agency also require disclosures of :

- personal interest the agent has in a transaction (such as owner or buyer)
- personal benefit the agent will derive from a service referral
- required property and market information
- information about customers a client is entitled to have

Duties. A licensee who acts for a principal in a real estate transaction is required by law to assume certain responsibilities toward the parties to the transaction. Whether a state applies the fiduciary duties of agency law or specifies its own duties toward clients and consumers, the basic duties remain:

To all parties

- honesty
- fairness
- reasonable care and skill
- disclosures

To clients

- skill
- care
- diligence
- loyalty
- obedience
- confidentiality

- accounting
- full disclosure

The duty to exercise **skill, care and diligence** means that licensees may not be casual or negligent in their actions. Licensee negligence is actionable when principals are harmed by the licensee's failure.

The duty of **loyalty** requires the agent to *put the client's interests above those of everyone else*, including his or her own.

The duty of **obedience** requires the agent to act on the principal's wishes regarding the transaction as long as they do not result in any illegal action. The duty of obedience never overrides the legal obligation of agents to deal fairly and honestly with all parties.

The duty of **confidentiality** requires the agent to hold in confidence any information that would harm the client's interests or bargaining position or anything else the client wishes to keep secret, unless the law requires disclosure. The duty of confidentiality survives the termination of the listing contract.

The duty of **accounting** applies to all funds involved in a real estate transaction. Accounts must be maintained as required by law, and escrow funds are to be handled strictly in accordance with the law.

The duty of **disclosure** applies to both parties to a transaction, although usually with some differences. Proper disclosure to customers primarily concerns agency, property condition, and environmental hazards. To the client, it generally concerns all known facts regarding the property and the transaction, including information about the other transaction party. State laws prescribe what may, must, and must not be disclosed. Licensees must be vigilant to avoid oversights and conflicts of interest that can lead to a disclosure to the wrong party or disclosure of information that is confidential.

Conflicts of interest. Conflicts of interest arise when an agent forgets to put the best interests of a client ahead of those of everyone else. This can happen in situations involving undisclosed dual agencies, broker-owned listings, licensees buying for their own account, vendor referrals, and property management subcontracting of services, among many others. Even ordinary, everyday transactions carry a built-in risk of conflict of interest. Consider the fact that a licensee usually receives no compensation for a failed transaction. Therefore, it is in the licensee's interest to see the transaction completed, even if it may not be in the client's best interest. A negative result from a home inspection or other test has the potential to cause a buyer to back out of a contract. A licensee who has forgotten whose best interest should be primary might be tempted to recommend inspectors who will overlook problems in exchange for receiving referrals. Licensees must always disclose any self-interest they have in a transaction, and always remember their duties to clients and consumers.

Confidentiality. Licensees have a responsibility to maintain the confidentiality of certain kinds of information they obtain concerning clients and customers. The duty to maintain confidentiality generally survives the termination of a listing agreement into perpetuity. If it seems that revealing confidential information might benefit the client, the licensee should obtain the client's written permission to proceed.

Confidential information generally includes information about a client's motivations in a transaction, financial and personal details, and information specifically designated as confidential by the client. Public information, such as that contained in public records, information that becomes known without the licensee's participation, or that the client reveals to another, is not considered confidential.

State laws often require businesses to provide security for the personal information they obtain about consumers. Security procedures should protect personal information from unauthorized access, destruction, use, modification, or disclosure. Confidential information, when it is not to be retained, must be disposed of in a secure manner.

Penalties. Possible penalties for breach of agency relationships include:

- rescission of transaction
- loss of compensation
- fees and costs
- punitive damages
- ethics discipline
- license discipline

PROPERTY DISCLOSURES

Property condition. Most states require the seller of a residential property to deliver to the buyer a written disclosure or disclaimer about the property's condition, including any material defects the owner knows about. The disclosure is usually required before any purchase contract is accepted.. A second disclosure may be required at closing. The licensee should always obtain the parties' signatures acknowledging receipt of these disclosures.

Depending on the state, the licensee may have no further duty to disclose property condition after properly informing parties of their rights and obligations. However, the licensee may still be subject to legal action for

- deliberately distorting the facts (intentional misrepresentation)
- cheating any party (fraud)
- concealing or failing to disclose adverse facts which the licensee knew about or should have known about (intentional or unintentional misrepresentation)

Lead-based paint and other disclosures. Federal law requires sellers of houses built before 1978 to make a lead-based paint disclosure before accepting an offer to purchase. The licensee must tell the seller about this requirement, give the seller the proper disclosure form, and make sure that the buyer receives it.

The licensee must also make sure the seller discloses any other circumstances the situation and the law require, which may include:

- wood infestation inspection report
- soil test report
- subsurface sewage disposal system permit disclosure
- impact fees or adequate facilities taxes disclosure
- mold and radon reports or treatments

LISTING AND SELLING PROCESS

Nature and accuracy of the listing agreement. In most states, a listing agreement is enforceable only if it is in writing. Most states forbid net listings, because they violate the requirement that a valid listing agreement must specify a selling price and the agent's compensation. The licensee, in accordance with the duty of due diligence, must verify the accuracy of the statements in the listing regarding the property, the owner, and the owner's representations. Especially important facts for a broker or agent to verify are:

- the property condition
- ownership status
- the client's authority to act

An agent who does not to act with a reasonable degree of due diligence in these matters may be exposed to liability if it turns out that the property is not as represented or the client cannot perform the contract as promised.

Comparative Market Analysis (CMA). In preparing a Comparative Market Analysis, licensees should guard against using the terms "appraisal" and "value," which are reserved for the use of certified appraisers. Misuse of these terms could lead to a charge of misrepresenting oneself as an appraiser. In discussing listed properties with clients or customers, real estate licensees should be careful to use guarded terms such as "recommended listing price," "recommended purchase price,' and "recommended listing price range."

Agents should make every effort to help the sellers find a reasonable listing price based on the current market. If the CMA leads the seller to list at a price that is too high, the seller may blame the agent when the transaction fails because of an appraisal that comes in below the selling price. To minimize this risk, it is best to be conservative in the CMA and retain documentation that the seller went above the recommended price in spite of the agent's advice.

Estimate of Closing Costs. In preparing an estimate of closing costs for a seller or buyer, there is the risk of forgetting something, leading to an unpleasant surprise when the consumer suddenly faces unexpected costs or conditions. Licensees should use their broker's form, if there is one, and make it clear to the consumer that it is only an estimate of likely costs, not a statement of actual costs. In some states, brokers and agents do not prepare closing cost estimates, leaving that task to the lender.

Advertising. State and federal laws regulate advertising, including the federal Fair Housing laws as they pertain to discriminatory advertising and providing of services. Advertising includes electronic communication, social media/networking, and internet marketing. Usage must be consistent with company image and legal requirements. The license laws of most states list illegal advertising actions subject to discipline such as:

- making any substantial and intentional misrepresentation

- making any promise that might cause a person to enter into a contract or agreement when the promise is one the licensee cannot or will not abide by

- making continued and blatant misrepresentations or false promises through affiliate brokers, other persons, or any advertising medium

- making misleading or untruthful statements in any advertising, including using the term "Realtor" when not authorized to do so and using any other trade name, insignia or membership in a real estate organization when the licensee is not a member.

Committing such acts may result in license suspension or revocation.

Authorizations and Permissions. Licensees should stay within the bounds of the authority granted by the agency agreement or must not do anything requiring permission without first getting that permission in writing. For instance, permission should be obtained before doing any of the following unless the listing agreement specifically grants the authority:

- post a sign on the property
- remove other signs
- show the property
- hand out the property condition disclosure
- distribute marketing materials
- advertise in various media
- use a multiple listing service
- cooperate with other licensees
- divide the commission or negotiate a commission split
- share final sales data with the MLS
- place a lock box on the property
- appoint subagents
- appoint a designated agent
- change agency status

Scope of expertise. Real estate licensees are not, by nature, financial consultants, accountants, appraisers, soil scientists, well diggers, lawyers, decorators, contractors, builders, plumbers, carpenters, inspectors, prognosticators, and a number of other kinds of expert. However, in today's competitive environment, consumers often demand much more from a licensee than the traditional basic services. An agent who fails to live up to prevailing standards may be held liable for negligence, fraud, or violation of state real estate license laws and regulations. At the same time, agents must be particularly careful about the temptation to misrepresent themselves as experts and offer inappropriate expert advice. Disclaimer and referral are always the best risk control procedures to forestall an accusation of misrepresentation from a consumer who claims to have been harmed by reliance on the licensee's non-existent expertise. The exact nature of the services to be provided should be stated as clearly as possible in the listing agreement.

CONTRACTING

According to the Statute of Frauds, all contacts for real estate must be in writing to be enforceable. Contracts that contain incorrect information or are inadequately prepared can pose a serious liability for a licensee. To avoid such a situation, it is imperative for the contract to reflect the terms that the parties have agreed upon in the most accurate and honest manner. The agent must also be careful to comply with the letter of the real estate law. Violations can jeopardize the enforceability of a listing or sales contract, in addition to resulting in criminal prosecution.

Common risks and errors in the contracting process include:

- using an illegal form

    - A licensee may be punished for using any real estate listing agreement form, sales contract form, or offer to purchase form that lacks a *definite termination date*.

- failing to state inclusions and exclusions

    - The parties should identify as included in or excluded from the transfer any ambiguous items. Unwritten agreements between the parties are a source of later dispute and trouble.

- failing to track the progress of contingency satisfaction

    - The time period for completing contingencies such as inspections is specific and limited. Failure to meet or waive a condition may terminate the contract. A "time is of the essence" clause in the standard agreement makes the time period for contingencies critical.

- mistakes in entering data in a form

    - All data should be checked and verified: dates, times, amounts, warranties, descriptions, names, representations, promises, procedures, authority, etc. One way to reduce risk in the contracting process is to use a checklist that covers all the contract items.

Unauthorized practice of law. The unintentional practice of law without a license is a great risk in the contracting process, as well as in the representation process. It is illegal for real estate professionals who are not attorneys to draw up contracts for transactions they are not involved in or to charge a separate fee for preparing a contract.

Such licensees may fill in blanks or make deletions on a preprinted contract form prepared by a lawyer. While a licensee may make deletions, additions to a form should be drafted by an attorney. The principals themselves can make changes as long as each change is signed or initialed by all signers. Preprinted riders can often be attached as addenda to a contract without an attorney.

It is also illegal for real estate licensees who are not lawyers to give legal advice or interpret contract language. Licensees, however, may express opinions. For instance, if a licensee believes that a party has grasped the meaning of a contract, it is permissible to say something like, "Though I am not an attorney, in my opinion your understanding of this contract is correct." It would be questionable to make a definitive statement like, "That's correct."

FAIR HOUSING

The risk of violating fair housing laws can be minimized through ongoing education that addresses both the content and the intent of the laws. It is especially necessary for paperwork and documentation to be accurate and concise in a situation where a fair housing issue could arise.

Advertising. The Fair Housing Act forbids real estate advertising that mentions race, color, religion, national origin, sex, handicap, or familial status in any way that suggests preference or discrimination. State laws may add other protected categories, such as creed and age.

Risk can be reduced by the use of street names or other non-biased geographical references when stating where the property is located, and by describing the property rather than the type of persons who might live in or around it. Even if a home appears "ideal for a young family," it is best not to advertise it as such. Such advertising would exclude other groups such as singles, the elderly, and older families.

In advertising the sale or rental of housing covered by the Fair Housing Act, HUD recommends using the Fair Housing Logo or phrase "Equal Housing Opportunity."

Answering questions. When faced with questions that might lead to a *steering* charge or other violation of fair housing laws, it is best for the licensee to limit the response to features of the home and to the process of selling, buying, and listing properties, and refer the questioner to someone else to answer questions about such matters as the demographic make-up of the neighborhood. It is illegal for the licensee to voice an opinion based on race, religion, color, creed, national origin, sex, handicap, elderliness, or familial status. The agent should explain this fact to

the buyer and be wary of any situation where the agent's behavior might be construed as discriminatory.

Listing agreements. Before entering into a listing agreement, a licensee should explain that it is necessary to comply with fair housing laws and obtain the potential client's acknowledgment and agreement. The agent should make it clear that the agent will

- reject the use of terms indicating race, religion, creed, color, national origin, sex, handicap, age or familial status to describe prospective buyers.

- terminate the listing if the seller uses race, religion, creed, color, national origin, sex, handicap, age, or familial status in the consideration of an offer.

- inform the broker if the seller makes any attempt to discriminate illegally.

Offers. A seller cannot refuse to sell a property to an individual based on the individual's belonging to a protected class, and if this is attempted, the real estate professional must not be involved. If the seller asks about the color, religion, creed, national origin, ethnicity, age, or familial status of a buyer, the agent must explain that it is illegal to give out such information. The best risk reduction procedure is to treat all buyers and sellers equally, showing no preference for one over another.

MISREPRESENTAITON

Misrepresentation may be unintentional or intentional.

Unintentional misrepresentation. This type of misrepresentation occurs when a licensee _unknowingly_ conveys inaccurate information to a consumer concerning a property, financing or agency service. False or inaccurate information that the licensee, as a professional, should have known to be false or inaccurate may be included in the definition. Those found guilty generally have to pay fines and may be disciplined by state real estate regulators and professional organizations.

Risky areas for unintentional misrepresentation include:

- making and reporting measurements
- describing property
- offering opinions about future growth and development of a neighborhood or neighboring property
- making declarative statements about the presence or absence of hazardous materials

The risks of unintentional misrepresentation are reduced if an agent

- learns to measure and calculate areas accurately
- relies on measurements reported by others only with extreme caution and specific disclaimers
- refrains from exaggeration
- avoids stating opinions a consumer might take for expertise

Intentional misrepresentation. Also known as fraud, this kind of misrepresentation occurs when a licensee _knowingly_ conveys false information about a property, financing or service. Fraud is a criminal act that may result in fines and incarceration, in addition to discipline from state regulators and professional organizations.

RECOMMENDING PROVIDERS

There are several risks attending the recommendation of vendors and service providers to a consumer. First, the consumer may not be satisfied with the performance of the recommended party and blame the licensee. Second, in cases where a recommended provider performs illegal acts, there may be legal consequences for the licensee. Third, if a licensee has a business relationship with a recommended vendor or provider and neglects to disclose the fact, there are license violation consequences.

The major risk management technique is to shift the responsibility for choosing a vendor to the consumer. This can be done by refusing to recommend vendors at all; by presenting a broad range of choices and allowing the consumer to select; or by presenting a short list of thoroughly vetted vendors and allowing the consumer to make the decision, always with the disclaimer that **to the best of the licensee's knowledge**, the vendors on the list are competent and honest, but that the consumer is responsible for investigating and making his or her own judgment before hiring or buying.

FINANCING AND CLOSING

In the financing and closing phases of a transaction, a consumer may feel that a licensee has been incompetent or misleading. Licensees have an obligation to inform and educate their clients throughout the transaction process. Surprises and accusations of incompetence or misrepresentation are among possible results of failing to keep the party informed.

Discrimination. Of course, it is important to comply with relevant laws. Licensees must be mindful of the requirements of ECOA and refrain from participating in any manner of discriminatory lending. It is illegal to:

- threaten, coerce, intimidate or interfere with a person who is exercising a fair housing right or assisting another other to exercise that right.

- indicate a limitation or preference based on race, color, national origin, religion, sex, familial status, or handicap in any advertisement or communication. Single-family and owner-occupied housing that is otherwise exempt from the Fair Housing Act is subject to this prohibition against discriminatory advertising.

Progress reporting. All inspections and tests must comply with local and state laws and with the purchase contract. Progress reports should be accurate, timely, in writing, and free of speculation. If a consumer has a question about the meaning of something in an inspection report, the licensee should refer the consumer to the person who wrote the report rather than trying to explain it. This method transfers some of the risk inherent in interpreting the report.

Qualifying buyers. Many transactions fail because a buyer has been improperly qualified before the offer is presented. Using a lender to qualify the buyer saves time and protects the agent against leading a seller to believe a purchaser is fully qualified when this may not be the case. Also, lenders and loan agents are better able to look into the buyer's qualifications than a real estate licensee is. If it becomes necessary to show a property to a potential buyer who has not been qualified by a lender, the licensee can gain some protection by performing an informal qualification and documenting the fact that it was based on the information provided by the buyer. The buyer's signature on this documentation indicates the buyer's acceptance of at least partial responsibility for the qualification.

Lending fees disclosure. The licensee should explain loan fees, charges,

amounts, timing, and responsibilities. Agents can assist in the loan decision by explaining how to compare loans with differing charges and interest rates. The fact that a high origination fee and points may make a loan with a low interest rate unattractive to a borrower is important information for the agent to provide, and providing it may protect the agent against a later complaint that the buyer suffered a loss because of the agent's failure to inform.

Appraisal problems. Delays and appraised value are the typical problem areas. Failure to inform parties about delays can compromise the transaction. An under-appraisal will require the buyer to make a larger down payment or the seller to lower the price. If the property appraises for more than the purchase price, the seller may blame the agent for suggesting the lower price. In such a case, the seller's agent's defense is that the seller agreed to the listing price and that the price was a factor in attracting the buyer to the property.

TRUST FUND HANDLING

State laws prescribe how licensees must handle any escrow or earnest money deposits they receive. Those laws usually state that a broker must hold money received in connection with the purchase or lease of real property in a trust fund account. The type of account and financial depository are specified. The broker must record receipt of the money and place that money in the trust account within a specified time period. Usually, the law allows the broker to hold an earnest money check uncashed until the offer is accepted, provided the buyer gives written permission and the seller is informed.

Typical trust fund handling requirements include:

- the broker named as trustee of the account
- a federally-insured bank or recognized depository located in the state
- an account that is not interest-bearing if the financial institution ever requires prior written notice for withdrawals
- maintenance of records in a particular accounting format
- separate records kept for each beneficiary, property, or transaction
- records of funds received and paid out regularly reconciled with bank statements
- withdrawals only by the broker-trustee or other specifically authorized person

Commingling and conversion. Mixing of personal or company funds with client funds is grounds for the revocation or suspension of a real estate license. Depositing client funds in a personal or business account, or using them for any purpose other than the client's business, is also grounds for suspension or revocation of a license. It is important for the broker to remove commissions, fees or other income earned by the broker from a trust account within the period specified by law to avoid committing an act of commingling.

MODULE 5 SNAPSHOT REVIEW:

RISK REDUCTION

RISK MANAGEMENT STRATEGIES

- two dimensions of risk: size, probability; risk management: structured approach to uncertainty

    Avoidance -- refrain from risky activity
    Reduction -- reduce probability; share responsibility
    Transference -- pass risk by contract; insurance
    Retention – accept risk; self-insurance

RISK MANAGEMENT PROCEDURES

Education -- train in laws, forms and procedures, job performance
Disclosures -- provide information to reduce misunderstanding & lawsuits; agency, property condition, duties, personal interest
Documentation, records -- maintain evidence of compliance; manuals, forms, records, contracts, accounting, other documents
Insurance -- general liability, E & O, fire and hazard, flood, casualty, workers, personal property, consequential loss, surety bond

PRIMARY RISK AREAS IN BROKERAGE
Agency

- main failures: to inform and disclose, to fulfill duties
- disclosures: verbal, written, signed receipt; agency relationship and duties; personal interest in transaction; required information
- duties: to all– honesty, fairness, care, skill, required disclosures; additional to clients– diligence, loyalty, obedience, confidentiality, accounting, full disclosure
- conflicts of interest arise from failing to put client's interest first
- confidentiality duty lasts forever; laws define what is confidential, how to treat and dispose of information
- penalties include loss of transaction, compensation, fees and costs, damages, license

Property disclosures

- property condition, lead-based paint, other conditions; disclosure may discharge liability; failure to disclose may be construed as misrepresentation

Listing and selling process

- areas of risk include listing agreement accuracy, Comparative Market Analysis results, closing cost estimates, advertising, authorizations and permissions, exceeding expertise

Contracting process

- contracts for real estate must be in writing; inaccuracy endangers contract; other risks: illegal form, omitted elements, lapsed contingencies, wrong data

- unauthorized practice of law: non-lawyers may fill in blanks and delete words on standard contract forms; no legal advice to public allowed

Fair Housing

- advertising may not state preference, limitation or discrimination based on race, color, religion, national origin, sex, handicap, familial status
- agent must not be involved with discriminatory actions of a client or customer

Antitrust

- government prosecutes cooperative arrangements that raise prices or reduce consumer choices: Sherman Antitrust Act outlaws restraint of trade; Clayton Act outlaws practices that harm competition; Federal Trade Commission Act outlaws unfair methods of competition
- violations punishable by government criminal and civil actions as well as by private lawsuits; fines, damages, and imprisonment possible

Rules and regulations

- violators of state rules and regulations risk license expiration, revocation, suspension, and other discipline
- prime causes of discipline include commission of prohibited acts, practicing with an expired license, disclosure failures, earnest money mishandling

Misrepresentation

- unintentional: inaccurate information conveyed unknowingly; subject to fines and license discipline; occurs most often in measurements, property descriptions
- intentional: fraud, knowingly conveying false information; criminal act subject to fines, license discipline, and incarceration

Recommending providers

- risks include consumer dissatisfaction, possible vicarious liability for illegal acts committed by a recommended provider, undisclosed business relationship (RESPA violation as well as license violation)
- best practice: do not recommend any vendors, or provide a list of trusted vendors with no recommendation and a disclaimer

Financing and closing

- risk areas include fair housing and ECOA violations; failed transactions because of agent failure to monitor contingency period; failure to ensure proper disclosure of closing costs; RESPA violations

Trust fund handling

- risk areas include mishandling of earnest money deposits; commingling and conversion of trust funds; errors in use of trust accounts

MODULE 5 – RISK REDUCTION

QUIZ

Carefully read each question and provide your best answer based on what you learned in this module. Then check your answers against the Answer Key which immediately follows the quiz questions.

1. Which risk management strategy involves refraining from an activity that carries risk?

   a. Reduction
   b. Avoidance
   c. Transference
   d. Retention

2. Which licensee duty requires the agent to act on the principal's wishes regarding the transaction?

   a. Loyalty
   b. Accounting
   c. Obedience
   d. Accommodation

3. An agent's duty to exercise _____ means that licensees may not be casual or negligent in their actions.

   a. obedience
   b. loyalty, disclosure and accountability
   c. confidentiality
   d. skill, care and diligence

4. According to the _____, all contracts for real estate must be in writing to be enforceable.

   a. Statute of Frauds
   b. Anti-trust Laws
   c. Written Contract Law
   d. Contract Validity Act

5. Which licensee duty applies to both parties to a transaction?

   a. Confidentiality
   b. Disclosure
   c. Obedience
   d. Accounting

6. The risks of unintentional misrepresentation are reduced if an agent _____.

   a. makes measurements.
   b. describes the property appropriately.
   c. refrains from exaggeration.
   d. makes declarative statements about the absence of hazardous materials.

7. It is important for a broker to remove commissions earned by the broker from a trust account within a specific time period to avoid committing an act of _____.

   a. conversion.
   b. commingling.
   c. mixing.
   d. tainting.

8. Which risk management strategy passes the risk to another party?

   a. Transference
   b. Reduction
   c. Transience
   d. Affiliation

9. Common risks in the contracting process include using an illegal form, failing to state inclusions, mistakes in entering a date in a form and _____.

   a. mixing funds.
   b. failing to track the progress of contingency satisfaction.
   c. steering.
   d. redlining.

10. Entering into an activity in spite of known risks and taking full responsibility for the consequences is known as _____.

    a. retention.
    b. education.
    c. disclosure.
    d. avoidance.

11. Which licensee duty applies to all funds involved in a real estate transaction?

    a. Accounting
    b. Monetary
    c. Financial
    d. Price duty

12. Which type of risk management strategy provides evidence of compliance with laws and regulations?

    a. Policy procedures
    b. Disclosures
    c. Transference
    d. Documentation and recordkeeping

13. Which type of issue might happen with an undisclosed dual agency?

    a. Dual agency is not allowed
    b. Unauthorized practice of law
    c. Conflict of interest
    d. No issue would occur

14. If an agent charges a fee to draw up a contract for a transaction they are not involved in, they can be charged with _____.

    a. the unauthorized practice of law.
    b. lack of expertise.
    c. illegal contracting.
    d. This practice is allowed.

15. Which risk management strategy is the first line of defense against risk?

    a. Disclosure
    b. Avoidance
    c. Education
    d. Documentation

16. Which statute forbids real estate advertising to mention religion, race, or familial status?

    a. The Discrimination Act
    b. The Civil Rights Act of 1999
    c. The Fair Housing Act
    d. The Steering Statute of 1876

17. Federal law requires sellers of houses built before _____ to make a lead-based paint disclosure.

    a. 1956
    b. 1978
    c. 1925
    d. 1989

18. The duty of _____ requires the agent put the client's interests above those of everyone else, including his or her own.

    a. loyalty
    b. care
    c. accounting
    d. obedience

19. What is the primary method for transferring the professional liability risks of brokers and licensees?

   a. General liability insurance
   b. Errors & omissions insurance
   c. Professional liability insurance
   d. Real estate insurance

20. What type of analysis does a listing agent run in order to determine an appropriate listing price?

   a. Appraisal
   b. Comparative market analysis
   c. Broker price opinion
   d. Market value analysis

21. Which of the following is a risky area for unintentional misrepresentation?

   a. Reading public records
   b. Facts about the local attractions
   c. Statements about the presence of hazardous materials
   d. Measurements reported by the builder of the property

22. Which insurance offers coverage against losses resulting from criminal acts of an employee?

   a. Surety bond
   b. Errors insurance
   c. Workers' compensation
   d. Hazard insurance

23. Which of the following is a duty a licensee has to all parties?

   a. Honesty
   b. Loyalty
   c. Diligence
   d. Accounting

24. Which type of misrepresentation occurs when a licensee unknowingly conveys inaccurate information to a consumer?

   a. Intentional fraud
   b. Misrepresentation of facts
   c. Unintentional misrepresentation
   d. Intentional misrepresentation

25. Which of the following is a duty a licensee has to clients but not to all parties?

   a. Fairness
   b. Reasonable care
   c. Disclosures
   d. Obedience

MODULE 5 – RISK REDUCTION

ANSWER KEY TO QUIZ

1. **b. Avoidance**
2. **c. Obedience**
3. **d. skill, care and negligence**
4. **a. Statute of Frauds**
5. **b. Disclosure**
6. **c. refrains from exaggeration.**
7. **b. commingling.**
8. **a. Transference**
9. **b. failing to track the progress of contingency satisfaction.**
10. **a. retention.**
11. **a. Accounting**
12. **d. Documentation & recordkeeping**
13. **c. Conflict of interest**
14. **a. the unauthorized practice of law.**
15. **c. Education**
16. **c. The Fair Housing Act**
17. **b. 1978**
18. **a. loyalty**
19. **b. Errors & omissions insurance**
20. **b. Comparative market analysis**
21. **c. Statements about the presence of hazardous materials**
22. **a. Surety bond**
23. **a. Honesty**
24. **c. Unintentional misrepresentation**
25. **d. Obedience**

MODULE 5 – RISK REDUCTION

CHECK YOUR UNDERSTANDING

Instructions:

Carefully read each challenge question, then provide your best answer based on what you learned in this module. Then check your answers against the Answer Key which immediately follows the questions.

1. The primary method for transferring the professional liability risks of brokers, managers and licensees is _____.

    A. professional liability insurance.
    B. licensee liability insurance.
    C. Errors & Omissions insurance.
    D. general liability insurance.

2. List three risk management strategies.

    1. _____

    2. _____

    3. _____

3. Federal law requires sellers of houses built before 1978 to make a lead-based paint disclosure. True or false?

4. Which type of misrepresentation occurs when a licensee unknowingly conveys inaccurate information to a consumer concerning a property?

    A. Unintentional misrepresentation
    B. Implied misrepresentation
    C. Intentional misrepresentation
    D. Fraudulent misrepresentation

5. List four common risks and errors in the contracting process.

    1. _____

    2. _____

    3. _____

    4. _____

6. The terms "appraisal" and "value" are reserved for the use of certified real estate agents. True or false?

7. List three risk management procedures.

    1. _____

    2. _____

    3. _____

MODULE 5 – RISK REDUCTION

CHECK YOUR UNDERSTANDING ANSWER KEY

1. The primary method for transferring the professional liability risks of brokers, managers and licensees is _____.

   C. Errors and Omissions insurance.

2. List three risk management strategies.

   1. Avoidance

   2. Reduction

   3. Transference

3. Federal law requires sellers of houses built before 1978 to make a lead-based paint disclosure.

   True

4. Which type of misrepresentation occurs when a licensee unknowingly conveys inaccurate information to a consumer concerning a property?

   A. **Unintentional misrepresentation**

5. List four common risks and errors in the contracting process.

   1. Using an illegal form

   2. Failing to state inclusions and exclusions

   3. Failing to track the progress of contingency satisfaction

   4. Mistakes in entering data in a form

6. The terms "appraisal" and "value" are reserved for the use of certified real estate agents.

   False

7. List three risk management procedures.

   1. Education

   2. Disclosure

   3. Documentation & recordkeeping

MODULE 5: RISK REDUCTION

CASE STUDY EXERCISE: Mitigating Risks

Situational data:

Abigail is a brand new real estate agent and is hungry for her first deal. She is hosting an open house at a foreclosure property and an investor stops by. They chat briefly and, as he tours the home, he starts asking her for the cost to renovate the kitchen and what the future of the neighborhood looks like. Abigail has no experience pricing renovations but she is very eager to land her first client.

Analysis Questions:

1. *What would you say if you were Abigail?*

   _____

   _____

   _____

   _____

   _____

   _____

Case Study Debrief Observations:

1. Since Abigail is not a contractor she should not speak on the repair estimates for the home.

2 Unintentional misrepresentation occurs when a licensee unknowingly conveys inaccurate information to a consumer concerning a property, financing or agency service. False or inaccurate information that the licensee, as a professional, should have known to be false or inaccurate may be included in the definition. Those found guilty generally have to pay fines and may be disciplined by state real estate regulators and professional organizations.

3. Instead of trying to win the client over with inaccurate estimates, Abigail should state that she is not a contractor but knows a few trusted contractors she could schedule to come out there for accurate estimates. This will show the potential client that she is resourceful and has his best interest at heart. It will also help protect her from any liability or misrepresentation issues.

Module 6: TENNESSEE REAL ESTATE COMMISSION LAWS, RULES & POLICIES

I. Broker Relationships & Responsibilities
II. Broker- Affiliate Relationship & Responsibilities
III. Broker – Brokerage Firm Regulations and Requirements

Module 6 Learning Objectives

Broker Relationships & Responsibilities

1. Define the regulations impacting a broker's management and maintenance of his or her trust accounts, specifically concerning deposits, disbursements, and record keeping.
2. Identify specific guidelines for handling transaction documents.

Broker- Affiliate Relationship & Responsibilities
1. Explain the different broker salesperson relationships
2. Demonstrate an awareness of compensation regulations

Broker- Brokerage Firm Regulations and Requirements
1. Identify the salient rules that apply for maintaining compliant branch locations and signage
2. Summarize the restrictions applicable to brokerage teams and personal assistants, both licensed and unlicensed; summarize what types of activity are (a) prohibited without a license, and (b) authorized as administrative tasks
3. Describe what to do in the case of death or incapacitation of brokers

I. Broker Relationships & Responsibilities

TRUST ACCOUNTS REGULATIONS

Depository and account requirements. Each broker is required to maintain a separate escrow account to hold any funds received by the broker as deposits, earnest money, or other similar funds, unless a waiver is obtained from the Commission.

Rental deposits held by a broker must be held in a separate account specifically for that purpose.

Escrow monies deposited with vacation lodging services must be in a federally-insured financial institution approved by the Commission and located in Tennessee.

Affiliate brokers pay to the broker with whom they are under contract all deposits and earnest money immediately upon receipt.

Licensees may not accept post-dated checks for payment of trust money unless specified in the offer.

The broker must always control the escrow account, even if he or she is not the owner.

Time requirements for deposit of funds. As indicated, affiliate brokers must give earnest money to their brokers immediately upon receipt.

Earnest money must be deposited into an escrow or trustee account promptly upon acceptance of the offer, unless the offer contains a statement such as "earnest money to be deposited by...."

Brokers are responsible for deposits and earnest money accepted by them or by their affiliate brokers, in compliance with the terms of the contract. If a contract authorizes the broker to place funds in an escrow or trustee account, the broker must clearly specify the following in the contract:

- the amount and form of earnest money (check, cash)
- the terms and conditions for disbursement
- the name and address of the person who will actually hold the funds

When a contract authorizes an individual or entity other than either broker to hold the funds in an escrow or trustee account, the broker is relieved of responsibility for the funds when the funds are received by the specified escrow agent.

Other general requirements. The broker must maintain for at least three (3) years accurate records of the escrow or trustee account showing

- the depositor of the funds
- date of deposit
- date of withdrawal
- the payee of the funds
- other pertinent information required by the Commission

Escrow account waiver. If the principal broker does not engage in activities that require the broker's acceptance of any funds belonging to others, he or she may receive a waiver to avoid the escrow account requirement. Upon receipt of a waiver by the Commission, a principal broker may close the firm's escrow account.

If the principal broker is authorized pursuant to a waiver to operate without an escrow account, he or she may accept funds belonging to another if the broker

- opens an escrow account within one (1) business day of accepting the deposit and deposits the funds into the account on the same day
- the broker notifies the Commission within one (1) business day after opening the new escrow account and provides the name and address of the bank, the name of the new account, and the account number

The principal broker who opens an escrow account after a waiver acknowledges his or her responsibility to operating under all the requirements of for escrow account.

Only one waiver may be obtained for a real estate firm for each license renewal period.

Permissible disbursement. Brokers may properly disburse funds from an escrow account

- upon a reasonable interpretation of the contract that authorizes the broker to hold the funds
- upon obtaining a written agreement signed by all parties having an interest in the funds, provided the agreement is separate from the contract that authorizes the broker to hold such funds
- at the closing of the transaction
- upon the rejection of an offer to purchase, sell, rent, lease, exchange or option real estate
- upon withdrawal of an offer not yet accepted to purchase, sell, rent, lease, exchange or option real estate
- upon filing an interpleader action in a court of competent jurisdiction
- upon the order of a court of competent jurisdiction

Escrow or trustee account funds must be disbursed in a proper manner without unreasonable delay.

Funds should be disbursed or interpleaded within twenty-one (21) calendar days from the date of receipt of a written request for disbursement of earnest money. Post-dated checks may not be used for payment of a deposit or earnest money, unless agreed to in the offer by the parties.

Commingling/improper use. Commingling is maintaining funds belonging to others in the same bank account that contains the licensee's personal or business funds. Commingling is strictly prohibited and can result in disciplinary action.

Conversion is misappropriating the funds or property of others, that is, using the funds or property entrusted to the licensee for a purpose other than the purpose for which the licensee was authorized to use it. Conversion can result not only in disciplinary action by the Commission, but may also result in criminal charges.

RECORDKEEPING

Responsibility for keeping records

The broker is responsible for the maintenance of brokerage records, including escrow or trustee account records, and transaction records. Although record maintenance is the broker's responsibility, affiliated licensees should ensure that records for transactions in which they are involved are provided to the broker. This may include, in addition to other documents, emails or note regarding phone calls of significance.

These documents must be maintained by any broker negotiating the transaction or identified in sales contract, brokerage agreement, closing statement, lease, or other document related to the transaction.

Retention period

The broker must retain all required records for a minimum of three (3) years from consummation of the transaction, and they must be made available to the Commission upon request.

What must be retained

All escrow or trustee accounts must be retained, as well as brokerage transaction records. The following items would be retained by the broker:

- listing agreements and any accompanying addenda, amendments, and inspection reports
- buyer agreements
- agency disclosures
- property disclosures
- offers, including rejected offers
- paper trail on deposited escrow funds
- any other documents pertaining to listings, purchase agreements, agency disclosures, correspondence pertaining to listings (letters, emails, faxes, and any notes made relative to phone conversations)
- any property management or lease agreements

Other general requirements

In order to ensure proper document retention, the principal broker using electronic recordkeeping methods must use a retention schedule that safeguards the security, authenticity, and accuracy of all records for the entire required retention period, and also provides the use of technology and hardware to ensure record accessibility in a readable format.

HANDLING TRANSACTION DOCUMENTS

Licensees must furnish a copy of any listing, sale, lease or other contract relevant to a real estate transaction to all signatories of the contract at the time of execution of the document.

Written offers. A broker or affiliate broker must promptly present every written offer to purchase or sell (all offers and counter-offers) obtained on a property until a contract is signed by all parties. Licensees must also communicate to the parties regarding how the offer is progressing and any inspection reports.

Upon obtaining acceptance of an offer to purchase, or any counteroffer, a broker or affiliate broker must promptly deliver true executed copies, signed by the seller, to both the purchaser and the seller. Brokers and affiliate brokers must ensure that all terms and conditions of the real estate transaction are included in the contract to purchase. If an offer is rejected, the licensee must request that the seller note the rejection on the offer and return the noted copy to the offeror or the offeror's agent.

Multiple offers. Tennessee license law does not specifically address multiple offers. It is the option of the offeree. The agent can advise the offeree on options available. As an example, a seller receiving multiple offers may choose to let all offerors know, in hopes of obtaining a higher offer. However, in some situations, buyers decide they do not wish to get into a bidding war and withdraw their offer(s). The most prudent action for the agent is to give the offeree the options and let that person decide how to proceed. The agent would never disclose the amount of one offer to the other party or that party's agent.

Transaction records. Records may be maintained in any record storage system that utilizes paper, film, electronic, or other media if the licensee can produce true copies and if copies can be made available to the Commission's authorized representative upon reasonable request within 24 hours.

Falsifying documents or misleading representations prohibited. Licensees may not falsify any document involved in a real estate transaction. Licensees are prohibited from knowingly representing to a principal any false information. This includes indicating an amount other than the actual sale, lease or exchange price, or the true actual amount of down payment, earnest money, security deposit or any other trust funds. Licensees must also indicate only the types of trust funds actually used. Licensees are in violation if they indicate that the funds are in the form of cash when they are not. Failing to accurately disclose any of these is considered to be misrepresentation and could result in disciplinary action. Misleading a lender as to the true down payment or sale price could result in a charge of fraud.

The Commission or the Commission's authorized representatives may, at all reasonable hours, examine and copy brokerage books, accounts, documents, or records relevant in determining whether a developer or escrow agent has complied with the applicable rules and laws. The Commission randomly audits brokerage records.

All documents required to be retained must be readily accessible in a format that makes document identification easily discernable. Documents must be made accessible to the Commission within twenty-four (24) hours of any request for inspection by representatives of the Commission.

II. Broker – Affiliate Relationship & Responsibilities

BROKER-SALESPERSON RELATIONSHIPS

Permitted affiliations

Commingling is maintaining funds belonging to others in the same bank account that contains the licensee's personal or business funds. Commingling is strictly prohibited and can result in disciplinary action.

Conversion is misappropriating the funds or property of others, that is, using the funds or property entrusted to the licensee for a purpose other than the purpose for which the licensee was authorized to use it. Conversion can result not only in disciplinary action by the Commission, but may also result in criminal charges.

Brokers responsibilities

The principal broker must devote full time to the management of the office, and licensees may not engage in any real estate activity in any office unless there is a principal broker devoting full time to office management. He or she must be accessible during normal daytime working hours, and be engaged primarily in the real estate business.

Although the broker has possession of the affiliates' licenses, each licensee is responsible for satisfying all legal requirements for retention of the license, including payment of appropriate fees and completion of required real estate education.

The principal broker is responsible for overseeing all advertising to ensure compliance with local, state and federal laws, including fair housing laws. He or she is also responsible for supervising and training affiliated licensees. The broker's responsibility includes ensuring that all affiliates are properly licensed and that they maintain errors and omissions insurance coverage at all times.

Additionally, the broker is responsible for all contracts. Only the broker may pay licensees affiliated with the broker.

It is the responsibility of the broker to properly maintain and oversee the trust/escrow account, and to ensure that all monies received are properly and timely deposited and withdrawn. Trust accounts are covered in detail in a later unit.

Record maintenance. The broker is required to maintain all brokerage records for a minimum of three years from consummation of transaction but they should be retained for a minimum seven (7) years for risk management concerns. Records the broker would maintain include:

- all offers, including rejected offers
- sales contracts
- property disclosures and disclaimers
- any lead paint disclosures, radon disclosures, and inspection reports
- escrow records
- leases
- closing statements and accompanying documents
- agency disclosures

- other correspondence pertinent to listings, offers, leases, or other real estate contracts.

Advertising oversight. The broker is responsible for all advertising and must ensure that it complies with all laws.

COMPENSATION REGULATIONS

Licensees may be paid only by the broker with whom they are contracted. Licensees may not be paid by other brokers, any affiliate broker, or consumers. A licensee's commission is based on his or her independent contractor or employment agreement with the broker with whom the licensee is contracted.

The broker's compensation is negotiated and determined by the broker and the principal. Brokers may pay compensation to licensees no longer affiliated with the broker but who were licensed with the broker at the time the commission is earned (usually at the time of contract), and the contract closes, if the affiliated licensee

- transfers to a new broker
- retires his or her license
- is in broker release status
- allowed his or her license to expire
- has died

Commissions and other fees for real estate activity can be paid only to individuals licensed as brokers, affiliate brokers or time-share salespersons at the time the commission or fee was earned. No action or lawsuit may be instituted, nor recovery obtained, by any person in any court in Tennessee for compensation for any act or service rendered for licensing activity other than by those individuals licensed as a broker, affiliate broker or time-share salesperson at the time of performing or offering to perform a real estate act or service or procuring any promise or contract for the payment of compensation for doing so.

Referrals. A referral fee is a commission or any other type of compensation for the referral of a potential buyer, seller, lessor or lessee of real estate.

As indicated in a previously, a licensed broker may pay a commission to a licensed broker of another state if the nonresident broker does not conduct real estate negotiations in Tennessee.

If a licensee recommends to any party to a transaction the use of services of another individual or service provider in which the licensee has an interest or from whom the licensee may receive a referral fee or other compensation for the referral, he or she must timely disclose to the party who receives the referral the licensee's interests in the referral or the fact that a referral fee may be received. This requirement does not apply to referrals to other licensees to provide real estate services.

Reasonable cause must exist for a party to be eligible to collect a referral fee. Reasonable cause does not exist unless the party seeking the referral fee actually introduced the business to the real estate licensee from whom the referral fee is sought and one or more of the following conditions exists between the party seeking the referral fee and the real estate licensee:

- a sub-agency relationship
- a contractual referral fee relationship
- a contractual cooperative brokerage relationship

Reasonable cause allows a real estate licensee to solicit or request a referral fee but does not necessarily mean that the licensee has a legal right to be paid a referral fee.

It is illegal for any person or entity to solicit or request a referral fee from a real estate licensee without reasonable cause, or to threaten to reduce or withhold employee relocation benefits or to take other action adverse to the interests of a client of a real estate licensee because of an agency relationship.

III. Broker – Brokerage Firm Regulations & Responsibilities

BROKERAGE REGULATIONS, REQUIREMENTS

The broker and firm owner will determine the type of business entity, agency policies, compensation schedule, and what service the firm will offer (buyers and sellers, buyers only, sellers only, property management, etc.).

Business locations and signage requirements

Each brokerage office, including any branch office, is required to have a real estate firm license, a principal broker and a fixed location with adequate facilities for affiliated licensees. The office location must conform with zoning laws and ordinances. In making application for a license or for a change of location, the licensee must provide the Commission with written verification that the office conforms with zoning requirements.

Each office, including any branch office, must also have a sign conspicuously displayed on the outside of the place of business that contains the name of the firm as registered with the Commission.

A broker may have the main office or a branch office in his or her home. It must be licensed, have a principal broker, must display licenses, and must comply with sign requirements and local zoning ordinances. Although the requirement to have a sign outside the place of business is applicable to all offices, including an office maintained in the broker's home, this may be waived in cases of certain unusual geographical circumstances.

Affiliate brokers are not required to display signs at the office of their brokers.

Change of location

Within ten (10) days of any change of office location, all licensees registered at that office are required to notify the Commission in writing of their new business address and pay the fee delineated in TCA 62-13-308.

If the applicant for a broker's license maintains more than one place of business within the state, the applicant must apply for and obtain an additional firm license for each branch office. Each application must state the location of the branch office and the name of the person in charge. Each branch office must be under the direction and supervision of a broker licensed at that address.

Death or incapacitation of broker

The Commission must be notified within ten (10) days of the death, resignation, termination, or incapacity of the firm's principal broker. In an unexplained extended absence of a principal broker, the Commission must be notified within a reasonable time period. At the time of notification, a plan must be submitted addressing the continuation of operations without a principal broker.

The Commission may, at its discretion and based on the merits and circumstances of each case, permit a real estate firm to continue operating without a principal broker for up to thirty (30) days from the date of death, resignation, termination, or incapacity of a principal broker, subject to conditions that may be imposed by the Commission.

If, within the thirty (30) day period, the real estate firm contacts the Commission demonstrating compliance with their initial approved plan and circumstances which require additional time to continue operating without a principal broker, the executive director has the authority to grant a thirty (30) day extension to the period originally allowed by the Commission. In the event that a thirty (30) day extension is granted, a new principal broker must be in place no later than the sixty-first (61st) day from the date of death, resignation, termination, or incapacity of a principal broker.

Brokerage of two firms

A principal broker may act as a principal broker for two (2) firms if both firms are in the same location (are located at and use the same physical address).

Teams

As indicated, teams must advertise in the name of the broker.

Licensees who hold themselves out as a team, group, or similar entity within a firm must be affiliated with the same licensed firm. The team may not establish a physical location that is separate from the physical location of record of the firm with which they are affiliated.

The team members must receive all compensation for licensing activity only from their principal broker.

The principal broker cannot delegate his or her supervisory responsibilities to any licensees who are team members; the principal broker remains ultimately responsible for oversight and supervision of all licensees within the firm.

No team members within a firm are permitted to represent themselves as a separate entity from the licensed firm, and are prohibited from designating members as designated firm agents; only the principal broker of the firm may do so.

Personal assistants

Only licensees can legally perform licensing activity; however, employees of the firm or personal assistants to licensees are not required to be licensed if they perform no licensing activities in performing their duties. Affiliated licensees may hire personal assistants with authorization from the broker.

A licensed assistant or employee would have an affiliate broker or broker license and could perform any licensing activity. This individual could be paid a portion of commissions or receive a salary. The hiring licensee must have a written agreement with the assistant, and if the assistant is an employee, must adhere to any applicable labor laws. Licensed assistants must be licensed with and compensated by the broker.

An unlicensed assistant or employee may not be paid based on commissions or per transaction, or in any way be compensated based on or directly related to a real estate transaction.

Prohibited activities. An unlicensed assistant or employee is prohibited from

- showing properties for sale or lease to prospective purchasers

- making personal or phone cold calls to potential clients

- hosting open houses, home show booths, or fairs

- negotiating terms of a real estate transaction

- negotiating or agreeing to commissions or referral fees on behalf of a licensee

- discussing or explaining contracts, listings, offers or other similar matters with persons outside the firm

Authorized activities. Duties that may be performed by an unlicensed assistant or employee include

- completing and submitting listing information to the multiple listing service

- answering and forwarding phone calls to a licensee

- providing information on the listing agreement on phone calls received

- following up on loan commitments after contract negotiation; obtaining reports on progress of the loan

- obtaining public information available from utility services and court house records

- assembling documents as preparation for closing

- having keys made for listings

- placing ads, after approval by the principal broker

- accepting, recording and depositing security deposits and advance rents under direct supervision of the principal broker

- preparing flyers and other promotional materials for distribution, after approval by the principal broker

- typing contracts for approval by the hiring licensee and principal broker

- placing signs on property

- monitoring licenses and personnel files

- ordering repairs as directed by the hiring licensee

- calculating and distributing commission checks

MODULE 6 SNAPSHOT REVIEW:

TENNESSEE REAL ESTATE COMMISSION LAWS, RULES, POLICIES

BROKER RELATIONSHIPS AND RESPONSIBILITIES

Trust accounts

- broker must keep trust funds, deposits in separate escrow account; salespersons must give trust funds to broker upon receipt
- broker controls all aspects of the trust account; deposits must be deposited upon acceptance of the offer
- must maintain escrow records for 3 years

Recordkeeping

- broker responsible for all record maintenance; salespersons must ensure documents they are working with are transmitted to broker

Handling transaction documents

- must give signatories copies of all contracts upon execution
- written offers must be promptly presented; if accepted, executed copies promptly delivered; if rejected, licensee requests offeree to note on offer and promptly provides copy to offeror
- Commission may at reasonable hours examine and copy broker's records and accounts; record must be available within 24 hours

BROKER-AFFILIATE RELATIONSHIP & RESPONSIBILITIES

Permitted affiliations

- all licensees must be affiliated with a broker; broker must certify licensee's honesty and that broker will supervise and train licensees

Brokers' responsibilities

- managing full time, accessible during normal working hours, engaged primarily in real estate
- ensuring all affiliates are properly licensed and have E & O insurance
- overseeing trust fund, all advertising, and affiliates' real estate activity
- compensation of subordinates –may only be paid by the broker
- referrals – broker may pay fee to a licensed broker of another state; reasonable cause must exist for a party to receive a referral fee

BROKER – BROKERAGE FIRM REGULATIONS & RESPONSIBILITIES

Business locations; signage

- each brokerage office must have a real estate firm license, principal broker, and fixed location
- must display sign conspicuously outside of the office;
- may have office in home; affiliate brokers not required to display sign

Change of location

- must notify Commission of any change of office location within 10 days; all licensees must report new business address

Death of broker

- must notify Commission within 10 days if principal broker dies, resigns, leaves brokerage and submit plan of continued operations; may continue operating for 30 days with possible 30-day extension

Teams

- must advertise in name of broker; teams cannot have a separate location
- broker cannot delegate supervisory responsibilities; principal broker is ultimately responsible

Personal assistants

- do not require license if perform administrative tasks
- can be hired if principal broker authorizes; must execute written agreement and be paid by broker
- prohibited activities: showing properties; prospecting; open house hosting; negotiating terms or commissions; explaining contracts
- permitted activities: answering, forwarding phone calls; providing listing information; obtaining public information; general administrative duties; placing signs

MODULE 6 - TENNESSEE REAL ESTATE COMMISSION LAWS, RULES, POLICIES

QUIZ

Carefully read each question and provide your best answer based on what you learned in this module. Then check your answers against the Answer Key which immediately follows the quiz questions.

1. Maintaining funds belonging to others in the same bank account that contains the licensee's personal or business funds is also called _____.

    a.   commingling.
    b.   conversion.
    c.   fraud.
    d.   money laundering.

2. The broker is required to maintain all brokerage records for a minimum of _____ for risk management concerns.

    a.   1 year
    b.   5 years
    c.   7 years
    d.   10 years

3. How long does a broker have to present every written offer to the sellers?

    a.   3 days
    b.   7 days
    c.   24 hours
    d.   The broker must present written offers immediately.

4. A licensee's commission is based on his or her _____.

    a.   expertise.
    b.   services offered.
    c.   independent contractor agreement with the broker.
    d.   contractor agreement with the client.

5. The broker must retain all required records for a minimum of _____ from consummation of the transaction.

    a.   5 years
    b.   3 years
    c.   1 year
    d.   7 years

6. Using escrow funds for a purpose other than which the licensee was authorized to use it is called _____.

   a. retention.
   b. conversion.
   c. revocation.
   d. commingling.

7. A licensed broker may pay a commission to a licensed broker of another state. This commission is also called a _____.

   a. referral fee.
   b. transaction fee.
   c. finder's fee.
   d. recommendation fee.

8. Where must a brokerage display its sign?

   a. Above the broker's desk
   b. On the outside of the place of business
   c. On the office door
   d. There are no signage rules for brokerages.

9. Who is responsible for overseeing all advertising to ensure compliance with local and federal laws?

   a. The principal broker
   b. The team leader
   c. NAR
   d. The local government real estate division

10. Which of the following is an authorized activity for an unlicensed employee?

    a. Hosting open houses
    b. Following up on loan commitments
    c. Negotiating terms of a real estate transaction
    d. Discussing contracts

11. Earnest money must be deposited into an escrow account _____.

    a. promptly upon acceptance of the offer.
    b. with the initial offer.
    c. within 14 days of acceptance of the offer.
    d. within 5 days of the closing date.

12. A principal broker may act as a principal broker for _____.

    a. 1 firm only.
    b. as many firms as they choose to.
    c. up to 5 firms.
    d. 2 firms if both firms are in the same location.

13. Escrow funds should be disbursed within _____ calendar days from the date of receipt of a written request for disbursement.

    a. 5
    b. 21
    c. 7
    d. 30

14. The Commission may permit a real estate firm to continue operating without a principal broker for up to _____ from the date of death of a principal broker.

    a. 30 days
    b. 3 months
    c. 6 months
    d. 1 year

15. What is the name of the length of time a broker must hold onto all records?

    a. Recordkeeping period
    b. Commingling period
    c. Retention period
    d. Transaction period

16. How can an unlicensed assistant be paid?

    a. Hourly
    b. Per transaction
    c. Commissions
    d. In a way that's directly related to real estate transactions

17. Who determines the broker's compensation?

    a. The licensee according to regulatory commission schedules
    b. The broker and the principal via negotiation
    c. The seller
    d. The broker

18. Who pays team members compensation?

    a. The team leader
    b. The Commission
    c. The principal broker
    d. The seller

19. If the Commission requests to see transaction records, how long does a broker have to provide them?

    a. 12 hours
    b. 48 hours
    c. 1 week
    d. 24 hours

20. The broker's responsibility includes ensuring that all licensees are properly licensed and that they
    _____.

    a. sell multiple homes a year.
    b. maintain errors and omissions insurance coverage at all times.
    c. can recite all of the fair housing laws.
    d. have compliant advertising.

21. Who controls the escrow account?

    a. The broker
    b. The licensee
    c. The seller
    d. The buyer

22. Within _____ days of any change of office location, all licensees registered at that office are
    required to notify the Commission of their new business address.

    a. 5
    b. 7
    c. 10
    d. 15

23. Who is NOT entitled to a real estate commission?

    a. Broker
    b. Time-share salesperson
    c. Affiliate broker
    d. Vendor

24. Which of the following activities is an unlicensed assistant prohibited from?

    a. Completing listing information
    b. Showing properties for sale
    c. Having keys made for listings
    d. Placing signs on property

25. If the principal broker does not engage in activities that require the broker's acceptance of any
    funds belonging to others, he or she may receive a(n) _____.

    a. earnest money forgiveness.
    b. Commission designated escrow account.
    c. escrow account waiver.
    d. All brokers are required to have an operable escrow account.

MODULE 6 - TENNESSEE REAL ESTATE COMMISSION LAWS, RULES, POLICIES

ANSWER KEY TO QUIZ

1. a. commingling.
2. c. 7 years
3. d. The broker must present written offers immediately.
4. c. independent contractor agreement with the broker.
5. b. 3 years
6. b. conversion.
7. a. referral fee.
8. b. On the outside of the place of business
9. a. The principal broker
10. b. Following up on loan commitments
11. a. promptly upon acceptance of the offer.
12. d. 2 firms if both firms are in the same location.
13. b. 21
14. a. 30 days
15. c. Retention period
16. a. Hourly
17. b. The broker and the principal via negotiation
18. c. The principal broker
19. d. 24 hours
20. b. maintain errors and omissions insurance coverage at all times.
21. a. The broker
22. c. 10
23. d. Vendor
24. b. Showing properties for sale
25. c. escrow account waiver.

MODULE 6 - TENNESSEE REAL ESTATE COMMISSION LAWS, RULES, POLICIES

CHECK YOUR UNDERSTANDING

Instructions:

Carefully read each challenge question, then provide your best answer based on what you learned in this module. Then check your answers against the Answer Key which immediately follows the questions.

1. The broker is required to maintain all brokerage records for a minimum of _____ from consummation of transaction.

    A. 3 years

    B. 6 months

    C. 5 years

    D. 7 years

2. List three authorized activities for an unlicensed assistant.

    1. _____

    2. _____

    3. _____

3. If the principal broker does not engage in activities that require the broker's acceptance of any funds belonging to others, he or she may receive a waiver to avoid the escrow account requirement. True or false?

4. What is it called when funds belonging to others are in the same account as a licensee's personal or business funds?

    A. Mixing

    B. Commingling

    C. Transitioning

    D. Comixing

5. The _____ is the time period a broker must keep all required records.

    A. maintenance period

    B. recordkeeping period

    C. transaction period
    D. retention period

6. Each broker is required to maintain a separate escrow account to hold any funds received by the broker as deposits or earnest money. True or false?

7. List three prohibited activities for an unlicensed assistant.

    1. _____

    2. _____

    3. _____

8. The Commission must be notified within 3 days of death of the firm's principal broker. True or false?

9. What is the name of the type of compensation for introducing a buyer to a licensee?

    A. Kickback
    B. Commission

    C. Referral fee
    D. This type of compensation is not allowed.

10. List four items a broker must retain.

    1. _____

    2. _____

    3. _____

    4. _____

MODULE 6 - TENNESSEE REAL ESTATE COMMISSION LAWS, RULES, POLICIES

CHECK YOUR UNDERSTANDING ANSWER KEY

1. The broker is required to maintain all brokerage records for a minimum of _____ from consummation of transaction.

   A. 3 years

2. List three authorized activities for an unlicensed assistant.

   1. Completing and submitting listing information to the multiple listing service

   2. Answering and forwarding phone calls to a licensee

   3. Having keys made for listings

3. If the principal broker does not engage in activities that require the broker's acceptance of any funds belonging to others, he or she may receive a waiver to avoid the escrow account requirement.

   True

4. What is it called when funds belonging to others are in the same account as a licensee's personal or business funds?

   B. Commingling

5. The _____ is the time period a broker must keep all required records.

   D. retention period

6. Each broker is required to maintain a separate escrow account to hold any funds received by the broker as deposits or earnest money.

   True

7. List three prohibited activities for an unlicensed assistant.

   1. Negotiating terms of a real estate transaction

   2. Hosting open houses

   3. Making phone cold calls to potential clients

8. The Commission must be notified within 3 days of death of the firm's principal broker.

   False

9. What is the name of the type of compensation for introducing a buyer to a licensee?

   C. Referral fee

10. List four items a broker must retain.

    1. Buyer agreements

    2. Listing agreements

    3. Agency disclosures

    4. Property disclosures

Module 7: RESIDENTIAL/COMMERCIAL/RENTAL PROPERTY MANAGEMENT

I. Essential Dynamics of Property Management
II. Advanced Considerations in Property Management
III. Property Management Specializations and Tennessee Law

Module 7 Learning Objectives

Essential Dynamics of Property Management

1. Describe the essential aspects and underlying tasks associated with property management including reporting, budgeting, renting, property maintenance and construction.
2. Summarized the salient tasks involved in proficient property maintenance including management objectives; routine maintenance, and what is entailed in preventive maintenance.
3. Define what is meant by tenant improvements and differentiate from renovations and environmental concerns.

Advanced Considerations in Property Management

1. Identify the best methods to manage risks encountered in property management in terms of strategy; safety and insurance.
2. Define the foundations of leasing
3. List the central provisions of the conventional property management agreement.
4. Explain how to specialize in the management business including property specializations, securing business, and professional development.

Property Management Specializations and Tennessee Law

1. Demonstrate an understanding of timeshares including the mechanics of registration, the public offering statement, and rights of cancellation.
2. Summarize the primary thrusts of the Rental Location Act of 1978, including license particulars; licensing requirements; and required disclosures.
3. Define the practice of 'vacation lodging services', and the licensing mechanics associated with its practice; highlight the central responsibilities entailed in compliant practice.
4. Summarize the salient rights and responsibilities of the landlord and the tenant as proscribed by the Universal Residential Landlord Tenant Act (URLTA).

I. Essential Dynamics of Property Management

PROPERTY MANAGEMENT FUNCTIONS

Property management is a specialty within the real estate profession. Many states require persons who manage real estate on behalf of other persons or entities to be licensed as real estate brokers. Other states license such persons specifically as property managers. Real estate firms that handle the sale of commercial and investment properties are in a natural position to manage those properties for their owners. Some property managers work for firms that manage multiple properties under blanket management contracts; others are independent agents and some are employees of the owner.

Reporting

Financial reporting to the principal is a fundamental responsibility of the property manager. Reports may be required monthly, quarterly, and annually. Required reports typically include an annual operating budget (see below); monthly cash flow reports indicating income, expenses, net operating income, and net cash flow; profit and loss statements based on the cash flow reports and showing net profit; and budget comparison statements showing how actual results match the original budget.

Budgeting

An operating budget based on expected expenses and revenues is a necessity for management. The budget will determine rental rates, amounts available for capital expenditures, required reserve funds, salaries and wages of employees, amounts to be paid for property taxes and insurance premiums and mortgage or debt service. It will indicate the expected return, based on the previous year's performance. A typical budget will contain a projection, also based on past performance and on current market information, of income from all sources, such as rents and other services, and of expenses for all purposes, such as operating expenses, maintenance services, utilities, taxes, and capital expenditures. Operating statements itemizing income and expenses are then presented to the owner on a regular basis so that the owner can evaluate the manager's performance against the budget.

Income. The total of scheduled rents plus revenues from such sources as vending services, storage charges, late fees, utilities, and contracts is the *potential gross income*. Subtracting losses caused by uncollected rents, vacancies and evictions gives *effective gross income*. Operating expenses are subtracted from this total to show *net operating income*. When debt service and reserves (which are not counted as operating expenses) are subtracted, the result is *cash flow*.

Expenses. Expenses may be fixed or variable. Fixed expenses are those that remain constant and may include operating expenses, regular maintenance costs, and administration. Variable expenses are those that may change from month to month or occur sporadically, such as specific repairs or capital expenditures.

Capital expenditures. Expected expenditures for major items such as renovation or expansion should be included as a budgeting item. Large-scale projects are typically budgeted over a period of years.

Cash reserve. A cash reserve is a fund set aside from operating revenues for variable expenses, such as supplies, redecorating, and repairs. The amount of the reserve is based on experience with variable expenses in previous years.

Renting

The property manager, whose full responsibilities include maintaining and managing the property in accordance with the owner's financial goals, include seeing that the property is properly rented and tenanted. The manager may use the services of a leasing agent, whose concern is solely to rent the space. In such a situation, some of the manager's tasks may be performed by the leasing agent. Renting the property includes the following tasks, regardless of which party is actually performing them.

Controlling vacancies. There are many possible reasons for vacancies in a building:

- rent too high or too low
- ineffective marketing
- management quality
- poor tenant-retention program
- image and appearance problems
- high market vacancy rate

Successful managers look for these factors and take steps to limit or counteract their effects.

Marketing. Finding and attracting the right kind of tenants for a property is the aim of a marketing program. A marketing plan based on the property's features and the relationship between supply and demand in the market area, and consonant with the money available, will determine the best mix of advertising and promotional activities. Marketing methods include:

- billboard advertising
- brochures and fliers
- meetings and presentations
- networking
- newspaper ads
- radio and television advertising
- signs
- tenant referrals
- websites and online services

The efficiency of marketing activities can be judged in terms of how many prospects per completed lease they generate. The lower the cost per prospect per lease, the more effective and efficient the program.

Setting rents. Rental income must be sufficient to cover fixed expenses, operating expenses, and desired return on investment. But rental rates must also be realistic, taking into account what is happening in the market. The manager must consider prevailing rents in comparable properties as well as vacancy rates in the market and in the property. The manager makes a detailed survey of competitive space and makes adjustments for differences between the subject property and competing properties before setting the rental rates for the property. Residential apartment rates are stated in monthly amounts per unit, while commercial rates are usually stated as an annual or monthly amount per square foot. If vacancy rates in the managed property are too high, the manager may have to lower rates or identify problems in the property or its management that are contributing to vacancy level. On the other hand, if the property's vacancy rate is significantly lower than market rates, the manager may conclude that higher rental rates are called for.

Selecting tenants. To ensure that the property produces the desired level of income from rent, it is essential to find the most suitable tenants. For commercial space, the manager must determine that:

- the space meets the tenant's needs for size, configuration, location, and quality.
- the tenant will be able to pay for the space.
- the tenant's business is compatible with that of other tenants.
- there is room for expansion if the tenant's need for space is likely to grow.

For residential space, in addition to ascertaining the tenant's creditworthiness, the manager must be careful to comply with all federal and local fair housing laws. A manager should collect the same type of information on all prospective tenants. However, even though the law prohibits discrimination on the basis of race, sex, age and other protected classes, a manager may discriminate in certain other ways. For example, a manager has the right to refuse to rent to a person who has a history paying rent late, damaging property, fighting with other tenants, or spotty employment.

Collecting rents. The lease agreement should clearly specify the terms of rental payment. The manager must establish a system of notices and records as well as a method of collecting rents on schedule. Compliance with all state laws and regulations concerning collecting and accounting for rents is a necessity to avoid unwanted legal complications. As for monies received, the manager must follow trust fund handling procedures established by law and laid out in the rental and management agreements. If authorized by the management agreement, the manager may also collect security deposits and handle them as required by law.

Maintaining tenant relations. Happy tenants remain in a rented space longer than unhappy tenants. High tenant turnover adds to increased advertising and redecorating expenses. For these reasons, it is incumbent on the manager to

- communicate regularly with tenants
- respond promptly and satisfactorily to maintenance and service requests
- enforce rules and lease terms consistently and fairly
- comply with all relevant laws, such as fair housing and ADA (Americans with Disabilities Act) regulations

Legal issues (Fair Housing, ADA, and ECOA)

Fair housing laws govern landlords and tenants just as they do sellers and buyers. They ensure that persons receive fair treatment regardless of race, color, religion, national origin, sex, handicap, or familial status. Families with children must receive equal treatment with those who do not have children. Landlords cannot charge higher rents or security deposits because of the presence of children. Managers must make sure that their marketing and leasing practices are in accordance with fair housing laws.

The Americans with Disabilities Act similarly requires landlords in certain circumstances to make housing and facilities available to disabled persons without hindrance. Familiarity with this law and with the latest state, federal, and local fair housing laws is essential.

The Equal Credit Opportunity Act, which prohibits discrimination in lending, applies to how property managers evaluate potential tenants. The manager must be consistent in evaluating the creditworthiness of applicants. The same application forms and the same credit requirements should be used with all applicants.

Property maintenance

Physical maintenance of the property is one of the property manager's primary functions. The costs of services provided must always be balanced with financial objectives and the need to satisfy tenant needs. The manager will also be concerned with staffing and scheduling requirements, in accordance with maintenance objectives.

Maintenance objectives. The foremost maintenance objective is generally to preserve the value of the physical asset for the owner over the long term. Although not every property is best served by vast expenditures on top-level maintenance, it is almost always important to maintain the viability of the property as a rental. Three general types of maintenance are required to keep a property in serviceable condition: routine, preventive, and corrective.

Routine maintenance. Routine maintenance activities are those necessary for the day-to-day functioning of the property. Regular performance of these activities helps to keep tenants satisfied as well as forestall serious problems requiring repair or correction. Routine activities are such things as:

- regular inspections
- scheduled upkeep of mechanical systems-heating, air-conditioning, rest rooms, lighting, landscaping
- regular cleaning of common areas
- minor repairs
- supervision of purchasing

Preventive maintenance. Preventive maintenance goes beyond the routine in attempting to deal with situations that can become serious problems if ignored. Seasonal or scheduled replacement of appliances and equipment, regular painting of exterior and interior areas, and planned replacement of a roof are a few examples.

Corrective maintenance. When routine and preventive maintenance fail, repairs and replacements become mandatory to keep the property operational. A boiler may develop a leak, an air-conditioning unit may break down, an elevator may cease to function properly.

Maintenance contracting. Depending on building type and size, tenant needs, and budgetary constraints, a manager may decide to hire an outside firm to handle maintenance services rather than hiring on-site employees. Efficiency, competence, responsiveness, and effective cost will be major deciding factors.

Construction

Commercial and industrial property managers are regularly called upon to make alterations to existing space to accommodate a tenant's needs. They may also have to undertake or oversee construction that alters or expands common areas or the entire building itself. Again, such work may be contracted out or done by in-house employees.

Tenant improvements. Alterations made specifically for certain tenants are called build-outs or tenant improvements. The work may involve merely painting and re-carpeting a rental space, or erecting new walls and installing special electrical or other systems. In new buildings, spaces are often left incomplete so that they can be finished to an individual tenant's specifications. In such cases, it is important to clarify which improvements will be considered tenant property (trade fixtures) and which will belong to the building.

Renovations. When buildings lose functionality (become functionally obsolescent), they generally also lose tenants, drop in class, and suffer declining rental rates. Maintenance becomes more expensive because of the difficulties of servicing out-of-date building components. Renovation may solve some of these problems, but the manager will have to help the owner determine whether the costs of renovation can be recovered by increased revenues resulting from the renovation.

Environmental concerns. A variety of environmental concerns confronts a property manager, ranging from air quality to waste disposal, tenant concerns, and federal, state and local environmental regulations. The managed property may contain asbestos, radon, mold, lead, and other problematic substances. Tenants may produce hazardous waste. The manager must be aware of the issues and see that proper procedures are in place to deal with them, including providing means for proper disposal of hazardous materials, arranging for environmental audits and undertaking possible remediation. For instance, an audit may show that a building is causing tenants to become sick because of off-gassing from construction materials combined with a lack of ventilation. Remediation may consist of nothing more than replacing carpets and improving ventilation, and the manager, if empowered to do so, should take the necessary steps.

Legal concerns (ADA). The Americans with Disabilities Act requires managers to ensure that disabled employees and members of the public have the same level of access to facilities as is provided for those who are not disabled. Employers with at least fifteen employees must follow nondiscriminatory employment and hiring practices. Reasonable accommodations must be made to enable disabled employees to perform essential functions of their jobs. Modifications to the physical components of the building may be necessary to provide the required access to tenants and their customers, such as widening doorways, changing door hardware, changing how doors open, installing ramps, lowering wall-mounted telephones and keypads, supplying Braille signage, and providing auditory signals. Existing barriers must be removed when the removal is "readily achievable," that is, when cost is not prohibitive. New construction and remodeling must meet a higher standard, Managers must be aware of the laws and determine whether their buildings meet requirements. If not, the manager must determine whether restructuring or retrofitting or some other kind of accommodation is most practical.

II: Advanced Considerations in Property Management

RISK MANAGEMENT

Many things can go wrong in a rented property, from natural disaster to personal injury to terrorism to malfeasance by employees. Huge monetary losses for the owner, in the form of civil and criminal penalties, legal costs, fines, damages, and costs of remediation can be the result. A manager must consider the possibility of such events and have a plan for dealing with them.

Risk management strategies. Depending on the nature of the risk, the size of the potential losses, the likelihood of its happening, and the costs of doing something about it, a manager and owner will generally choose one or more of the following risk management strategies:

- avoidance-removing the source of the risk, such as by closing off a dangerous area of the building

- reduction-taking action to forestall the event before it happens, such as by installing fire alarms, sprinklers, and security systems

- transference-shifting the risk to someone else by buying an insurance policy

- retention-taking the chance that the event is not likely enough to occur to justify the expense of one of the other strategies; self-insurance

Security and safety. A court may hold a manager and owner responsible for the physical safety of employees, tenants, and customers in leased premises. In addition to standard life safety and security systems such as sprinklers, fire doors, smoke alarms, fire escapes, and door locks, a manager may have to provide electronic and human monitoring systems (security cameras, security guards) and be prepared to take action against tenants who allow, conduct or contribute to dangerous criminal activities such as assault and drug use.

Insurance. Many types of insurance are available to allow for the shifting of liability away from the owner. An insurance audit by a competent insurance agent will indicate what kind of and how much coverage is advisable. Common types of insurance coverage for income and commercial properties include:

- casualty-coverage for specific risks, such as theft, vandalism, burglary, illness and accident, machinery damage

- liability-coverage for risks incurred by the owner when the public enters the building; medical expenses resulting from owner negligence or other causes

- workers' compensation-hospital and medical coverage for employees injured in the course of employment, mandated by state laws

- fire and hazard-coverage for damage to the property by fire, wind, hail, smoke, civil disturbance, and other causes

- flood-coverage for damages caused by heavy rains, snow, drainage failures, and failed public infrastructures such as dams and levies; flood insurance is not included in regular hazard policies

- contents and personal property-coverage for building contents and personal property when they are not actually on the building premises

- consequential loss, use, and occupancy-coverage for the business losses resulting from a disaster, such as loss of rent and other revenue, when the property cannot be used for business

- surety bond-coverage against losses resulting from criminal or negligent acts of an employee

The owner may opt for a multi-peril policy which combines standard types of commercial policies and may allow special coverage for floods, earthquakes, and terrorism.

The amount of coverage provided by certain types of policies may be based on whether the property is insured at depreciated value or current replacement value. Depreciated value is its original value minus the loss in value over time. Current replacement value, which is more expensive, is the amount it would cost to rebuild or replace the property at current rates.

Commercial policies include coinsurance clauses requiring the insured to bear a portion of the loss. Fire and hazard policies usually require the coverage to be in an amount equal to at least 80 percent of the replacement value.

Owner's policies do not cover what is owned by the tenant. Tenants should obtain their own renter's or tenant's insurance to cover personal belongings. Residential and commercial or business variants are available. The question of who owns tenant improvements is not only important when it is time for the tenant to leave the premises. It is also likely to determine whether the tenant's or the landlord's insurance company will be paying if the improvements are damaged or destroyed.

Handling of trust funds. Managers are responsible for proper handling of monies belonging to other parties that come into the manager's hands in the course of doing business. For property managers, such funds include rents collected from tenants, security deposits, and capital contributions from the property owner. State laws, usually incorporated into real estate commission rules and the state's real estate law, specify how a property manager is to manage trust funds. In general, the agent is to maintain a separate bank account for these funds, with special accounting, in a qualified depository institution. The rules for how long an agent may hold trust funds before depositing them, and how the funds are to be disbursed, are spelled out. The fundamental requirements are that the owners of all funds must be identified, and there must be no commingling or conversion of client funds and agent funds. Mishandling carries heavy penalties.

THE MANAGEMENT AGREEMENT

The management agreement establishes an agency agreement between manager and owner as well as specifying such essentials as the manager's scope of authority, responsibilities, objectives, compensation, and the term of the agreement. Property managers are usually considered to be general agents empowered to perform some or all of the ongoing tasks and duties of operating the property, including the authority to enter into contracts. The agency relationship creates the fiduciary duties of obedience, care, loyalty, accounting, and disclosure. The contractual relationship ensures that the manager will strive to realize the highest return for the owner consistent with the owner's objectives and instructions. The agreement should be in writing and include at least the basics of any real estate contract, as follows.

- **Names of the parties**--owner, landlord, manager, tenant or other party to be bound by the contract

- **Property description**--street address, unit number and location, square footage, and other information that specifies the leased premises

- **Term**--time period (months, years) covered by the contract; termination conditions and provisions

- **Owner's purpose**--maximize net income, maximize asset value, maximize return, minimize expenditure, maintain property quality, etc.; long-term goals for the property

- **Owner's responsibilities**--management fees, plus any management expenses such as payroll, advertising and insurance that the manager will not be expected to pay

- **Manager's authority**--the scope of powers being conveyed to the manager: hiring and staffing, setting rents, contracting with vendors, ordering repairs, limits on expenditures without seeking owner permission

- **Manager's responsibilities**--specification of duties, such as marketing, leasing, maintenance, budgeting, reporting, collecting and handling rents; the manager should be included as an additional insured on the liability policy for the property

- **Budget**--amounts, or percentages of revenues, allotted for operations, taxes, insurance, capital expenditures, etc.

- **Allocation of costs**--who is to pay certain expenses, that is, which will be treated as expenses of the manager vs. which will be paid directly by the owner

- **Reporting**--how often and what kind of reports are to be made

- **Compensation**--the management fee or other means of compensation to the manager; there may be a flat fee based on square footage, a rental commission based on a percentage of annual rent, a combination of these, or some other arrangement; in compliance with anti-trust laws, management fees are not standardized but must be negotiated by agent and principal

- **Equal opportunity statement**--the HUD statement or equivalent concerning availability to all persons and classes protected by law, incorporated into the agreement in the case of a residential property

FOUNDATIONS OF LEASING

Recall from the prelicense chapter on leases that a leasehold estate may grant tenancy for years, from period-to-period, at will, and at sufferance.

For years. An estate for years may be for any definite period—years, months, weeks, days. When the estate expires, the lessee must return the premises to the lessor and vacate the premises. Most commercial leases grant this type of estate.

Periodic. An estate from period-to-period does not have any definite period. Such an estate begins as a lease for a definite period but continues after the expiration of the lease, as long as the lessee continues to pay rent at the regular interval, the lessor accepts it, and no one gives notice to terminate the lease. This type of leasehold is common with residential properties.

At will. A tenancy at will is similar to the periodic tenancy, except that it does not begin with a definite period. It continues, with the consent of the lessor, as long as the tenant pays rent at regular intervals. It is terminated by the death of either party. The tenancy at will is rarely, if ever, used in a written lease.

At sufferance. A tenancy or estate at sufferance comes into existence when a tenant stays beyond the expiration of another type of lease without the lessor's permission. This type of tenancy is never intentionally used in a written lease.

Leases, depending on how rent is determined, are also defined as gross, net, percentage leases, and graduated leases.

Gross. In a gross lease, the tenant pays an established, fixed rent, and the landlord pays all property operating expenses, such as taxes, insurance, utilities, and other services. This is the arrangement commonly used in residential leases.

Net. Net leases have the tenant paying rent plus some or all of the operating expenses attributable to the rented space. This arrangement is commonly used in office and industrial leases.

Percentage. A percentage lease may be gross or net, but the rent is not fixed, but depends on the income generated by the tenant in the leased property. A common

arrangement is to set a fixed base rent plus a percentage of the tenant's gross income or sales at the site. The percentage calculation may take effect only when the income reaches a certain level. This arrangement is commonly used in retail leases.

Graduated. Either a gross or a net lease may also be a graduated lease, in which

the rental rate increases at specified times over the lease term.

Owned and leased inclusions

The lease should set forth items that are excluded or included in the leased property. For instance, a residential lease may include built-in appliances such as dishwashers but exclude freestanding ones, such as refrigerators. Furniture may be included or excluded. At issue for the landlord is the cost of maintenance. If a refrigerator is not included, it does not have to be maintained by the property manager.

Ownership also relates to insurance policies: one can only insure what one owns, so if a property item is destroyed by fire, the owner's policy will not provide any coverage for an item that is not included in the lease as belonging to the property. This may be of critical importance in a commercial lease where certain improvements might be owned by either the landlord or the tenant, according to the lease.

The lease should also have clear rules about making alterations. If the tenant is not satisfied with an item that is part of the property, the lease may provide for the tenant to make changes only with permission or with the obligation to return the premises to their original condition on termination, or that any alterations made to fixtures become the property of the landlord. Trade fixtures, by definition, belong to the tenant and can be removed when the tenant leaves.

Inclusions may also be of a financial nature-what is included in the rent. Principal and interest on a mortgage loan, homeowner's association dues, common area maintenance charges, liability and hazard insurance, and various operating expenses are items that might be included in the lease as the owner's or the tenant's responsibilities.

Landlord rights and responsibilities

State law, often incorporating or modeling the Universal Residential Landlord Tenant Act (see below) prescribes rights and responsibilities for residential landlords and tenants.

Rights. Commonly, the landlord retains a right of entry into the premises in order to perform needed repairs and maintenance on a property. The lease and/or the law may specify that a landlord may enter the tenant's property only under one or more of the following conditions:

- An emergency requires the landlord to enter.

- The tenant gives consent to enter.

- The landlord enters during normal business hours and only after giving notice to either make repairs or to show the property to prospective tenants, purchasers or contractors.

- The tenant has abandoned or surrendered the property.

- The landlord has a court order allowing the entry.

Likewise, the landlord has the right to expect prompt payment of rent and adherence to building rules. At the end of the lease term, the landlord has the right to retake possession of the premises. In case of tenant breach or default, the landlord has the right to pursue the remedies provided by law, such as eviction, to take possession.

Responsibilities. The landlord (by way of the property manager), is expected to deliver a property that is habitable. This means that the landlord at the very least must:

- keep the heating, cooling, electrical, and plumbing systems in good working condition

- keep floors, stairways and railings safe and in good repair

- provide pest control as needed

- repair roof leaks and broken windows promptly.

Tenant rights and responsibilities

Rights. Beyond the right to quiet enjoyment (privacy) of a property received and maintained in a habitable condition, the tenant has other rights, depending on state law. For instance, a tenant may be able to take any of the following actions if a landlord fails to correct a problem that is the landlord's responsibility:

- move out without liability for back rent or the unexpired portion of the lease
- refer the problem to mediation, arbitration or small claims court
- after giving the owner written notification of an emergency situation, call a professional repair person and deduct the cost from the next month's rent.

Responsibilities. Depending on state law, a tenant generally must:

- pay rent on time
- follow the rules and regulations set out by the landlord
- give a 30-day notice when terminating a month-to-month lease
- return all door and mailbox keys when leaving the property
- leave the unit in as clean a condition as it was at the start of the lease
- keep the unit clean and sanitary
- dispose of all rubbish, garbage and other waste in a sanitary manner
- use and operate all electrical, gas and plumbing fixtures properly
- refrain from destroying or damaging the property
- prevent others from destroying or damaging the property
- use the property and the rooms only for their intended purposes

Evictions

An *actual eviction* follows a procedure prescribed in state law and stated in the lease contract. The landlord must serve notice on the tenant a specified number of days before beginning the eviction suit. A court issues a judgment for possession, which requires the tenant to vacate. A court officer, such as a sheriff, may forcibly remove the tenant and possessions if the tenant refuses to vacate. The landlord can then enter and take possession.

A *constructive eviction* occurs when a tenant vacates the leased premises and declares the lease void, claiming that the landlord's actions have made the premises unfit for the purpose described in the lease. The tenant must prove that it was the landlord's actions that were responsible and may be able to recover damages.

Termination of a lease

Like contracts in general, leases may terminate in a number of ways. Principal among these are the following.

Expiration. A lease with a term (estate for years) automatically expires at the end of the term.

Performance. Any contract terminates when all parties have performed their obligations.

Agreement. The parties may agree to terminate the lease before the end of the term.

Abandonment. The landlord may retake possession and pursue the tenant for default if the tenant abandons the premises and fails to fulfill lease obligations. The tenant's obligation to pay rent continues.

Default or Breach. A default occurs when either the tenant or landlord violates any of the terms or covenants of the lease. The damaged party may sue for damages, specific performance (of the breached obligation), or cancellation of the lease. When the default arises from the tenant's failure to pay rent or maintain the premises, the landlord may sue for possession and for eviction.

Notice. A periodic leasehold or tenancy at will may be terminated by proper notice given by either party.

Destruction. Property destruction is grounds for termination of the lease.

Condemnation. Eminent domain proceedings terminate leases.

Foreclosure. Foreclosure actions terminate lease obligations.

Death. A tenancy at will terminates on the death of either party. The landlord's death terminates any lease if the landlord held the leased property under a life estate, since the landlord cannot convey an interest that extends beyond the landlord's life.

Security deposit procedures

As previously mentioned in the context of handling trust funds, state laws, real estate commission rules, and the state's real estate law, usually specify how a property manager is to manage security deposits. Such funds are normally held in a special trust account and may not be used for any purpose other than the intended one. Whether the deposit can earn interest, and to whom that interest belongs, are likewise prescribed by law. The law also prescribes when the deposit must be returned to the tenant, and under what circumstances any of it may be withheld. The contract language should clearly state the rules, among other things, governing what happens to the deposit when the lease terminates.

Unit III: Property Management Specializations and Tennessee Law

SPECIALIZING IN THE MANAGEMENT BUSINESS

Property management is increasingly a specialization within real estate. There is a growing need for skilled managers because of the increasing number and complexity of properties.

Specialist opportunities. Property managers with specialized training are in demand in a wide variety of property types, including shopping centers, commercial buildings, residential properties, and industrial parks. Within these property specialties are opportunities to specialize even further in such areas as:

- leasing
- asset management
- corporate property management
- resort management
- association management
- housing program management
- mobile home park management
- office building management

Owners and investors in these various property types are among the consumers of management services who represent potential clients for a professional property manager. Such owners and investors may be individuals, corporations, developers, landlords, banks, trusts, homeowners' associations, condominium associations, or investment syndicates

Professional development. A number of organizations provide valuable information and training in subjects related to property management. The certifications and designations provided by these organizations are often viewed as valuable signs of competence and can be a significant factor in getting hired as a manager. Important associations include:

- IREM-The Institute of Real Estate Management, offering the CPM (Certified Property Manager) designation

- BOMA and BOMI-The Building Owners and Managers Association International and the affiliated Building Managers and Owners Institute International, offering the RPA (Real Property Administrator), SMA (Systems Maintenance Administrator), and FMA (Facilities Management Administrator) designations

- NAA-The National Apartment Association, offering designations in apartment building management, maintenance, leasing, portfolio supervision and other related areas

- NARPM-The National Association of Residential Property Managers, offering the RPM (Residential Property Manager), MPM (Master Property Manager) and other related designations

- ICSC-The International Council of Shopping Centers, offering designations in retail property leadership, management, marketing, leasing, and development

- NACM-The National Association of Condominium Managers, offering the RCM (Registered Condominium Manager) designation

RENTAL LOCATION AGENTS

Rental location agents are governed by the Rental Location Agent Act of 1978, TCA 62-25, and Rule 1260 3.

A rental location agent assists individuals by providing assistance or furnishing information concerning the location or availability of real property, including apartment housing, that may be leased or rented as a private dwelling or place of residence and who receives or solicits a fee or other valuable consideration from the prospective tenant. The "Rental Location Agent" includes the licensed rental location agent and all employees and agents of the Rental Location Agent.

Rental location agency license (Rule 1260-3). Every individual or firm is required to obtain a special license to operate as a rental location agency. The license expires two (2) years from the date it is issued or renewed.

Each rental location agency employee is required to obtain a separate license prior to beginning employment, and the license will be issued, renewed, or transferred on the same basis as all other licenses issued by the Commission.

Agency license applicants and individual applicants for license are subject to a credit, criminal, and background investigation by authorized agents of the Commission before license approval. Office inspections are made periodically to assure compliance with the Act and Rules. (Rule 1260-3-.03)

A change of business address is considered to be a transfer of license; retirements are not permitted.

Requirements. A rental location agent must obtain a surety bond of ten thousand dollars ($10,000) executed to the state by a surety company authorized to do business in Tennessee; if the agent is employed by a firm that is licensed as a rental location agent, a bond of two thousand five hundred dollars ($2,500) must be posted. Any person who is injured or aggrieved may bring an action in the person's own name on the bond without assignment.

Each prospective tenant who pays full or partial consideration must be provided with a contract or receipt that includes a statement that any amount over ten dollars ($10) will be refunded if he or she, after a bona fide effort, does not obtain a rental through the listing furnished by the rental location agent. The contract or receipt must conform to rules adopted by the Commission designed to affect material information regarding the services to be provided (Rule 1260-3-.05).

If provided rental information provided is not current or accurate regarding to the type of rental requested, the prospective tenant is entitled to receive a full refund.

Agents are prohibited from advertising housing unless its availability for rental has been verified the day the ad is submitted to the advertising medium. Availability must be verified daily as long as the ads continue. If the agent becomes aware the property is unavailable, he or she must immediately take steps to cancel the ad.

Any property that is not being advertised may not be represented as available for rental unless availability has been verified within 72 hours of when it is presented as available.

The agent must disclose the following information accurately and clearly regarding any property represented as available:

- the date it is available for occupancy if not currently available

- the monthly rent, number of bedrooms, and whether a lease is required

- the existence (and the amount, if known) of any damage deposit, security deposit, clean-up fees, rent prepayment, or similar charges required in addition to the monthly rent

- restrictions other than legal restrictions, such as no pets

- the types of housing (i.e., single family, duplex or trailer)

- the location of the rentals with reference to the areas defined by the agent

- the utilities paid by renter and by lessor

- the telephone number of the landlord.

VACATION LODGING SERVICES

"Vacation lodging service" (TCA 62-13) refers to a person, corporation, company, partnership, firm or association that provides services of management, marketing, booking and rental of residential units owned by others as sleeping accommodations furnished for pay to transients or travelers staying no more than fourteen (14) days.

Licensing requirements for the firm and the designated agent were covered previously. Briefly: the service and the designated agent must be licensed; exemptions are the same as those exemptions to be licensed as a real estate broker or affiliated broker.

For reissuance of the firm license and the designated agent license every two (2) years, the firm is required to furnish certification that the designated agent has completed eight (8) classroom hours in training programs approved by the Commission. No exam is required for the issuance or renewal of a firm license for a vacation lodging service. The designated agent's license is issued or renewed so that it expires on the date the license of the firm expires.

The Commission may to refuse a license for cause or to suspend or revoke a license if obtained by false representation or by fraudulent act or conduct.

A qualified individual may serve as a designated agent for multiple offices of the same vacation lodging service firm, but may serve in that capacity with only one firm at any time.

Designated agent responsibilities (Rule 1260-07-.03). The designated agent is responsible for supervising all employees of the firm and must be reasonably available to manage and supervise each vacation lodging service office during regular business hours. The designated agent is also responsible for maintaining the escrow/trustee account.

If the designated agent leaves the firm or moves from the firm, the firm or designated agent must notify the Commission within ten (10) days. The vacation lodging service must replace the designated agent within sixty (60) days and inform the Commission of the name of the new designated agent.

Office required. The vacation lodging service must have an office at a fixed location with adequate facilities and located to conform with zoning. The Commission must be notified of the new address within ten (10) days after any change of location of the office.

Escrow/trustee account. When applying for a firm license and for each renewal, the firm must provide proof of having established an escrow account satisfactory to the Commission. Every firm must keep an escrow or trustee account in a federally insured institution for funds deposited with the firm related to vacation lodging services.

Vacation lodging services are required to maintain at least three (3) years of accurate records of the account showing depositor, date of deposit, payee, and other pertinent information the Commission may require.

No funds may be distributed from the account until the customer's stay is complete or according to terms disclosed to the renter in writing at the time of making the reservation or within three (3) days, mailed to the renter through the United States postal service or transmitted to the renter via electronic mail, facsimile or other tangible form of communication. Commissions earned by the firm and the revenue due owners must be disbursed at least monthly. Funds held in escrow must be disbursed in a prompt manner with no unreasonable delay.

When a lodging rental customer or owner claims to have been injured or damaged by the dishonesty or misconduct of a licensee files suit in this state and recovers judgment, the court may revoke the certificate of license which will not be reissued except with the consenting vote of six (6) Commission members.

COMMERCIAL/INDUSTRIAL REAL ESTATE

"Commercial real estate" means any real estate other than:

- real estate containing one (1) to four (4) residential units
- real estate on which no buildings or structures are located and is zoned for no more than one (1) to four (4) family residential units

It does not include single family residential units such as condominiums, town houses or homes in a subdivision when sold, leased or otherwise conveyed on a unit-by-unit basis, even though these units may be a part of a larger building or parcel of real estate containing more than four (4) residential units.

Commercial transactions are exempt from agency disclosure requirements and do not require use of the Tennessee Residential Property Condition Disclosure form.

As indicated previously, a separate license is not required to participate in commercial real estate transactions; licensed real estate brokers and affiliate brokers are qualified to do so.

LICENSING AND URLTA

Property managers in Tennessee must have a real estate broker's license to solicit or negotiate, or attempt to solicit or negotiate, the rental or leasing, or options to rent or lease real estate.

Property managers must comply with the Uniform Residential Landlord and Tenant Act (TCA 66-28), in addition to the Real Estate License Act. The Uniform Residential Landlord and Tenant Act governs the rental of dwelling units and covers obligations and rights of both the landlord and the tenant, eviction proceedings, lease contracts, and escrow funds.

This is a brief overview of some of the key points in the Act. If an individual desires to be a property manager, the Act should be reviewed in its entirely: TCA 66-28- 101 through -521.

Application/exemptions. The Act does not apply to hotel and motel tenants, condos and cooperatives, occupancy under a contract for deed, or lease agreements entered into prior to July 1, 1975. It does not apply to counties with a population of less than seventy-five thousand (75,000), or rental agreements covering primarily agricultural use.

Specifically, unless created to avoid the application of the Uniform Residential Landlord and Tenant Act, the Act does not apply to the following:

- residence at a public or private institution, if incidental to detention or the provision of medical, geriatric, educational, counseling, religious, or similar service

- occupancy under a contract of sale of a dwelling unit or the property of which it is a part, if the occupant is the purchaser or a person who succeeds to the purchaser's interest

- transient occupancy in a hotel, or motel or lodgings subject to city, state, transient lodgings or room occupancy under the Excise Tax Act

- occupancy by an owner of a condo unit or a holder of a proprietary lease in a cooperative

- occupancy under a rental agreement covering premises used by the occupant primarily for agricultural purposes

The Act does not apply to any occupancy in a public housing unit or other housing unit that is subject to regulation by HUD and owned by a governmental entity or non-profit corporation to the extent that the regulation conflicts with state law, but applies to the extent that the regulations defer to the application of state law.

RIGHTS AND DUTIES

Security deposits. Security deposits for both residential and commercial properties must be maintained in a special account solely for that purpose in a lending institution subject to regulation by the state or any agency of the United States government. Landlords of residential property are required to notify tenants at the time the lease is signed and the security deposit is submitted of the location of the account required to be maintained, but is not required to provide the account number.

Residential landlord registration (TCA 66-28-107). Each landlord of one (1) or more dwelling units is required to furnish certain information with the agency or department of local government that is responsible for enforcing building codes in the jurisdiction where the dwelling units are located, including the landlord or the landlord's agent's name, telephone number, and physical address, which does not include a post office box; and the street address and unit number, as appropriate, for each dwelling unit the landlord owns, leases, or subleases or has the right to own, lease, or sublease.

Grace period for tenant (TCA 66-28-201). The tenant must be given a late rent payment grace period of five (5) days upon prior to late fees being assessed, not including Sundays or legal holidays. If the fifth day falls on Sunday or a legal holiday, the tenant has until the following day to pay the rent. Late fees may not exceed ten percent (10%) of the past due rent.

Termination of periodic tenancy -- holdover remedies (TCA 66-28-512). The landlord or tenant may terminate tenancies as indicated:

- a week-to-week tenancy by a written notice given to the other at least ten (10) days prior to the termination date specified in the notice

- a month-to-month tenancy by a written notice given to the other at least thirty (30) days prior to the periodic rental date specified in the notice

If the tenant remains in possession without the landlord's consent after expiration or termination, the landlord may bring an action for possession and if the tenant's holdover is willful and not in good faith, the landlord may also recover actual damages sustained by the landlord, plus reasonable attorney's fees.

Abandonment and landlord retaking possession. If the tenant has been absent for (thirty) 30 days and failed to pay the rent, or if the tenant is fifteen (15) days late with rent and circumstances indicate the tenant has vacated, the landlord may retake possession of the property.

Termination and possession by landlord. If the tenant remains in possession beyond the termination date stated in the lease or rental agreement, the landlord may sue for possession and damages. The landlord may not discontinue services unless the tenant has abandoned or surrendered the property.

Inspection of property and security deposits. Landlords of residential property requiring security deposits prior to occupancy must deposit security deposits in an account used only for that purpose, in a bank or other lending institution subject to regulation by the state or federal agency.

The tenant has a right to inspect the premises to determine liability for physical damages that are the basis for any charge against the security deposit, unless the tenant abandoned or surrendered the property, or was evicted. The landlord and tenant inspect the premises and compile a listing of a damage to the unit that will be a charge against the security deposit. Both parties sign the listing of damages.

If the tenant vacates with unpaid rent or other amounts owed, the landlord may remove the deposit from the account and apply it to the unpaid debt. If the tenant leaves with a refund due, the landlord must send notification to the last known or reasonably determinable address, of the amount of any refund due the tenant. If the landlord does not receive a response from the tenant within sixty (60) days, the landlord may remove the deposit from the account and retain it free from any claim of the tenant or any person claiming it on behalf of the tenant.

Effect of unsigned or undelivered agreement. If the landlord does not sign a written rental agreement, acceptance of rent without reservation by the landlord binds the parties on a month to month tenancy.

Anyone taking possession without payment of rent and failing to sign a written rental agreement delivered to them by the landlord, or who enter without oral agreement, are considered trespassers and may be evicted and held liable for damages and rent for the term of the trespass and reasonable attorney's fees. If that person pays rent which is accepted by the landlord, he or she will become a tenant of the landlord.

Maintenance by landlord. The landlord must:

- comply with requirements of applicable building and housing codes affecting health and safety
- make all repairs and keep the premises habitable
- keep all common areas clean and safe
- in multi-unit complexes of four (4) or more units, provide and maintain appropriate receptacles and conveniences for removal of ashes, garbage, and rubbish

Default of landlord. If the landlord fails to provide essential utility services or any other obligations which materially affect the health or safety of the tenant, the tenant may give written notice to the landlord and do one of the following:

- obtain essential services during the period of the landlord's non-compliance and deduct their actual and reasonable costs from the rent
- recover damages based on the reduced fair rental value of the unit, provided the tenant continues to occupy premises
- procure reasonable substitute housing during the period of the landlord's noncompliance; in this case the tenant is not required to pay rent for the period of the landlord's noncompliance

Additionally, the tenant may recover the actual and reasonable value of the substitute housing and reasonable attorney's fees.

Landlord access to premises. The landlord may enter premises for emergencies, maintenance or repairs, and showing to future tenants (with 24-hour notice). The landlord may not harass the tenant or abuse the right to enter.

MODULE 7 SNAPSHOT REVIEW:

PROPERTY MANAGEMENT

ESSENTIAL DYNAMICS OF PROPERTY MANAGEMENT

Property management functions
- main manager types: individual broker or firm managing for multiple owners; building manager, employed by owner or other manager to manage a single property; resident manager, employed by owner, broker, or management firm to live and manage on site.
- manager is a fiduciary of the principal; duty to act in principle's best interests; may specialize in a property type
- needed skills: marketing, accounting, finance, construction; financial, physical, administrative services; specific functions determined by management agreement

Reporting
- monthly, quarterly, or annually; annual operating budget, cash flow reports, profit and loss statements, budget comparison statements

Budgeting
- manage and control income, expenses, capital expenses and cash

Renting
- control vacancies; conduct marketing activities to locate tenants; establish the proper rent levels; screen, interview, qualify tenants; collect rents and maintain tenant relations

Legal issues
- maintain compliance with fair housing, ADA and ECOA laws

Property maintenance
- manage ongoing physical condition of property; conduct preventive maintenance measures; complete corrective maintenance as needed; oversee maintenance contracting

Construction
- includes renovation, environmental projects to maintain safety
- hazards to manage include air quality; waste disposal; contamination prevention; manage radon, mold, lead and other issues
- manage ADA compliance and accommodations

ADVANCED CONSIDERATIONS IN PROPERTY MANAGEMENT

Risk management
- risk ranges from natural disaster to personal injury, terrorism, and employee malfeasance; handled by avoiding or removing the source, installing protective systems, buying insurance, self-insuring (risk retention)
- life safety systems include sprinklers, fire doors, smoke alarms, fire escapes, monitoring systems
- insurance includes casualty, liability, workers' comp, fire and hazard, flood, contents, consequential loss, surety bonds, multi-peril; tenants need their own insurance
- handling of trust funds is a major risk area; mishandling carries heavy penalties

The management agreement
- establishes agency agreement between manager and owner; should be in writing
- sets forth job essentials of scope of authority; tasks; duties; authorities
- specific provisions include parties; property description; responsibilities; budget; compensation; reports required

Foundations of leasing
- lease types: for years; periodic; at will; at sufferance; gross; net; percentage
- what is included and excluded from the leased premises definition
- landlord rights and responsibilities, including rights to enter premises, receive payments, retake premises upon termination, remedy default; responsibilities: provide habitable conditions; maintain heating, cooling, electrical, plumbing; keep clean and in repair
- tenant rights, responsibilities: quiet enjoyment, habitable premises, right to take action for default; responsibilities: pay rent, obey rules, give proper notice, return property in prescribed condition, use only for intended purpose
- evictions -- actual: prescribed legal procedure; notice, suit, judgment, taking of premises; constructive eviction: tenant vacates for landlord failure to maintain premises

Termination of a lease
- causes: expiration, performance, agreement, abandonment, breach, notice, destruction of premises, condemnation, foreclosure, death of either party (tenancy at will), death of landlord (life estate)

Security deposits
- state laws dictate how deposits are held, returned, and limits on withholding

PROPERTY MANAGEMENT SPECIALIZATIONS AND TENNESSEE LAW

SPECIALIZING IN THE MANAGEMENT BUSINESS

Specialist opportunities
- can vary by property types – retail; office ; residential; industrial
- can vary by activity, including leasing; asset management; corporate property management; resort management; association management; housing program management; mobile home parks; and office building management

Professional development
- key trade groups: IREM; BOMA; NAA; NARPM; ICSC; NACM

Rental location agents
- provide information regarding availability of property for rent or lease for dwellings; agent must have $10,000 bond; if employed by licensed firm must have $2,500 bond
- prohibited from giving information on property not for lease, not meeting tenant specifications, property already leased or rented, or listed without owner consent; using false information, showing financial irresponsibility are violations
- rental information must be current; advertising must be kept current and contain agent's name and status as agent; certain information required to be disclosed
- violations are Class C misdemeanors

Vacation lodging services
- provides management, marketing, booking, rental of residential units to transients or travelers staying up to 14 days; firm and designated agent must be licensed; license must be renewed every 2 years
- requirements: designated agent to manage employees, fixed office location, escrow account or irrevocable letter of credit
- violations: misleading/untruthful advertising, making false promise or substantial misrepresentation, failing to account for funds or furnishing contract copy, using contracts without specific termination date, unauthorized practice of law

Commercial / industrial real estate
- real estate other than one to four residential units or vacant land zoned for one to four units
- agency disclosure requirements and residential property disclosure form to do apply to commercial property
- broker who has contact and earned commission due may enforce contract against subsequent owner if notice given to that owner prior to owner receiving title

Licensing and URLTA
- property manager must be licensed real estate broker
- manager must comply with Uniform Landlord and Tenant Act and Real Estate License Act; must have separate escrow account

Rights and duties under URLTA
- landlords of dwelling units required to furnish name, address, rental unit address to local government agency that enforces building codes
- tenant must receive in writing prior to tenancy: name of managing agent and owner or person authorized to accept notices and demands, and institution holding security deposit
- landlord or tenant may terminate week-to-week tenancy with ten days written notice; month-to-month with 30-day written notice
- tenant may inspect property to determine liability for damages that are charged against security deposit
- if tenant is absent 30 days and rent unpaid, or 15 days late with rent and vacated or surrendered premises, landlord may retake possession
- if tenant stays after termination date, landlord may sue for possession and damages but cannot discontinue services unless property abandoned or surrendered

MODULE 7 – PROPERTY MANAGEMENT

QUIZ

Carefully read each question and provide your best answer based on what you learned in this module. Then check your answers against the Answer Key which immediately follows the quiz questions.

1. Funds for improvements to major items such as new bedrooms and enlarged garages, as opposed to periodic repairs and maintenance, are called _____.

   a. operating cash flows.
   b. capital expenditures.
   c. business expenses.
   d. business fees.

2. Which risk management strategy shifts the risk to someone else by buying an insurance policy?

   a. Transference
   b. Retention
   c. Reduction
   d. Avoidance

3. Which of the following items is defined as preventative maintenance?

   a. Minor repairs
   b. Landscaping
   c. Cleaning of common areas
   d. Regular painting of exterior areas

4. Which type of eviction occurs when a tenant vacates the leased premises and declares the lease void?

   a. Actual eviction
   b. Constructive eviction
   c. Terminated eviction
   d. False eviction

5. Which of the following is a landlord's responsibility?

   a. Keeping the unit sanitary
   b. Disposing of all rubbish
   c. Providing pest control as needed
   d. Preventing others from destroying the property

6. When routine and preventative maintenance fail, _____ needs to be done to keep the property operational.

   a. corrective maintenance
   b. maintenance contracting
   c. immediate maintenance
   d. construction maintenance

7. Vacation lodging service records must be maintained at least _____.

   a. one year
   b. three years
   c. five years
   d. seven years

8. A rental location agency license expires _____ from the date it is issued.

   a. 5 years
   b. 3 years
   c. 2 years
   d. 1 year

9. Efficiency, competence, responsiveness and _____ are major deciding factors when choosing an outside firm to handle maintenance contracting.

   a. effective cost
   b. tenant needs
   c. budgetary constraints
   d. supplies

10. What is the formula for deriving effective gross income?

    a. Total scheduled rents + revenues
    b. Potential gross income – vacancy losses
    c. Debt services + reserves
    d. Gross income – net operating income

11. Which type of lease allows the rental rate to increase at specified times over the lease term?

    a. Graduated
    b. Exponential
    c. Net
    d. Rising

12. Which insurance type provides coverage for damage to the property by wind, hail, smoke and other causes?

   a. Fire and hazard insurance
   b. Liability insurance
   c. Flood insurance
   d. Casualty insurance

13. What is the name of the fund sets aside moneys from operating revenues for supplies and repairs?

   a. Capital expenditures
   b. Emergency fund
   c. Cash reserve
   d. Maintenance fund

14. Which type of lease allows the tenant to pay rent plus a portion of the operating expenses?

   a. Percentage lease
   b. Net lease
   c. Gross lease
   d. Office lease

15. Which statute applies to how property managers evaluate potential tenants?

   a. The ADA
   b. The Fair Housing Act
   c. The Equal Credit Opportunity Act
   d. The Landlord Tenant Act

16. Which risk management strategy involves taking action to forestall the event before it happens?

   a. Avoidance
   b. Reduction
   c. Transference
   d. Retention

17. The tenant must be given a grace period of _____ following the rent-due date before late fees can be assessed for unpaid rent.

   a. one week
   b. three days
   c. twenty-four hours
   d. five days

18. What is the name of the service that refers to a person, corporation or firm that provides services of management, marketing, booking, and rental of residential units?

    a. Vacation lodging service
    b. Timeshare service
    c. Asset management
    d. Condo-hotel

19. Alterations made specifically for certain tenants are called _____.

    a. capital expenditures.
    b. tenant improvements.
    c. tenant concerns.
    d. renovations.

20. Which statute governs the rental of dwelling units and covers obligations and rights of both the landlord and tenant?

    a. The Uniform Residential Landlord and Tenant Act
    b. The ECOA
    c. TILA
    d. The Landlord Act

21. Which of the following is a determining factor for choosing a suitable tenant for a given residential space?

    a. The tenant's creditworthiness
    b. The tenant's business is compatible with that of other tenants
    c. The tenant will be able renew the lease for the space
    d. There is room for expansion if the tenant's need for space is likely to grow

22. A landlord may enter one's rented premises for maintenance and repairs with _____ notice to tenants.

    a. 12-hour
    b. 48-hour
    c. 24-hour
    d. no

23. Which type of insurance provides coverage for business losses resulting from a disaster?

    a. Casualty insurance
    b. Consequential loss, use, and occupancy insurance
    c. Hazard insurance
    d. Workers' compensation insurance

24. Which statute requires modifications such as widening doorways and installing ramps for tenants?

   a. Americans with Disabilities Act
   b. Nondiscrimination Act
   c. Tenant Accessibility Act
   d. Fair Housing Law

25. A _____ comes into existence when a tenant stays beyond the expiration of another type of lease without the lessor's permission.

   a. tenancy at will
   b. periodic tenancy
   c. tenancy at sufferance
   d. holdover tenancy

MODULE 7 – PROPERTY MANAGEMENT

ANSWER KEY TO QUIZ

1. b. capital expenditures.
2. a. Transference
3. d. Regular painting of exterior areas
4. b. Constructive eviction
5. c. Providing pest control as needed
6. a. corrective maintenance
7. b. three years
8. c. 2 years
9. a. effective cost
10. b. Potential gross income – vacancy losses
11. a. Graduated
12. a. Fire and hazard insurance
13. c. Cash reserve
14. b. Net lease
15. c. The Equal Credit Opportunity Act
16. b. Reduction
17. d. five days
18. a. Vacation lodging service
19. b. tenant improvements.
20. a. The Uniform Residential Landlord and Tenant Act
21. a. The tenant's creditworthiness
22. c. 24-hour
23. b. Consequential loss, use, and occupancy insurance
24. a. Americans with Disabilities Act
25. c. tenancy at sufferance

MODULE 7 – PROPERTY MANAGEMENT

CHECK YOUR UNDERSTANDING

Instructions:

Carefully read each challenge question, then provide your best answer based on what you learned in this module. Then check your answers against the Answer Key which immediately follows the questions.

1. What do property managers call the expenditures for major items such as renovations?

    A. Reserves
    B. Capital expenditures
    C. Budget
    D. Expenses

2. List three types of tenancies.

    1. _____

    2. _____

    3. _____

3. A percentage lease has fixed rent. True or false?

4. Which statute requires managers to ensure that disabled employees have the same level of access to facilities as those who are not disabled?

    A. ECOA
    B. ADA
    C. TILA
    D. RESPA

5. A constructive eviction occurs when a tenant vacates the leased premises and declares the lease void. True or false?

6. Which type of insurance provides coverage against losses resulting from criminal acts of an employee?

    A. Surety bond-coverage
    B. Consequential loss
    C. Liability-coverage
    D. Criminal-coverage

7. List three possible reasons for vacancies in a building.

1. _____

2. _____

3. _____

8. Fire and hazard-coverage insurance covers damage to the property by wind, hail and civil disturbance. True or false?

9. A tenancy at will is similar to _____.

    A.   tenancy at sufferance.
    B.   net lease.
    C.   periodic tenancy.
    D.   graduated tenancy.

10. List four marketing methods for a property manager.

1. _____

2. _____

3. _____

4. _____

MODULE 7 – PROPERTY MANAGEMENT
CHECK YOUR UNDERSTANDING ANSWER KEY

1. What do property managers call the expenditures for major items such as renovations?

   B. Capital expenditures

2. List three types of tenancies.

   1. Periodic
   2. At sufferance
   3. For years

3. A percentage lease has fixed rent.

   False

4. Which statute requires managers to ensure that disabled employees have the same level of access to facilities as those who are not disabled?

   B. ADA

5. A constructive eviction occurs when a tenant vacates the leased premises and declares the lease void.

   True

6. Which type of insurance provides coverage against losses resulting from criminal acts of an employee?

   A. Surety bond-coverage

7. List three possible reasons for vacancies in a building.

   1. Rent is too high

   2. Ineffective marketing

   3. Image problems

8. Fire and hazard-coverage insurance covers damage to the property by wind, hail and civil disturbance.

   True

9. A tenancy at will is similar to _____.

   C. periodic tenancy.

10. List four marketing methods for a property manager.

    1. Networking

    2. Newspaper ads

    3. Signs

    4. Brochures

Module 8: ETHICS AND REAL ESTATE

I. Ethics
II. Professional Etiquette

Module 8 Learning Objectives

Ethics

1. Summarize the purpose, role, and four parts of the National Association of Realtors' Code of Ethics
2. Paraphrase the central theme identified for each of the Code's 17 Articles.

Professional Etiquette

1. Explain how Realtors® resolve disputes in terms of the structured process.
2. Define the standards established in the Realtors®' Pathways to Professionalism, including what is entailed in demonstrating respect for public, property, and peers in real estate practice.

I. Ethics

NATIONAL ASSOCIATION OF REALTORS' CODE OF ETHICS

Historical abstract

In the early 1900s, real estate agents were given licenses by county judges, and often they were "peddlers" licenses. The 1900s was a time of land scams and speculation. In 1908, the National Association of Realtors® (NAR) formed to eliminate the notion of "Caveat emptor" or let the buyer beware. Their goal was to protect the public and promote homeownership in the United States.

In 1913, NAR introduced the Code of Ethics for Realtors® to follow in their dealings with their clients, the public, and other Realtors®. This document has been fluid and ever-changing over the years. Today, Realtors® have one of the strongest professional Code of Ethics in the United States.

The Code of Ethics also provides standard practices and procedures setting forth how Realtors® should react in their dealings with specific individuals and others in their field. The Code of Ethics, however, is not law. Rather, the Code of Ethics enhances local, state, or federal laws.

A quote in the 2020/2021 Code of Ethics and Arbitration Manual reads, "Because the Code is a living document and real estate is a dynamic business and profession, the law need never be its substitute. So long as the aspiration to better serve the public remails the underlying concept of the code, it must evolve and grow in significance and importance consonant with but independent of the law."

Structure of the Code of Ethics

The Code of Ethics has four parts:

- The Preamble
- Duties to Clients and Customers (Articles 1 – 9)
- Duties to the Public (Articles 10 – 14)
- Duties to Realtors® (Articles 15 – 17)

The Articles within the Code of Ethics define the broad statements about the licensee's behavior and duties. The Standards of Practice, within each Article, gives more specific guidance to the licensee. The Standards of Practice support and interpret the Articles.

In resolving ethics complaints, complainants are to cite only the Article(s) violated and not the Standard of Practice. It will be up to the Professional Standards Committee to give the specific Standard of Practice violated in their final report.

The Preamble

"Under all is the land."

This statement is a powerful start to NAR's Code of Ethics. It means that everything we do, are, or aspire to become, begins with the land beneath our feet. The quote shows the importance of the role each Realtor® holds in our society. Real estate impacts everything.

The Preamble of the Code of Ethics serves as a vision statement on how licensees should conduct themselves and represent their profession to the public. The Preamble calls for Realtors® to "maintain and improve the standards of their calling." It also states that it is the Realtor's responsibility to "act with integrity and honesty."

As of January 1, 2021, the Board of Directors of NAR changed the Preamble. It added that licensees should not dishonor the profession or do anything that will hurt the organization's public trust. The Board of Directors altered the Preamble wording to reflect the changes in Article 10 of the Code of Ethics (see also Chapter 5).

SECTION 1: DUTIES TO CLIENTS AND CUSTOMERS.

ARTICLE 1

> *"When representing a buyer, seller, landlord, tenant, or other client as an agent, REALTORS® pledge themselves to protect and promote the interests of their client. This obligation to the client is primary, but it does not relieve REALTORS® of their obligation to treat all parties honestly. When serving a buyer, seller, landlord, tenant or other party in a non-agency capacity, REALTORS® remain obligated to treat all parties honestly."*

Central themes. Article 1 of the Code of Ethics promotes honesty as a critical virtue of any licensee. The 16 Standards of Practices within Article 1 describes the different duties a licensee may have and how they must act in specific situations. The basis of the Standards of Practices is the duties owed to our customers and clients based on Tennessee's Agency Law.

Article 1 Standards of Practice. The central thrust of Article 1 is reflected in its Standards of Practices 1.1 through 1.16. These are as follows:

SP 1.1 – Be careful to abide by the Code when you are representing yourself in a transaction.
SP 1.2 – The Code of Ethics applies to all transactions.
SP 1.3 – Do not mislead the owner as to the real market value of a piece of property.
SP 1.4 – Do not mislead the savings or benefits of utilizing the services of a Realtor®.
SP 1.5 – No dual agency. An agent cannot have a fiduciary relationship with both parties in a transaction.
SP 1.6 – Submit all offers and counteroffers promptly.
SP 1.7 – When working as the listing agent, present all offers until closing, unless waived in writing.
SP 1.8 – When working as the buyer's agent, present all offers until contract acceptance, unless waived in writing.
SP 1.9 – Maintain confidentiality even after termination of a relationship.
SP 1.10 – In property management, the licensee must comply with the management agreement and ensure their tenants' rights, safety, and health.

SP 1.11 – Use skill, care, and diligence in all transactions.

SP 1.12 - Disclose to sellers and landlords cooperation policy and compensation to all parties.

SP 1.13 – Disclose cooperation with other brokers.

SP 1.14 – Appraisal fees must not be based on the market value of the property.

SP 1.15 – Disclose any other offers already presented or any expected offers.

SP 1.16 – Do not enter the property without permission or authorization from the owner.

Article 1 illustration. A broker was preparing a CMA for a listing appointment. The broker knew the seller was interviewing several other brokers. He decided to increase the property's market value to show the seller how much more money they could earn from hiring him. The violation in this example is of Article 1, Standard Practice 1.3 and 1.4.

ARTICLE 2

"REALTORS® shall avoid exaggeration, misrepresentation, or concealment of pertinent facts relating to the property or the transaction. REALTORS® shall not, however, be obligated to discover latent defects in the property, to advise on matters outside the scope of their real estate license, or to disclose facts which are confidential under the scope of agency or non-agency relationships as defined by state law."

Central theme. Article 2 of the Code of Ethics discusses the need for transparency in all transactions. While a licensee is not required to seek out defects in the property, they must disclose any defects they know exists. This duty is necessary no matter the type of agency relationship the broker has established.

Article 2 Standards of Practice. Article 2 has five Standards of Practice:

SP 2.1 – A Realtor® must disclose any latent defects they know about or that are readily observable to a lay-person. They are not required to be experts in fields other than their own.

SP 2.2 – Moved to Standard of Practice 1.12

SP 2.3 – Moved to Standard of Practice 1.13

SP 2.4 – A Realtor® must not participate in doctoring the numbers on any contract.

SP 2.5 – Realtors® must not disclose non-material items not pertinent to the transaction.

Article 2 illustration. Susie is showing a potential buyer a house. The MLS stated that the roof was 25 years old and had a few leaks. During the showing, Susie's customer asked about the condition of the roof. Susie stated she was not aware of any problems. Susie has violated Article 2, Standard 2.1.

ARTICLE 3

"REALTORS® shall cooperate with other brokers except when cooperation is not in the client's best interest. The obligation to cooperate does not include the obligation to share commissions, fees, or to otherwise compensate another broker."

Central theme. Article 3 promotes cooperation among brokers unless it is not in their client's best interest.

Article 3 Standards of Practice. Article 3 has eleven Standards of Practice as follows:

SP 3.1 – Realtors® must establish terms of cooperation.

SP 3.2 - Realtors® who change the compensation in a transaction must communicate it to other licensees.

SP 3.3 – Realtors® may change the cooperative compensation.

SP 3.4 – Realtors® must disclose variable rate commissions.

SP 3.5 – Realtors® must disclose all pertinent facts before and after the sale.

SP 3.6 - Realtors® should disclose any current accepted offers.

SP 3.7 – Realtors® must disclose their status when calling other Realtors® about a listed property.

SP 3.8 – Realtors® must not give false information about the availability of property to be shown.

SP 3.9 – Realtors® must not provide access to a listed property in any way other than what is agreed upon by the seller.

SP 3.10 – Realtor should share information on listed property and make the property available to other brokers.

SP 3.11 – Realtors® may not violate Fair Housing laws and refuse to show a piece of property to someone in a protected class.

Article 3 illustration. Janet's seller told her that they did not want to sell their home to anyone who was not white. Janet told potential buyers who were not white that the house was no longer available or was not available to be shown. The violation in this example is of Article 3, Standards of Practice 3.8 and 3.11.

ARTICLE 4

"REALTORS® shall not acquire an interest in or buy or present offers from themselves, any member of their immediate families, their firms, or any member thereof, or any entities in which they have any ownership interest, any real property without making their true position known to the owner or the owner's agent or broker. In selling property, they own, or in which they have any interest, REALTORS® shall reveal their ownership or interest in writing to the purchaser or the purchaser's representative."

Central theme. Article 4 requires Realtors® to disclose that they have a real estate license when buying or selling property for themselves. If they do not disclose this fact, then they have an unfair advantage over the average consumer. By telling them, the Realtor® is giving them a chance to obtain representation in the transaction. Thus, keeping it an arms-length transaction.

Article 4 Standard of Practice. The one Standard of Practice for Article 4 requires the Realtor® to reveal their ownership or interest in the property in writing before entering into any contract.

ARTICLE 5

"REALTORS® shall not undertake to provide professional services concerning a property or its value where they have a present or contemplated interest unless such interest is specifically disclosed to all affected parties."

Central theme. Article 5 requires Realtors® to disclose any conflict of interest before providing any professional services. The only time this would be allowed is with the written permission of all parties involved in providing the service.

Article 5 illustration. ABC Realty shares office space with a lender and a title company. They recommend that all their buyers use these companies since they are in the same location, and it allows them to communicate with the lender and title company to ensure the closing goes smoothly. What the Realtor® did not disclose to their customers is the fact that family members own these companies.

ARTICLE 6

"REALTORS® shall not accept any commission, rebate, or profit on expenditures made for their client, without the client's knowledge and consent.

When recommending real estate products or services (e.g., homeowner's insurance, warranty programs, mortgage financing, title insurance, etc.), REALTORS® shall disclose to the client or customer to whom the recommendation is made any financial benefits or fees, other than real estate referral fees, the REALTOR® or REALTOR®'s firm may receive as a direct result of such recommendation."

Central theme. Article 6 states a Realtor® may not accept any compensation in the form of a commission, rebate, kickback, etc., without the client's written consent. This requirement includes gifts from home inspectors, appliance companies, plumbers, etc.

Article 6 illustrated. A Realtor® hired Ace Home Inspection to inspect a home for a buyer. The Realtor did not tell the buyer that he received a $50 gift card for the referral. The Realtor® violates Article 6 of the Code of Ethics.

ARTICLE 7

"In a transaction, REALTORS® shall not accept compensation from more than one party, even if permitted by law, without disclosure to all parties and the informed consent of the REALTOR®'s client or clients."

Central theme. Article 7 states that a Realtor® cannot accept compensation from more than one person without disclosing the fact to all parties. The Realtor should also have that consent in writing.

Article 7 illustrated. A broker has a Buyer's Broker Agreement with a buyer. The agreement states that the broker will get a 3% commission on a home valued at $350,000. The broker finds a home for $300,000 that the buyer likes, and they enter a contract. The broker is getting 3% from the listing broker and then asks the buyer to pay him a 3% commission. The broker tells the buyer he is not getting any commission from the seller's side. This type of action would be a violation of Article 7 of the Code of Conduct. The broker may not receive compensation from more than one party in a transaction unless he has written all the parties' written consent.

ARTICLE 8

"REALTORS® shall keep in a special account in an appropriate financial institution, separated from their own funds, monies coming into their possession in trust for other persons, such as escrows, trust funds, clients' monies, and other like items."

Article 8 central themes. Article 8 addresses escrow funds and how to handle other people's money. A Broker must be careful not to commingle funds. Commingle is mixing their personal money with money held in trust for others. The only time commingling is legal is when a Broker puts up to $1,000 of personal funds for a Sales Escrow Account or $5,000 in a Tenant Escrow Account to stop the possibility of conversion.

.

ARTICLE 9

"REALTORS®, for the protection of all parties, shall assure whenever possible that all agreements related to real estate transactions including, but not limited to, listing and representation agreements, purchase contracts, and leases are in writing in clear and understandable language expressing the specific terms, conditions, obligations, and commitments of the parties. A copy of each agreement shall be furnished to each party to such agreements upon their signing or initialing."

Central themes. Article 9 states Brokers must ensure all documents related to a real estate transaction be in clear, concise language. The contracts must also clearly represent the terms and conditions of the agreement between the parties. Tennessee law requires that the broker keep all contracts and real estate related transaction documents for three years.

Article 9 Standards of Practice. Article 9 has 2 Standards of Practice as follows:

SP 9.1 – Realtors® should use reasonable care to ensure extensions and amendments.
SP 9.2 – Realtors® should make a reasonable effort to explain the different parts of a contract to clients when working electronically.

Article 9 illustrated. Broker Jane is working with a buyer in another state. She sends them an electronic contract and indicates where the buyer needs to sign. Jane does not review the Sales and Purchase Agreement with them or go over any of the disclosures. Upon return of the contract, Jane does not send a copy to the buyer. Broker Jane violates Article 9 of the Code of Articles.

SECTION 2 – DUTIES TO THE PUBLIC.

DEFINITIONS

Demographic information. Information gathered on customers or clients. May include information such as age, sex, race, color, or national origin. This information is collected only to assist in operating the brokerage and identifying advertising avenues, not discriminating against anyone in a protected class.

Professional services. The eight professional services a Realtor® may perform are advertising, buying, auctioning, renting, selling, appraising, leasing, and exchanging.

NAR's protected classes. The NAR Code of Ethics' protected classes includes race, color, religion, sex, handicap, familial status, national origin, sexual orientation, or gender identity.

Public trust. Public Trust refers to misappropriation of client or customer funds or property, discrimination against the protected classes under the Code of Ethics, or fraud.

Duties to the public. The third section of NAR's Code of Ethics covers how Realtors® should behave when interacting with the public. Articles 10 to 14 and their Standards of Practices identify specific behavior and guidelines for dealing with the public. This section restates many of the same ideas expressed in Articles 1 through 9; however, it explicitly identifies the duties owed to the member of the public.

ARTICLE 10

> *"REALTORS® shall not deny equal professional services to any person for reasons of race, color, religion, sex, handicap, familial status, national origin, sexual orientation, or gender identity. REALTORS® shall not be parties to any plan or agreement to discriminate against a person or persons on the basis of race, color, religion, sex, handicap, familial status, national origin, sexual orientation, or gender identity."*

> *"REALTORS®, in their real estate employment practices, shall not discriminate against any person or persons on the basis of race, color, religion, sex, handicap, familial status, national origin, sexual orientation, or gender identity."*

Central theme. Article 10 of the Code of Ethics prohibits Realtors® from discrimination against the protected classes identified in the Code of Ethics. NAR has added protected classes to their Code of Ethics, making it stricter than the Federal Fair Housing Laws and the State of Tennessee's Fair Housing Laws.

Article 10 Standards of Practice. Article 10 has 5 Standards of Practices as follows:

SP 10.1 – Realtors® may provide necessary demographic information of a neighborhood; however, they cannot provide information about the neighborhood's racial, religious, or ethnic composition.

SP 10.2 – Realtors® may gather demographic information; however, they must be careful how the information is used and distributed.

SP 10.3 – Realtors® should be cautious with any advertisement that indicates a neighborhood's racial or ethnic makeup or targets one of the protected classes.

SP 10.4 –Realtors® must follow fair employment practices of employees or independent contractors.

SP 10.5 – Realtors® may not use harassing speech, hate speech, epithets, or slurs against someone in one of the protected classes.

Amendments to SP 10.5. In November 2020, the NAR Board of Directors made changes to Standard Practice 10.5. After extensive research, the Professional Standards Committee recommended changes that effectively broadened the context of this standard. In the past, the Code of Ethics only covered Realtors'® activities during a real estate transaction. The applicability of the new Standard of Practice 10,5 covers all activities of a Realtor.®

Under the changes made in November 2020, a Realtor® can be found guilty of a Code of Ethics violation whether the infraction related to a transaction, or other membership-related context. Presently, any potential breach of Article will be looked at individually to see if it is in violation of Article 10 or if it is someone expressing their First Amendment rights.

The new wording of Article 10, SP 10.5 became:
> "Realtors® must not use harassing speech, hate speech, epithets, or slurs" based upon an individual or group that falls under one of the protected classes."

Article 10 illustration. A Realtor® created an advertisement using models and demographic information about a neighborhood's racial makeup. The purpose was primarily to steer specific individuals to a particular community. This action is a violation of Article 10, Standards of Practice 10.2 and 10.3.

ARTICLE 11

> *"The services which REALTORS® provide to their clients and customers shall conform to the standards of practice and competence which are reasonably expected in the specific real estate disciplines in which they engage; specifically, residential real estate brokerage, real property management, commercial and industrial real estate brokerage, land brokerage, real estate appraisal, real estate counseling, real estate syndication, real estate auction, and international real estate."*

> *"REALTORS® shall not undertake to provide specialized professional services concerning a type of property or service that is outside their field of competence unless they engage the assistance of one who is competent on such types of property or service, or unless the facts are fully disclosed to the client. Any persons engaged to provide such assistance shall be so identified to the client, and their contribution to the assignment should be set forth."*

Central theme. Realtors® should only work within real estate areas in which they have sufficient knowledge to protect their customer or client. One agent can't know everything about all areas of specialization within the industry.

Article 11 Standards of Practice. Article 11 has four Standards of Practice as follows:

SP 11.1 – When preparing an opinion of value on a piece of property, they must know that specific area of real estate and provide detailed information to the customer or client.

SP 11.2 – A Realtor® should perform only in an area that they have reasonable competence.

SP 11.3 – When providing consulting services or advice, they shall objectively present the material. The fee shall be contingent on the level of difficulty and the market value of the real property.

SP 11.4 – Competency required under Article 11 is based on the services agreed to by the customers or clients and follows the Code of Ethics and state law.

Article 11 illustration. A Realtor® is asked to prepare an appraisal for a bank on a commercial building's short sale. The agent had no experience in doing an appraisal or in commercial real estate. This agent would be guilty of violating Article 11 Standards of Practice 11.1, 11.2, and 11.4.

ARTICLE 12

> *"REALTORS® shall be honest and truthful in their real estate communications and shall present a true picture in their advertising, marketing, and other representations. REALTORS® shall ensure that their status as real estate professionals is readily apparent in their advertising, marketing, and other representations and that the recipients of all real estate communications are, or have been, notified that those communications are from a real estate professional."*

Central theme. Realtors® should be honest in all their advertising and marketing.

Article 12 Standards of Practice. Article 12 has 13 Standards of Practices:

SP 12.1 – Realtors® who advertise something as free must disclose if they will receive any compensation and from whom they are going to receive the payment.

SP 12.2 – Deleted in January 2020.

SP 12.3 – Realtors® should use care if offering a prize or other compensation for real estate services. They must fully disclose the requirement to receive the compensation.

SP 12.4 – Realtors® should not advertise a property they are not authorized to market.

SP 12.5 – Realtors® must be careful not to practice Blind Advertising. The brokerage name must always appear in all advertising.

SP 12.6 – When selling their own property, a Realtor® must disclose their license status.

SP 12.7 – Only the brokers directly involved in a transaction may advertise that they sold or have a contract on the property with permission from the owner.

SP 12.8 – A Realtors® website should present current, accurate information, and they should keep the information current.

SP 12.9 – A Realtors® website shall disclose the brokerage's name and licensure state in a readily apparent manner.

SP 12.10 – Realtors® must advertise truthfully and give correct information and not deceptive the public in their URLs, websites, or the images they use.

SP 12.11 – Realtors® who intend to sell consumer information should disclose this wherever they gather the data.

SP 12.12 – Realtors® shall not use URL or domain names that may mislead the public.

SP 12.13 - Realtors® are only allowed to use designations, certifications, and other credentials they have earned and have maintained membership.

Article 12 illustration.

A Realtor® developed a website in which he promoted himself as the top producing agent in his area. He also stated that he had the following designations, Certified International Property Specialist (CIPS) and Graduate Realtor Institute (GRI). He had earned these designations; however, he did not keep up the designations' annual renewal. He also did not put the name of the brokerage on his website. The Realtor® has violated Article 12 and Standards of Practices 12.5, 12.9, and 12.13.

ARTICLE 13

"REALTORS® shall not engage in activities that constitute the unauthorized practice of law and shall recommend that legal counsel be obtained when the interest of any party to the transaction requires it."

Central theme. Realtors® must not represent themselves as attorneys nor give legal advice.

Article 13 illustration. While filling out an offer to buy a piece of real property, Realtor® John was asked by his customer how they should take title to the property. John asked the question without telling his customer that they should seek legal advice. John was practicing law by answering the question and thus in violation of Article 13.

ARTICLE 14

"If charged with unethical practice or asked to present evidence or to cooperate in any other way, in any professional standards proceeding or investigation, REALTORS® shall place all pertinent facts before the proper tribunals of the Member Board or affiliated institute, society, or council in which membership is held and shall take no action to disrupt or obstruct such processes."

Central theme. Realtors® must assist the Professional Standards Committee in any investigation or hearing. They must always present the truth and not interfere with the process.

Article 14 Standards of Practice. Article 14 has four Standards of Practice:

SP 14.1 – Only one board may hear any case of alleged violations of the Code of Ethics.
SP 14.2 – A Realtor® should not disclose any information they learned at an ethics hearing.
SP 14.3 – A Realtor® should not threaten or intimidate a witness or respondent in an ethics case.
SP 14.4 – A Realtor® should not mislead the investigation into an Ethics case, nor can they file multiple charges based on the same transaction.

Article 14 illustration: Broker Alicia was named in a Code of Ethics violation. She denies the allegations. Trying to get the case canceled, Alicia threatens the person who filed the charges against her and refuses to turn over information to the Professional Standards Committee. Alicia violates Article 14 Standards of Practices 14.3 and 14.4.

SECTION 3 –DUTIES TO REALTORS®

DEFINITIONS

Arbitration. A voluntary process where an independent third party listens to the individuals involved in the dispute and makes a binding decision on who is the winner.

Mediation. A voluntary process where an independent third person helps the parties agree to resolve their dispute. Mediation is considered a win-win option; the idea is that both sides will walk out feeling they got something from the mediation. In 90 days, if no resolution is met, the parties must move on to another dispute resolution method, preferably arbitration.

Ombudsman. A voluntary process where an individual appointed by a local Board of Realtors® receives assistance to resolve disputes through constructive communication and advocating for consensus and understanding.

Procuring cause. The agent who starts the uninterrupted chain of events leading to the sale or rental of a listing.

Public trust. Public trust refers to misappropriation of client or customer funds or property, discrimination against the protected classes under the Code of Ethics, or fraud.

Duties to Realtors®:

The fourth section of NAR's Code of Ethics covers how Realtors® should behave when interacting with other Realtors®. Articles 15 to 17 and their Standards of Practices identify specific behavior and guidelines for dealing with other Realtors®. This section restates many of the same ideas expressed in Articles 1 through 14; however, it explicitly identifies the duties owed to NAR members.

ARTICLE 15

> " *REALTORS® shall not knowingly or recklessly make false or misleading statements about other real estate professionals, their businesses, or their business practices.* "

Central theme. Article 15 of the Code of Ethics prohibits Realtors® from making a false or misleading statement about other real estate professionals, their own business, or their business practices.

Article 15 Standards of Practices: Article 15 three Standards of Practices as follows:

SP 15.1 – Realtors® may not file false or misleading statements about their business.
SP 15.2 – Realtors® may not make a false or misleading statement about other Realtor®. This Standard covers the false statements no matter what medium they are presented, i.e., digital, written, in person, etc.
SP 15.3 – Realtors® publish clarification if they discover a previous statement is false or misleading.

Article 15 Illustration: A Realtor® told everyone at her office that a competitive brokerage broker was not doing well financially. She even posted these statements on her Facebook page. She was trying to get agents from the other brokerage to join her company. She then boasted about how great her business was doing when in fact, it was struggling. This violation is of Article 15, Standard of Practices 15.1 and 15.2.

ARTICLE 16

> " REALTORS® shall not engage in any practice or take any action inconsistent with exclusive representation or exclusive brokerage relationship agreements that other REALTORS® have with clients."

Central theme. Realtors® must not try to steal away another broker's client. If they know someone is already working with a Realtor®, they must not try and get that client to come to them.

Article 16 Standards of Practice. Article 16 has 20 Standards of Practice as follows:

SP 16.1 – This Standard of Practice serves to set boundaries a Realtor® should not cross with respect to other practitioners. It is not trying to eliminate aggressive or innovative business practices.

SP 16.2 – A Realtor® may make general statements about their business and participate in marketing campaigns without infringing on other licensees' client relationships. Standard of Practice 16.2, however, outlines two unethical types of solicitation:
1.) Telephone or personal solicitation of sellers identified by yard signs or through MLS information; and,
2.) Mail or other written solicitation sent to customers or clients of other Realtors® that are not part of a mass marketing campaign.

SP 16.3 – A Realtor® may contact a client or customer of another Realtor® to offer different services than those the client is already under contract. Realtors® cannot use MLS information to target potential customers.

SP 16.4 & 16.5 – A Realtor® should not try to steal listings or represented buyers from another agent. The only time a Realtor® may contact another Realtors® client is to get specific information not available by the other agent or not listed in the MLS.

SP16.6 – If someone under contract with another Realtor® contacts a Realtor®, the Realtor® may discuss how they would work with the customer once their contract is up with the other real estate agent.

SP16.7 – The fact that a customer has worked with a specific Realtor® in the past does not prohibit another Realtor® from trying to get hired once any existing contract has expired. People do not have to return to the same Realtor® for every transaction they complete.

SP 16.8 – The fact that an exclusive agreement existed in the past does not prohibit another Realtor® from entering into a similar agreement once the first contact expires.

SP 16.9 – Before entering into an agreement with a client, a Realtor® must ensure that the client is not already in another contract with a different Realtor®.

SP 16.10 – A buyer's agent should disclose that the agreement exists between them when they begin to negotiate a contract.

SP 16.11 – For unlisted property, Realtors® must disclose any relationship between themselves and other customers. They should also request any desired compensation at the first meeting.

SP 16.12 – All contractual relationships should be disclosed before entering into a Purchase agreement.

SP 16.13 – Realtors® should communicate to the co-broking Realtor® and not the customer or client.

SP 16.14 – A Realtor® may enter into any representation but may not require them to pay compensation if the other party is contracted to pay compensation.

SP 16.15 – All monies and compensation must be paid broker to broker.

SP 16.16 – A Realtor® may not use the terms of an offer to modify the compensation terms already laid out.

SP16.17 – Realtors® shall not attempt to extend a listing broker's offer of cooperation without the listing broker's consent.

SP 16.18 – A Realtor® shall not use information obtained from another agent or the MLS to negotiate the client away from the firm.

SP 16.19 – Realtors® must have the owner's permission before placing signs on the property.

SP 16.20 – When a Realtor® leaves a brokerage, their listing stays with the brokerage. Agents are not allowed to entice customers to follow them to another agency.

Article 16 Illustration: A Realtor® is holding an open house. A couple comes in and begins looking around. They start asking the Realtor® questions and state they want to put an offer in on the house. The agent writes up an offer and presents it to the seller, who accepts it. Only after the offer is accepted does it come out that the buyers have a Buyer's Broker Agreement with another Realtor.

The Realtor holding the open house should have asked if they were under contract with another Realtor. This is a violation of Article 16 under the Code of Ethics.

ARTICLE 17

" In the event of contractual disputes or specific non-contractual disputes as defined in Standard of Practice 17-4 between REALTORS® (principals) associated with different firms, arising out of their relationship as REALTORS®, the REALTORS® shall mediate the dispute if the Board requires its members to mediate. If the dispute is not resolved through mediation, or if mediation is not required, REALTORS® shall submit the dispute to arbitration in accordance with the policies of the Board rather than litigate the matter.

In the event clients of REALTORS® wish to mediate or arbitrate contractual disputes arising out of real estate transactions, REALTORS® shall mediate or arbitrate those disputes in accordance with the policies of the Board, provided the clients agree to be bound by any resulting agreement or award.

The obligation to participate in mediation and arbitration contemplated by this Article includes the obligation of REALTORS® (principals) to cause their firms to mediate and arbitrate and be bound by any resulting agreement or award. "

Central theme. Realtors® should first commit to mediation if there are unsettled disputes. If mediation does not settle the conflicts, then the agents will move to binding arbitration.

Article 17 Standards of Practices: Article 17 has five Standards of Practices:

SP 17.1 – Realtors® who file litigation and refuse to withdraw in an arbitrable issue will constitute a refusal to arbitrate.

SP 17.2 – Parties to a dispute are not required to commit to mediation, but they are not relieved of the duty to arbitrate by not entering mediation.

SP 17.3 – Realtors®, when acting solely as principals, are not obligated to arbitrate disputes with other Realtors®.

SP 17.4 – This Standard of Practice lays out specific times when non-contractual disputes are subject to arbitration. Procuring cause disputes fall under this category.

SP 17.5 – The requirement to arbitrate includes disputes between Realtors® from different states. It also states which association will have jurisdiction over the disputes.

Article 17 illustration. Whenever there is a dispute among Realtors® or the parties to a real estate transaction, the parties, per our contract, should first go to mediation and then to binding arbitration. Realtors should work to keep disputes out of the legal system whenever they are able.

II. Professional Etiquette

REALTOR DISPUTE RESOLUTION

Anyone can file a complaint. It can be Realtor® vs. Realtor® or client/customer against Realtor®. Once filed with a local association of Realtors®, the complaint is then forwarded to the Grievance Committee to determine if there is a violation of the code of ethics and an arbitrational issue. If the Grievance Committee believes there is sufficient evidence of an Ethics violation, a hearing will be scheduled with the Professional Standards Committee to hear the case and recommend the Board of Directors on outcome and punishment.

If there is a monetary issue, then the matter will be sent to the local Board's Ombudsman program to help the parties decide. If the Ombudsman does not settle the dispute, the parties will be offered the opportunity to enter mediation and then go on to arbitration to resolve the dispute.

PATHWAYS TO PROFESSIONALISM

While the Code of Ethics establishes enforceable standards that Realtors® must follow, it does not set out standards of common courtesy or etiquette that a Realtors® should use in their dealings with other Realtors® or the public. This is accomplished with NAR's set of professional courtesy standards called the Pathways to Professionalism.

There are three sections to the Pathways to Professionalism:

1. Respect for the Public
2. Respect for Property
3. Respect for Peers

These Professional courtesies are intended to be used by REALTORS® voluntarily.
They cannot form the basis for a professional standards complaint.

Pathways to Professionalism

Respect for the Public

1. Follow the "Golden Rule": Do unto others as you would have them do unto you.
2. Respond promptly to inquiries and requests for information.
3. Schedule appointments and showings as far in advance as possible.
4. Call if you are delayed or must cancel an appointment or showing.
5. If a prospective buyer decides not to view an occupied home, promptly explain the situation to the listing broker or the occupant.
6. Communicate with all parties in a timely fashion.
7. When entering a property, ensure that unexpected situations, such as pets, are handled appropriately.
8. Leave your business card if not prohibited by local rules.
9. Never criticize property in the presence of the occupant.
10. Inform occupants that you are leaving after showings.

11. When showing an occupied home, always ring the doorbell or knock—and announce yourself loudly before entering. Knock and announce yourself loudly before entering any closed room.
12. Present a professional appearance at all times; dress appropriately and drive a clean car.
13. If occupants are home during showings, ask their permission before using the telephone or bathroom.
14. Encourage the clients of other brokers to direct questions to their agent or representative.
15. Communicate clearly; don't use jargon or slang that may not be readily understood.
16. Be aware of and respect cultural differences.
17. Show courtesy and respect to everyone.
18. Be aware of—and meet—all deadlines.
19. Promise what you can deliver—and keep your promises.
20. Identify your REALTOR® and your professional status in contacts with the public.
21. Do not tell people what you think—tell them what you know.

Respect for Property

1. Be responsible for everyone you allow to enter listed property.
2. Never allow buyers to enter listed property unaccompanied.
3. When showing property, keep all members of the group together.
4. Never allow unaccompanied access to the property without permission.
5. Enter property only with permission, even if you have a lockbox key or combination.
6. When the occupant is absent, please leave the property as you found it (lights, heating, cooling, drapes, etc.) If you think something is amiss (e.g., vandalism), contact the listing broker immediately.
7. Be considerate of the seller's property. Do not allow anyone to eat, drink, smoke, dispose of trash, use bathing or sleeping facilities, or bring pets. Leave the house as you found it unless instructed otherwise.
8. Use sidewalks; if weather is bad, take off shoes and boots inside the property.
9. Respect sellers' instructions about photographing or videographing their properties' interiors or exteriors.

Respect for Peers

1. Identify your REALTOR® and professional status in all contacts with other REALTORS®.
2. Respond to other agents' calls, faxes, and e-mails promptly and courteously.
3. Be aware that large electronic files with attachments or lengthy faxes may be a burden on recipients.
4. Notify the listing broker if there appears to be inaccurate information on the listing.
5. Share important information about a property, including pets, security systems, and whether sellers will be present during the showing.
6. Show courtesy, trust, and respect to other real estate professionals.
7. Avoid the inappropriate use of endearments or other denigrating language.
8. Do not prospect at other REALTORS®' open houses or similar events.
9. Return keys promptly.
10. Carefully replace keys in the lockbox after showings.
11. To be successful in the business, mutual respect is essential.

12. Real estate is a reputation business. What you do today may affect your reputation—and business—for years to come.

The above is from the 2021 NAR Code of Ethics and Arbitration Manual, Pathways to Professionalism, page vii. https://www.nar.realtor/code-of-ethics-and-arbitration-manual/pathways-to-professionalism

COMMITMENT TO EXCELLENCE

The Commitment to Excellence (C2EX) program from the National Association of REALTORS® is a professional development resource that empowers REALTORS® to evaluate, enhance and showcase their highest professional levels. It's not a course, class, or designation—it's an Endorsement that REALTORS® can promote when serving clients and other REALTORS®.

The NAR Board of Directors has requested that all Board of Directors, committee members, and leadership complete the C2EX program. To date, over 50,000 Realtors® have completed this program.

MODULE 8 SNAPSHOT REVIEW:

ETHICS AND ETIQUETTE

I. ETHICS

NATIONAL ASSOCIATION OF REALTORS' CODE OF ETHICS

- established in 1913; primary goal is to protect the public from land scams and to promote homeownership.

Structure of the Code

- The Code of Ethics has four parts: The Preamble, Duties to Clients and Customers, Duties to the Public, and Duties to Realtors.

The Preamble

- serves as a vision statement and lays out the duties and responsibilities for Realtors®·

PART 1: DUTIES TO CLIENTS AND CUSTOMERS

ARTICLE 1 --promotes honesty to all.

ARTICLE 2-- Realtor's® actions must have transparency to them.

ARTICLE 3 -- promotes cooperation among brokers unless it is not in their client's best interest.

ARTICLE 4 -- Realtors® must disclose that they have a real estate license when buying, selling, or renting their own property.

ARTICLE 5 -- Realtors® must disclose any conflict of interest before providing professional services.

ARTICLE 6 -- Realtors® may not accept any compensation without the written consent of all parties.

ARTICLE 7 -- Realtors may not accept compensation from more than one person without disclosing the fact to all parties.

ARTICLE 8 -- addresses the handling of escrow funds.

ARTICLE 9 -- states that all documents must be in clear and concise language.

PART 2: DUTIES TO THE PUBLIC

ARTICLE 10 -- Realtors® must give equal professional service to all clients and customers irrespective of race, color, religion, sex, handicap, familial status, national origin, sexual orientation, or sexual identity; Realtors do not discriminate in their employment practices

ARTICLE 11 -- Realtors® must be knowledgeable and competent in their fields of practice; If not competent, must get assistance from a knowledgeable professional or disclose any lack of experience to their client

ARTICLE 12 -- Realtors® must be honest and truthful in their communications; must present accurate descriptions in advertising, marketing, other public representations

ARTICLE 13 -- Realtors® must not engage in the unauthorized practice of law

ARTICLE 14 -- Realtors® must willingly participate in an ethics investigation and enforcement actions.

PART 3 : DUTIES TO REALTORS

ARTICLE 15 -- Realtors® must be truthful, make objective comments about other real estate professionals
ARTICLE 16 -- respect exclusive brokerage relationships of other Realtors® with their clients
ARTICLE 17 -- arbitrate financial disagreements with other Realtors® and with their clients.

II. PROFESSIONAL ETIQUETTE

REALTOR DISPUTE RESOLUTION
- **complaint process** begins with filing of a complaint by anyone against a Realtor®
- First, **Grievance Committee** reviews complaint, forwards to Professional Standards Committee if a violation of Code of Ethics occurred.
- **Professional Standards Committee** decides on punishment if a violation.
- recommendations forwarded to the Board of Directors to enforce

PATHWAYS TO PROFESSIONALISM
- sets forth etiquette standards Realtors® should follow
- three categories of etiquette: Respect for the Public, Respect for Property, Respect for Peers

COMMITMENT TO EXCELLENCE
- new program introduced by NAR to showcase, enhance professionalism; to date, 50,000+ Realtors® have completed program.

MODULE 8 – ETHICS AND ETIQUETTE

QUIZ

Carefully read each question and provide your best answer based on what you learned in this module. Then check your answers against the Answer Key which immediately follows the quiz questions.

1. Which of the following is considered to be ethical behavior?

    a. Buying a listed property as a licensee without proper disclosure to the seller.
    b. Refusing to rent the basement apartment of your home to a gay couple.
    c. Discriminating against a client based on race
    d. Disclosing all the defects of a home you are selling

2. C2EX is a new program _____.

    a. required by every Realtor.
    b. developed by local Tennessee boards.
    c. that confers NAR's new C2EX designation.
    d. encourages agents to show a high level of professionalism.

3. What is the name of NAR's set of professional courtesy standards?

    a. Golden Standard of Real Estate
    b. Professionalism in Real Estate
    c. Pathways to Professionalism
    d. The Etiquette Principals

4. Once a complaint against a Realtor® is filed with a local association of Realtors, it is then forwarded to the _____.

    a. Grievance Committee.
    b. State Board of Realtors.
    c. National Association of Realtors' Mediation Committee.
    d. Department of Real Estate.

5. You know that it is illegal and unethical to buy shares of a company you represent and receive information not available to the public. However, you have invested your children's college fund in the stock of your husband's company. Your husband tells you the company is about to go through an IRS audit, and he is worried about the outcome.

    The next morning you call your stockbroker to protect your children's college fund and ask him to sell all your stock and reinvest it in another company. This is an example of _____.

    a. business ethics.
    b. situational ethics.
    c. Code of Ethics.
    d. bad morals.

6. According to Article 13, a licensee should be careful not to practice _____.

    a. medicine.
    b. law.
    c. accounting.
    d. assessments.

7. Realtors® can do appraisals. If they do an appraisal, they _____.

    a. must follow USPAP rules and only do appraisals on Federally related transactions.
    b. need not follow USPAP rules and only do appraisals on Federally related transactions.
    c. must follow USPAP rules and not appraise any Federally related transactions.
    d. need not follow USPAP rules and not appraise any Federally related transactions.

8. The central theme of Article 1 of the NAR Code of Ethics is to _____.

    a. deal honestly with everyone no matter what type of relationship.
    b. disclose all defects of a home you are selling.
    c. use skill, care, and diligence if working with exclusive clients.
    d. not violate fair housing laws.

9. Articles 15 to 17 of the NAR Code of Ethics focus on how Realtors® should behave when interacting with _____.

    a. the public.
    b. other Realtors®.
    c. their clients.
    d. their customers.

10. Realtors follow the Pathway to Professionalism to show respect for _____ .

    a. the public, their peers, and their customers.
    b. the public, the property, and their clients.
    c. the public, the property, and their peers.
    d. the property, their peers, and their customers.

11. An individual appointed by a local Board of Realtors® to assist in resolving disputes through constructive communication is called _____.

    a. mediation.
    b. ombudsman.
    c. arbitration.
    d. procuring cause.

12. Realtors® may not advertise themselves as having _____.

    a. designations they have not obtained.
    b. property they have listed.
    c. a college degree.
    d. an award they won.

13. When was the Code of Ethics introduced?

    a. 1988
    b. 1964
    c. 1913
    d. 2021

14. According to Article 17, a licensee should be ready to _____ any complaints filed against them.

    a. deny
    b. ombudsman
    c. arbitrate
    d. litigate

15. Procuring cause of a sale goes to the Realtor® who _____.

    a. listed the property.
    b. started the chain of events that lead to the sale of the property.
    c. held the open house where the buyers first saw the home.
    d. had a fiduciary duty to their client.

16. A broker is selling his home as a For Sale by Owner. A potential buyer comes to look at the house, and the broker shows him around. The buyer puts in a 95% offer, and the seller accepts it. After closing, the buyer finds out the seller is a real estate broker and never disclosed it. Has this broker violated the Code of Ethics, and if so, why?

    a. No, since the buyer is only a customer
    b. No, since the offer was ultimately accepted
    c. Yes, since one must disclose his or her licensed status according to Article 4
    d. Yes, since the property was a For Sale by Owner

17. After attending a Professional Standards Hearing, Realtor Adam went home and discussed the case with his wife. He told her about all the parties involved and what had happened. Then he shared his opinion on what the outcome of the hearing should be. Which Article did Adam violate?

    a. Article 10
    b. Article 11
    c. Article 12
    d. Article 14

18. The Articles of the NAR Code of Ethics deal with all of the following duties, EXCEPT _____.

    a. Duties to your neighbors
    b. Duties to clients and customers
    c. Duties to the public
    d. Duties to other Realtors ®

19. When is an agent able to violate Federal Fair Housing Laws?

    a. Whenever it suits them
    b. Never
    c. Only if it is needed to make them money
    d. Only if no one suffers monetary damages

20. Jill completed a deal with Broker Jack. She was upset with the way Jack handled the transaction. She started spreading false rumors about Jack. Jill is guilty of violating _____ of the Code of Ethics.

    a. Article 10
    b. Article 15
    c. Article 16
    d. Article 17

MODULE 8 – ETHICS AND ETIQUETTE

ANSWER KEY TO QUIZ

1. d. Disclosing all the defects of a home you are selling
2. d. allows agents to show a high level of professionalism.
3. c. Pathways to Professionalism
4. a. Grievance Committee.
5. b. situational ethics.
6. b. law.
7. c. must follow USPAP rules and not appraise any Federally related transactions.
8. a. Deal honestly with everyone no matter what type of relationship.
9. b. other Realtors.
10. c. the public, the property, and their peers.
11. b. ombudsman.
12. a. designations they have not obtained.
13. c. 1913
14. c. arbitrate
15. b. started the chain of events that lead to the sale of the property.
16. c. Yes, since one must disclose his or her licensed status according to Article 4
17. d. Article 14
18. a. Duties to your neighbors
19. b. Never
20. b. Article 15

MODULE 8: ETHICS AND ETIQUETTE

CASE STUDY EXERCISE: Ethics on Social Media

Situational data:

A real estate agent is involved in local politics. During the County Commission meeting, the agent made a racist comment to a black member of the Commission. After the meeting, she went to her social media accounts and made additional derogatory comments against the Commissioner. She also suggested that the county would be better off if the County Commissioner died. Based on this information, discuss this scenario and answers the questions below.

Analysis Questions:

1. Which Article of the Code of Ethics do you feel was violated in this example?

   _____

   _____

2. What specific Standard of Practice do you feel was violated?

   _____

   _____

3. How could the situation be handled without violating the Code of Ethics?

   _____

   _____

CASE DEBRIEF:

1. Article 10 of the Code of Ethics was violated.

2. The agent violated Standard of Practice 10.5.

3. The agent may state their mind in the public forum; however, she may not use slurs or hate speech. She should have remained civil and not use derogatory comments against the County Commissioner. She would be guilty because she advocated violence against the Commissioner.

Module 9: FINANCE AND CLOSING

I. Real Estate Finance
II. Closings

Module 9 Learning Objectives

Real Estate Finance

1. Summarize the key steps involved in generating a mortgage loan, using both a mortgage and deed of trust, including the documents involved and the flow of borrowed funds between principal parties.
2. Describe the key aspects of loan qualification including income, cash and debt ratios.
3. Summarize the key provisions of ECOA, and the Fair Credit Reporting Act.
4. Identify the key organizations involved in secondary mortgage market activity, and what they do. Include FNMA, GNMA, and FHLMC.

Closings

1. Identify the key phases in the loan process from contract inception to recording.
2. Summarize the purposes of RESPA and how lenders achieve these by implementing the provisions the Act sets forth.
3. Summarize the mechanical aspects of a transaction's financial settlement process.

I. Real Estate Finance

MECHANICS OF THE MORTGAGE LOAN TRANSACTION

It is common to use borrowed money to purchase real estate. When a borrower gives a note promising to repay the borrowed money and executes a mortgage on the real estate for which the money is being borrowed as security, the financing method is called mortgage financing. The term "mortgage financing" also applies to real estate loans secured by a deed of trust. The process of securing a loan by pledging a property without giving up ownership of the property is called **hypothecation**.

States differ in their interpretation of who owns mortgaged property. Those that regard the mortgage as a lien held by the mortgagee (lender) against the property owned by the mortgagor (borrower) are called **lien-theory** states. Those that regard the mortgage document as a conveyance of ownership from the mortgagor to the mortgagee are called **title-theory** states (Tennessee is a title theory state). Some states interpret ownership of mortgaged property from a point of view that combines aspects of both title and lien theory.

A valid mortgage or trust deed financing arrangement requires

- a *note* as evidence of the debt
- the *mortgage or trust deed* as evidence of the collateral pledge

Note. In addition to executing a mortgage or trust deed, the borrower signs a promissory note for the amount borrowed. The amount of the loan is typically the difference between the purchase price and the down payment. A promissory note creates a personal liability for the borrower to repay the loan.

Mortgage. A mortgage is a legal document stating the pledge of the borrower (the **mortgagor**) to the lender (the **mortgagee**). The mortgage document pledges the borrower's ownership interest in the real estate in question as collateral against performance of the debt obligation. The flow of funds and obligations in a mortgage transaction is as follows:

Exhibit 9.1 Flow of a Mortgage Transaction

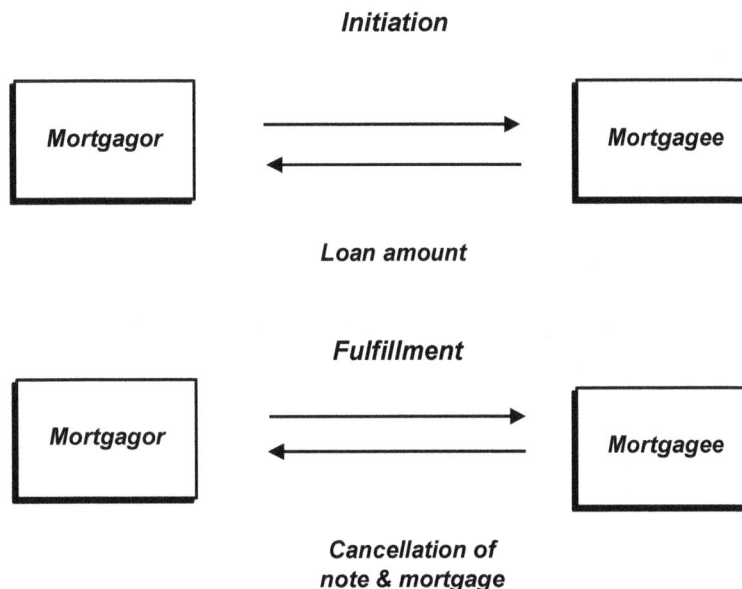

Initiation

| Mortgagor | $\longrightarrow$ | Mortgagee |

Loan amount

Fulfillment

| Mortgagor | $\longrightarrow$ | Mortgagee |

*Cancellation of
note & mortgage*

The deed of trust. A deed of trust conveys title to the property in question from the borrower (**trustor**) to a **trustee** as security for the loan. The trustee is a third party fiduciary to the trust. While the loan is in place, the trustee holds the title on behalf of the lender, who is the **beneficiary** of the trust. On repayment of the loan, the borrower receives the title from the trustee in the form of a deed of reconveyance.

The flow of funds and obligations in a trust deed transaction is as follows:

Exhibit 9.2 Flow of a Trust Deed Transaction

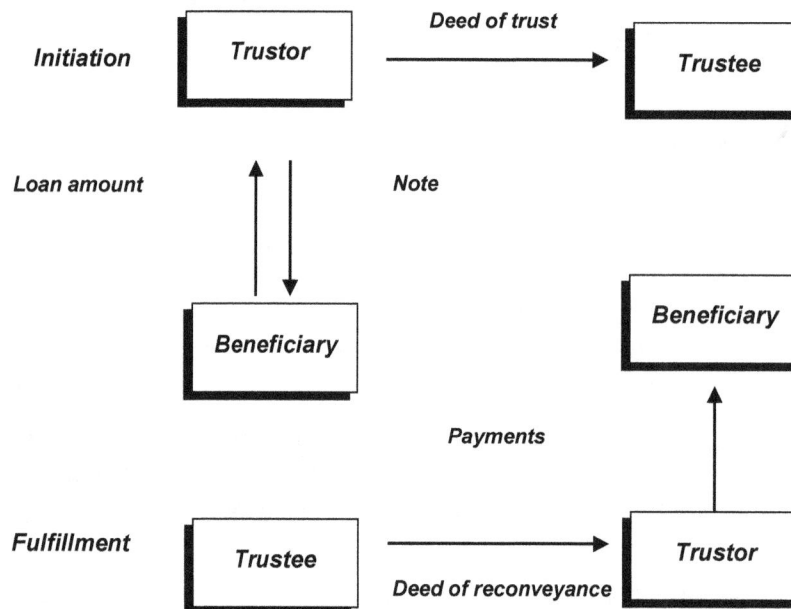

FINANCIAL QUALIFICATION

Income qualification

Lenders want to be assured that the borrower has adequate means to make all necessary periodic payments on the loan in addition to other housing expenses and debts such as credit card payments and car payments. Most lenders use two ratios to estimate an applicant's ability to fulfill a loan obligation: an *income ratio,* or *housing ratio*, and a *debt ratio*, or *housing plus debt ratio*. They also consider the stability of an applicant's income. Please note that the income and debt ratios in the discussion below do not necessarily reflect the latest ratios used by FHA, VA, or other lenders. Check for updates on the websites of those agencies.

Income ratio. The income ratio, or housing expense ratio, establishes borrowing capacity by limiting the percent of gross income a borrower may spend on housing costs. Housing costs include principal, interest, taxes, and homeowner's insurance, and may include monthly assessments, mortgage insurance, and utilities. The income ratio formula is:

Income Ratio

$$\frac{monthly\ housing\ expense}{monthly\ GROSS\ income} = income\ ratio$$

To identify the maximum monthly housing expense an income ratio allows, modify the formula as follows:

monthly gross income x income ratio = monthly housing expense

Most conventional lenders require that this ratio be *no greater than 25-28%*. In other words, a borrower's total housing expenses cannot exceed 28% of gross income. For an FHA-backed loan, the ratio is 31%. VA-guaranteed loans do not use this qualifying ratio.

For example, if a couple has combined monthly gross income of $12,000, and a lender's maximum income ratio is 28%, the couple's monthly housing expense cannot exceed $3,360:

$12,000 x 28% = $3,360

Debt ratio. The debt ratio considers all of the monthly obligations of the income ratio *plus any additional monthly payments the applicant must make for other debts*. The lender will look specifically at minimum monthly payments due on revolving credit debts and other consumer loans. The debt ratio formula is:

Debt Ratio

$$\frac{monthly\ housing\ expense + monthly\ debt\ obligations}{monthly\ GROSS\ income} = debt\ ratio$$

To identify the housing expenses plus debt a debt ratio allows, modify the formula as follows:

monthly gross income x debt ratio = monthly housing expense + monthly debt obligations

Most conventional lenders require that this debt ratio be *no greater than 36%*. For an FHA-backed loan, the debt ratio may not exceed 43%. The VA uses 41% and a variable "residual income" calculation. The FHA and VA include in the debt figure any obligation costing more than $100 per month and any debt with a remaining term exceeding six months.

Using the 36% debt ratio, the couple whose monthly income is $12,000 will be allowed to have monthly housing and debt obligations of $4,320:

$12,000 gross income x 36% = $4,320 expenses and debt

VA-guaranteed loans also require a borrower to meet certain qualifications based on net income after paying federal, state, and social security taxes, housing maintenance and utilities expenses. Such **residual income requirements** vary by family size, loan amount, and geographical region.

Income stability. A lender looks beyond income and debt ratios to assess an applicant's income stability. Important factors are:

- how long the applicant has been employed at the present job
- how frequently and for what reasons the applicant has changed jobs in the past
- how likely secondary income such as bonuses and overtime is to continue on a regular basis
- how educational level, training and skills, age, and type of occupation may affect the continuation of the present income level in the future.

Cash qualification and loan to value

A lender will usually lend only a portion of the property's value. The relationship of the loan amount to the property value, expressed as a percentage, is called the **loan-to-value ratio, or LTV**. If the lender's loan to value ratio is 80%, the lender will lend only $80,000 on a home appraised at $100,000. The difference between what the lender will lend and what the borrower must pay for the property is the amount the borrower must provide in cash as a down payment.

Since a lender lends only part of the purchase price of a property according to the lender's loan-to-value ratio, a lender will verify that a borrower has the cash resources to make the required down payment. If some of a borrower's cash for the down payment comes as a gift from a relative or friend, a lender may require a **gift letter** from the donor stating the amount of the gift and lack of any requirement to repay the gift. On the other hand, if someone is lending an applicant a portion of the down payment with a provision for repayment, a lender will consider this another debt obligation and adjust the debt ratio accordingly. This can lower the amount a lender is willing to lend.

Loan commitment

When a lender's underwriters have qualified an applicant and the lender has decided to offer the loan, the lender gives the applicant a written notice of the agreement to lend under specific terms. This written promise is the **loan commitment**. The commitment may take a number of common forms, including *a firm commitment, a lock-in commitment, a conditional commitment, and a take-out commitment.*

A **firm commitment** is a straight forward offer to make a specific loan at a specific interest rate for a specific term. This kind of commitment is the one most commonly offered to home buyers.

A **"lock-in" commitment** is an offer to lend a specific amount for a specific term at a specific interest rate, *but the interest rate is subject to an expiration date*, for instance, sixty days. This guarantees that the lender will not raise the interest rate during the application and closing periods. The borrower may have to pay points or some other charge for the lock-in.

A **conditional commitment** offers to make a loan if certain provisions are met. This kind of commitment generally applies to construction loans. A typical condition for funding the loan is completion of a development phase.

A **take-out commitment** offers to make a loan that will "take out" another lender's loan, i.e., pay it off and replace it. The take-out loan is most often used to retire a construction loan. The take-out lender agrees to pay off the short-term construction loan by issuing a long-term permanent loan.

Loan closing

Closing of a mortgage loan normally occurs with the closing of the real estate transaction. At the real estate closing, the lender typically has deposited the funded amount with an escrow agent, along with instructions for disbursing the funds. The borrower deposits necessary funds with the escrow agent, executes final documents, and receives signed copies of all relevant documents.

Title to the mortgaged property is transferred and recorded according to legal procedures in effect at the time of closing. The borrower receives a package containing copies of all documents relevant to the transaction.

FAIR FINANCING LAWS

ECOA

Equal Credit Opportunity Act prohibits discrimination in extending credit based on race, color, religion, national origin, sex, marital status, age, or dependency upon public assistance. A creditor may not make any statements to discourage an applicant on the basis of such discrimination or ask any questions of an applicant concerning these discriminatory items. A real estate licensee who assists a seller in qualifying a potential buyer may fall within the reach of this prohibition. A lender must also inform a rejected applicant in writing of reasons for denial within 30 days. A creditor who fails to comply is liable for punitive and actual damages.

Fair Credit Reporting Act

The FCRA ensures that all credit reporting agencies provide accurate information to the consumer. This statute lists every entity that can have access to the credit report. Thanks to the FCRA, consumers have a right to see their credit score and credit report.

SAFE Act

Secure and Fair Enforcement for Mortgage Licensing Act was established to create a national standard for residential mortgage loan originators to be licensed and registered.

PRIMARY, SECONDARY MORTGAGE MARKETS

The primary mortgage market consists of lenders who originate mortgage loans directly to borrowers. Primary mortgage market lenders include:

- savings and loans
- commercial banks
- mutual savings banks
- life insurance companies
- mortgage bankers
- credit unions

Mortgage brokers are also part of the primary mortgage market, even though they do not lend to customers directly. Rather, they are instrumental in procuring borrowers for primary mortgage lenders.

The primary lender assumes the initial risk of the long-term investment in the mortgage loan. Primary lenders sometimes also **service** the loan until it is paid off. Servicing loans entails collecting the borrower's periodic payments, maintaining and disbursing funds in escrow accounts for taxes and insurance, supervising the borrower's performance, and releasing the mortgage on repayment. In many cases, primary lenders employ mortgage servicing companies, which service loans for a fee.

Portfolio lenders. A primary mortgage market lender may or may not sell its loans into the secondary market. Many lenders originate loans for the purpose of retaining the investments in their own loan *portfolio.* These loans are referred to as *portfolio loans*, and lenders originating loans for their own portfolio are called *portfolio lenders*. Portfolio lenders are less restricted by the standards and forms imposed on other lenders by secondary market organizations. In retaining their portfolio loans, portfolio lenders may vary underwriting criteria and hold independent standards for down payment requirements and the condition of the collateral.

Secondary market

Lenders, investors and government agencies that buy loans already originated by someone else, or originate loans indirectly through someone else, constitute the **secondary mortgage market**.

Secondary mortgage market organizations include:

- Federal National Mortgage Association (FNMA, or Fannie Mae)
- Federal Home Loan Mortgage Corporation (FHLMC, or Freddie Mac)
- Government National Mortgage Association (GNMA, or Ginnie Mae)
- investment firms that assemble loans into packages and sell securities based on the pooled mortgages
- life insurance companies
- pension funds
- primary market institutions who also invest as secondary lenders

Secondary mortgage market organizations buy pools of mortgages from primary lenders and sell securities backed by these pooled mortgages to investors. By selling securities, the secondary market brings investor money into the mortgage market. By purchasing loans from primary lenders, the secondary market returns funds to the primary lenders, thereby enabling the primary lender to originate more mortgage loans.

Primary lenders make a profit on the sale of loans to the secondary market. The secondary market acquires a profitable long-term investment without having to underwrite, originate, and service the loans. Secondary market organizations customarily hire primary lenders or loan servicing companies to service mortgage pools.

Secondary market loan requirements. The secondary market only buys loans that meet established requirements for quality of collateral, borrower and documentation. Since many primary lenders intend to sell their loans to the secondary market, the qualification standards of the secondary market limit and effectively regulate the kind of loans the primary lender will originate.

Roles of FNMA; GNMA; FHLMC

As major players in the secondary market, the Federal National Mortgage Association (FNMA, "Fannie Mae"), Government National Mortgage Association (GNMA, "Ginnie Mae), and Federal Home Loan Mortgage Corporation (FHLMC, "Freddie Mac") tend to set the standards for the primary market.

Federal National Mortgage Association, or Fannie Mae. Fannie Mae is a government-sponsored enterprise, originally organized as a privately-owned corporation. As a secondary market player, it:

- buys conventional, FHA-backed and VA-backed loans
- gives banks mortgage-backed securities in exchange for blocks of mortgages
- offers lenders firm loan purchase commitments, provided they conform to Fannie Mae's lending standards
- sells bonds and mortgage-backed securities
- guarantees payment of interest and principal on mortgage-backed securities

Government National Mortgage Association, or Ginnie Mae. Ginnie Mae is a division of the Department of Housing and Urban Development. Its purpose is to administer special assistance programs and to help Fannie Mae in its secondary market activities. Specifically, GNMA

- guarantees payment on FNMA high-risk, low-yield mortgages and absorbs the difference in yield between the mortgages and market rates
- guarantees privately generated securities backed by pools of VA-and FHA-guaranteed loans

Federal Home Loan Mortgage Corporation, or Freddie Mac. Freddie Mac is a government-sponsored enterprise, originally chartered as an corporation in 1970. As a secondary market player, FHLMC buys mortgages and pools them, selling bonds backed by the mortgages in the open market. Freddie Mac guarantees performance on FHLMC mortgages.

A federal conservator, the Federal Housing Finance Authority (FHFA), now operates Fannie Mae and Freddie Mac as conservator with the U.S. Treasury a majority owner of both organizations

MORTGAGE-RELATED TENNESSEE LAWS

Title theory state, judicial and non-judicial foreclosure. Tennessee is primarily a title theory state. As indicated previously, in title theory states, the lender remains in control of the title until the loan is paid in full. In Tennessee, the title is held in trust until the loan is paid off. Lenders may also use judicial foreclosure in which the court issues the foreclosure judgment. But the most common method used by lenders in Tennessee is non-judicial using the power of sale clause in a deed of trust. So, Tennessee is both a judicial and non-judicial foreclosure state. (35-5-101 to 110; 21-1-803; 66-8-101 to 103)

When the deed of trust or mortgage includes a power of sale clause that specifies the terms and time of the sale, the sale must be carried out as specified. If not specified, Tennessee mortgage laws must be followed.

Deficiency judgments. Tennessee law permits lenders to obtain a deficiency judgment when a foreclosed property is sold and the sale price is less than the amount owed to the lender.

Right of redemption. Borrowers (mortgagors) have a statutory right of redemption for two years after a foreclosure, unless that right was waived in the original deed of trust. Real estate sold for debt is redeemable to the debtor and the debtor's creditors for two (2) years after the sale, regardless how often it had been previously redeemed. However, this right can be waived in the original mortgage documents.

Power of sale notices (TCA 35-5-101). In any sale to foreclose a deed of trust, mortgage or other lien under judicial order or process, advertisement of the sale must be made at least three (3) different times in a newspaper published in the county where the sale is to take place. The first publication must be at least twenty (20) days prior to the sale. The trustee or other party that sells the property must send the debtor and any co-debtor a copy of the required notice no later than the first date of publication by registered or certified mail, return receipt requested.

II. Closings

THE CLOSING PROCESS

The closing process consists of buyer and seller verifying that each has fulfilled the terms of the sale contract. If they have, then the mortgage loan, if any, is closed, all expenses are apportioned and paid, the consideration is exchanged for the title, final documents are signed, and arrangements are made to record the transaction according to local laws.

Exhibit 9.3 The Closing Process

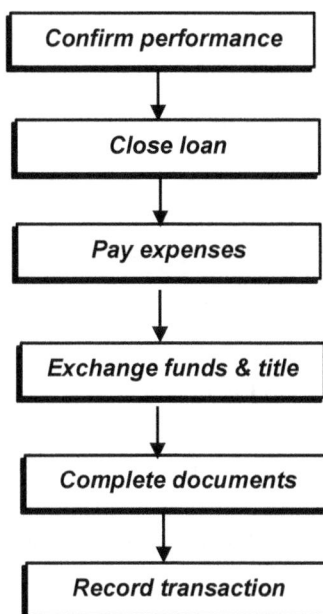

```
┌─────────────────────────┐
│  Confirm performance    │
└─────────────────────────┘
            │
            ▼
┌─────────────────────────┐
│      Close loan         │
└─────────────────────────┘
            │
            ▼
┌─────────────────────────┐
│     Pay expenses        │
└─────────────────────────┘
            │
            ▼
┌─────────────────────────┐
│  Exchange funds & title │
└─────────────────────────┘
            │
            ▼
┌─────────────────────────┐
│   Complete documents    │
└─────────────────────────┘
            │
            ▼
┌─────────────────────────┐
│   Record transaction    │
└─────────────────────────┘
```

TRANSFER OF TITLE

The seller must produce evidence of marketable title, such as a commitment for title insurance by a title insurer. Before making a title commitment, a title company performs a title search to discover any liens, encumbrances, restrictions, conditions, or easements attaching to the title.

If there are any encumbrances or liens that damage the title, the seller is expected to remove these prior to the date specified in the contract. The most common title cloud is an unpaid lien.

The seller may also be asked to execute an affidavit of title stating that, since the date of the original title search, the seller has incurred no new liens, judgments, unpaid bills for repairs or improvements, no unrecorded deeds or contracts, no bankruptcies or divorces that would affect title, or any other defects the seller is aware of.

The purchaser, purchaser's lender, or title company may require a survey to verify the location and size of the property. The survey also identifies any easements, encroachments, or flood plain hazard.

The buyer should inspect the property to make certain that the property is in the condition in which the seller states that it is, and that any repairs or other required actions have been performed. A final inspection, called a **buyer's walk-through**, should be conducted as close to the closing date as possible.

If the seller's mortgage lien(s) are to be satisfied at closing, the lender will provide a **payoff statement**, also called an **offset statement**, specifying the amount of unpaid principal and any interest due as of the closing date, plus fees that will be due the lender and any credits or penalties that may apply. The holder of a note secured by a trust deed will provide a similar statement, called a **beneficiary statement**, to show any unpaid balance. Even if the buyer is assuming the seller's mortgage loan, the buyer will want to know the exact amount of the unpaid balance as of the closing date.

Finally, the seller produces and/or deposits with the escrow agent the deed that conveys the property to the buyer.

Transfer of purchase funds

The buyer usually produces and/or deposits with the escrow agent the following:

- earnest money
- loan funds and documents
- any other cash needed to complete the purchase

ESCROW PROCEDURES

If the closing occurs "in escrow" rather than face-to-face, the principal parties deposit funds and documents with the appointed escrow agent, and the escrow agent disburses funds and releases documents to the appropriate parties when all the conditions of the escrow have been met. If for any reason the transaction cannot be completed, for instance if the buyer refuses the title as it is offered, or the buyer fails to produce the necessary cash, the escrow instructions usually provide a mechanism for reconveying title to the seller and funds to the buyer. In such a case, both parties return to their original status as if no sale had occurred.

LENDER CLOSING REQUIREMENTS

A lender is concerned about the quality of the collateral a borrower is providing in return for the mortgage loan. The collateral would be endangered by defects in the title, by liens that would take precedence over the mortgage lien, such as a tax lien, and by physical damage to the property which is not repaired. Consequently, the lender typically requires a survey; a property inspection; hazard insurance; a title insurance policy; a reserve account for taxes and insurance; and possibly, private mortgage insurance. In some cases the lender may also require a *certificate of occupancy* verifying that any new construction performed complies with local building codes.

BROKER'S ROLE

A broker usually continues to provide service between the signing of the sale contract and the closing by helping to make arrangements for pre-closing activities such as inspections, surveys, appraisals and repairs and generally taking steps to ensure that the closing can proceed as scheduled.

A broker may conduct proceedings at the closing meeting, or may have no further role in the transaction after the sale contract is signed, depending on local practices and the transaction in question. In many states, the broker is charged with the responsibility for accuracy and timely delivery of the closing documents to the principal parties. A broker may also have the responsibility for reporting the transaction to the Internal Revenue Service.

Finally, if the seller of the property is a non-resident alien, U.S. law may require the broker to withhold and transmit to the Internal Revenue Service a portion of the sale proceeds to cover the alien seller's income tax liability. There are also special reporting requirements when the transaction involves a non-resident alien.

REAL ESTATE SETTLEMENT PROCEDURES ACT

The **Real Estate Settlement Procedures Act** (RESPA) is a consumer protection statute enacted in 1974. Its purpose is to clarify settlement costs and to eliminate kickbacks and fees that increase settlement costs. RESPA specifies certain closing procedures when a purchase:

- involves a residential property, including one- to four-family residences, cooperatives and condominiums;

- involves a first or second mortgage lien; and

- is being financed by a "federally-related" mortgage loan, which includes loans made by a federally-insured lender; loans insured or guaranteed by the VA or FHA, loans administered by HUD, and loans intended to be sold to FNMA, FHLMC, or GNMA.

RESPA regulations do not apply to transactions being otherwise financed except in the case of an assumption in which the terms of the assumed loan are modified or the lender's charges for the assumption are greater than $50.

RESPA is directed at lenders and settlement companies, but licensees should be familiar with requirements and changes implemented as of January, 2014. The Dodd-Frank Act of 2010 granted rule-making authority under RESPA to the Consumer Financial Protection Bureau (CFPB) and generally granted the CFPB authority to supervise and enforce compliance with RESPA and its implementing regulations. In 2013, the CFPB made substantive and technical changes to the existing regulations. Substantive changes included modifying the servicing transfer notice requirements and implementing new procedures and notice requirements related to borrowers' error resolution requests and information requests. The amendments also included new provisions related to escrow payments, force-placed insurance, general servicing policies, procedures, and requirements, early intervention, continuity of contact, loss mitigation and the relation of RESPA's servicing provisions to State law. These RESPA amendments went into effect on January 10, 2014.

TILA/RESPA INTEGRATED DISCLOSURE RULE

Effective October 3, 2015, a TILA/RESPA Integrated Disclosure Rule (TRID) integrates the disclosure requirements of RESPA and Truth-in-Lending, replacing the old Good Faith Estimate form and HUD-1 Uniform Settlement Statement a new Loan Estimate form and Closing Disclosure form, respectively.

FINANCIAL SETTLEMENT OF THE TRANSACTION

Settlement process. The process of settlement consists of five basic steps:

1. Identify selling terms and closing costs.
2. Determine non-prorated debits and credits.
3. Determine prorated debits and credits.
4. Complete the closing statement.
5. Disburse funds.

Selling terms and closing costs. Selling terms are the price of the property, the buyer's deposit and downpayment, and the terms and amounts of the buyer's financing arrangements. Closing costs are final expenses that buyer or seller must pay at closing to complete the transaction. The sale contract identifies all selling terms and who pays which costs. The apportionment of expenses is subject to negotiation, and in the absence of a specific agreement, is determined by custom. Closing costs include such items as brokerage fees, mortgage-related fees, title-related expenses, and real estate taxes.

Debits and credits. The closing statement accounts for the debits and credits of the buyer and seller to settle and complete the transaction. A debit is an amount that one party must pay at closing or has already paid prior to closing. A credit is an amount that a party must receive at closing or that has already been received prior to closing.

The excess of the buyer's debits over the buyer's credits is the amount the buyer must bring to the closing. The excess of the seller's credits over the seller's debits is the amount the seller will receive at closing.

An individual expense item that one party owes to a party unrelated to the transaction, such as an attorney or the state, is treated as *a debit to that party only*. An income or expense item that affects both parties is apportioned, or **prorated**, to each party to reflect the proper amount that each owes or should receive. A prorated item is treated as *a debit to one party and a credit to the other party for the same amount*.

Buyer's debits and credits. To determine how much money the buyer owes at closing, the buyer's debits are totaled and compared with the total of the buyer's credits. The excess of debits over credits is the amount the buyer must bring to the closing, usually in the form of a cashier's check or certified check. The items typically debited and credited to the buyer are illustrated in the following exhibit.

$ Received or Receivable **Credit** » **Buyer or Seller** » Paid or Payable **Debit**

Exhibit 9.4 Buyer's Credits and Debits

Buyer's Credits

earnest money

loan amount (borrowed or assumed)

seller's share of prorated items the buyer will pay

Buyer's Debits

purchase price

expenses (per agreement or custom)

buyer's share of prorated items prepaid by seller

Seller's credits and debits. To determine how much the seller will receive at closing, the same procedure is followed for the seller's debits and credits. The excess of credits over debits is what the seller will receive. The items typically debited and credited to the seller are illustrated in the following exhibit.

Exhibit 9.5 Seller's Debits and Credits

Seller's Debits

expenses (per agreement or custom)

seller's share of prorated items the buyer will pay

loan balance or other lien to be paid off

Seller's Credits

purchase price

buyer's share of prorated items prepaid by seller

TRANSFER TAXES

Mortgage transfer tax (TCA 67-4-409). Prior to **recording** any instrument as evidence of a debt, such as mortgages, deeds of trust, conditional sales contracts, financing statements contemplated by the Uniform Commercial Code, and liens on personalty other than on motor vehicles, a mortgage transfer tax must be paid at the rate of eleven and one half cents ($.115) on each one hundred dollars ($100) of the indebtedness or fraction thereof, with the first two thousand dollars ($2,000) being exempt from the tax.

- **Example 1:** Mortgage amount $175,000 - $2,000 exemption = $173,000 ÷ 100 = 1,730 x $.115 = $198.95 mortgage transfer tax

- **Example 2:** Mortgage amount $205,050 - $2,000 exemption = $203,050 ÷ 100 = 2030.5; round to 2031 because of the "fraction thereof." Multiply 2031 x $.115 = $233.57 mortgage transfer tax

The tax is not required when recording judgment liens, contractors' and subcontractors' liens, furnishers' liens, laborers' liens, mechanics' and materialmen's liens, financing statements filed pursuant to the Uniform Commercial Code that secure an interest only in investment property as defined by law, and mortgages or deeds of trust issued under the Home Equity Conversion Mortgage Act.

Recordation (transfer) tax (TCA 67-4-409. Transfers of real estate pay 37 cents ($.37) per one hundred dollars ($100), and the tax is based on the consideration for the transfer or the value of the property, whichever is greater. "Value of the property," refers to the amount that the property would command at a fair and voluntary sale. No recordation transfer tax is paid on the transfer of a leasehold estate.

- **Example:** Sale price (or value of property) $425,000 ÷ $100 = 4,250 x $.37 = $1,572.50 recordation tax

The recordation tax is typically paid by the grantee, but is negotiable between the parties. It is collected by the register of the county in which the instrument is being recorded.

The grantee, the grantee's agent, or a trustee acting for the grantee is required to state under oath on the face of the instrument to be recorded in the presence of the register, or before an officer authorized to administer oaths, the actual consideration or value, whichever is greater, for the transfer of a freehold estate. A deliberate, false statement is punishable as perjury.

A person who obtains several deeds or other instruments of conveyance for the same transfer the same tract or parcel of real estate pays only one state tax with respect to that transfer.

The register is prohibited from recording the transfer until the recordation tax has been paid, and no transfer tax is due until the title to the property is transferred by deed.

Exemptions to transfer tax include the following transfers:

- transfers creating or dissolving a tenancy by the entirety

- conveyance from one spouse to the other

- conveyance from one spouse or both spouses to the original grantor or grantors in the instrument and the original grantor's spouse

- conveyance from one spouse or both spouses to a trustee and immediate reconveyance by the trustee in the same instrument as tenants in common, tenants in common with right of survivorship, joint tenants or joint tenants with right of survivorship

- deeds of division in kind of realty formerly held by tenants in common

- release of a life estate to the beneficiaries of the remainder interest

- deeds executed by an executor to implement a testamentary devise

- domestic settlement decrees or domestic decrees and/or deeds that are an adjustment of property rights between divorcing parties

- transfers by a transferor to a revocable living trust created by the same transferor or by a spouse of the transferor, or transfers by the trustee of a revocable living trust back to the same transferor or to the transferor's spouse

- deeds executed by the trustee of a revocable living trust to implement a testamentary devise by the trustor

For quitclaim deeds, the tax is based only on the actual consideration given for that conveyance.

CONVEYANCE OF PROPERTY

Tennessee forms of conveyance (TCA 66-5-103). The following or other equivalent forms of conveyance are used in Tennessee:

- deed in fee with general warranty

- covenants of seisin, possession, and special warranty

- quitclaim deed mortgage

- deed of trust

Although most lenders require a lender's title insurance policy, Tennessee law does not require title insurance or a title search. Surveys are not required, but lenders or purchasers may require one.

Effective date of conveyance (TCA 66-5-109). The effective day of any real property conveyance in Tennessee is presumed to be the date of the instrument of conveyance, and is not affected by notary acknowledgment in the conveyance dated prior to or subsequent to the date of conveyance.

If an instrument conveying real property is not dated, but contains a notary acknowledgment which is dated, the effective date is the date of the notary acknowledgment.

If the instrument is not dated, but contains more than one notary acknowledgment, containing more than one date, the latest date of a notary acknowledgment in the instrument will be the effective date.

Identification of specific mineral interests to be conveyed (TCA 66-5-111). In the absence of any law to the contrary, an owner of surface and mineral rights who enters into a contract to convey mineral rights resulting in a severance of those interests, the parties must identify the specific mineral interests to be conveyed. The purchaser of the mineral interests must identify the interests purchased by providing a deed reference number in accordance for the mineral interest with the property assessor in the county in which the interests are located. "Specific mineral interests" refers only to those minerals listed in the deed as contemplated by the parties. All rights to minerals not described in the deed remain with the surface owner

MODULE 9 SNAPSHOT REVIEW:

FINANCE & CLOSING

I. REAL ESTATE FINANCE

ESSENTIAL MECHANICS OF THE MORTGAGE LOAN
- Borrower gives note promising to repay borrowed money; executes mortgage on real estate for which money is being borrowed as security
- Lien-theory states- mortgage is lien held by mortgagee (lender) against property owned by mortgagor (borrower)
- Title-theory states- mortgage document is conveyance of ownership from mortgagor to mortgagee
- Valid mortgage requires note, mortgage/trust deed

Financial components
- Principal; interest/interest rate; points; term; payments

Income qualification
- Income/housing expense ratio
- Debt/housing plus debt ratio-
- Income stability

Cash qualification and loan to value
- LTV- loan amount to property value; percentage
- Lender verifies borrower has cash for required down payment

Loan commitment
- Written promise lender will offer loan
- Conditional commitment- offers to make loan if provisions met

Loan closing
- Lender deposits funded amount with escrow agent
- Borrower deposits necessary funds with escrow agents, executes final documents
- Title transferred and recorded

FAIR FINANCING LAWS
ECOA
- Prohibits discrimination in extending credit based on race, color, religion, national origin, sex, marital status, age, or dependency upon public assistance

Fair Credit Reporting Act
- Ensures credit reporting agencies provide accurate information to consumer

TILA/RESPA
- TILA/RESPA Integrated Disclosure Rule (TRID) integrates disclosure requirements of RESPA and Truth-in-Lending
- Clarifies settlement costs; eliminates kickbacks and fees increasing settlement costs
- RESPA prohibits kickback paid for service when party has not rendered service

SAFE Act
- Creates national standard for residential mortgage loan originators to be licensed/registered

PRIMARY & SECONDARY MORTGAGE MARKET

Primary market

- lenders who originate mortgage loans directly to borrowers
- Savings/loans; commercial banks; mutual savings banks; life insurance companies; mortgage bankers; credit unions
- Mortgage brokers
- Can sell loans to secondary market

Secondary market

- Lenders, investors, government agencies buy loans originated by someone else; originate loans indirectly through someone else
- FNMA; FHLMC; GNMA; investment firms that sell securities; life insurance companies; pension funds; primary market institutions investing as secondary lenders
- Qualifications limit loans primary lenders originate

Roles of FNMA, GNMA, FHLMC

- FNMA, GNMA, FHLMC set standards for primary market
- FNMA buys conventional, FHA, VA loans, etc.
- GNMA is division of HUD; guarantees payment on FNMA high-risk low-yield mortgages; guarantees privately generated securities backed by VA/FHA loans
- FHLMC guarantees FHLMC mortgages

MORTGAGE-RELATED TENNESSEE LAWS

- Tennessee is a title theory state; permits judicial and non-judicial foreclosure with power of sale clause; permits deficiency judgments
- borrowers have statutory right of redemption for two years after foreclosure, unless the right was waived in original deed

II. CLOSINGS

THE CLOSING PROCESS

- sale contract sets date, location, and who participates
- verify contract fulfillment; exchange consideration and title; pay expenses; sign final documents; arrange for recording the transaction

TRANSFER OF TITLE

- seller gives evidence of marketability-- title abstract or title insurance commitment; may also need affidavit stating no new encumbrances incurred; seller must remove encumbrances or liens prior to the specified date; if seller is paying off mortgage lien, lender provides a payoff statement

ESCROW PROCEDURES

- if closing "in escrow," escrow agent holds and disburses funds and releases documents when escrow conditions have been met

BROKER'S ROLE

- broker's role ranges from nil to conducting the proceedings to reporting the transaction

RESPA
- for residential property, first or second mortgage, federally-related mortgage, assumption modifying loan terms, lender charging over $50 for assumption

Information booklet
- lender must provide borrower with CFPB booklet, "Your Home Loan Toolkit"

Loan Estimate
- lender must provide CFPB's H-24 Loan Estimate of settlement costs

Mortgage servicing disclosure
- lender must disclose who will be servicing loan

Closing Disclosure
- lender must use CFPB's H-25 Closing disclosure

Disclosures after settlement
- loan servicers must provide annual escrow statements to borrowers

Limits on escrow accounts
- places ceiling on amounts lenders may compel borrowers to place in escrow

Referral fees and kickbacks
- RESPA prohibits payment of referral fees and kickbacks; business relationships between firms involved in the transaction must be disclosed

TILA/RESPA INTEGRATED DISCLOSURES RULE
- mandatory: Your Home Loan Toolkit booklet at loan application; Loan Estimate form 3 business days after loan application; Closing disclosure 3 business days before consummation

Good faith
- Loan Estimate costs based on best information available
- Closing Disclosure costs equal estimate costs within certain tolerances

Types of charges
- no limitation on increase over estimate
- 10% tolerance charges
- 0 tolerance charges

Applicable transactions
- most closed-end consumer mortgages, including: construction loans, loans secured by vacant land, loans to trusts
- not covered: home equity loans, reverse mortgages, loans on mobile homes, loans by small lenders (no more than 5 loans per year)

The H-25 form
- 5 pages, variable by loan type

FINANCIAL SETTLEMENT OF THE TRANSACTION
Settlement process
- identify closing costs; determine who pays what; do prorations; assign debits and credits; complete closing statement; disburse funds

Selling terms and closing costs
- price, deposits, downpayment, financing, final expenses to be paid at closing; apportionment of expenses determined by sale contract or custom

Debits and credits
- excess of buyer's debits over credits is amount buyer must produce at closing; excess of seller's credits over debits is amount seller must receive

Non-prorated items
- incurred by one party only; not shared

Prorated items
- incurred by buyer or seller in advance or arrears; shared by buyer and seller; typical: real estate taxes, insurance premiums, mortgage interest, rents

TRANSFER TAXES
- mortgage transfer tax $.115 per $100 (or portion thereof) of mortgage amount; recordation transfer tax $.37 per $100 of consideration or value (certain properties exempt)

CONVEYANCE OF PROPERTY
- forms of conveyance: deed in fee with general warranty; quitclaim deed; deed of trust;
- effective date of conveyance is date of instrument of conveyance if dated
- specific mineral rights being conveyed must be identified in deed

MODULE 9 – FINANCE & CLOSING

QUIZ

Carefully read each question and provide your best answer based on what you learned in this module. Then check your answers against the Answer Key which immediately follows the quiz questions.

1. The process of securing a loan by pledging property, without giving up ownership of the property, is called _____.

   a. trading.
   b. bartering.
   c. conveyance.
   d. hypothecation.

2. If the seller's mortgage lien(s) are to be satisfied at closing, the lender will provide a _____.

   a. lien amount.
   b. title commitment.
   c. payoff statement.
   d. loan commitment.

3. What is another name for income ratio?

   a. Housing expense ratio
   b. Monthly gross ratio
   c. Debt to income ratio
   d. Salary fraction

4. Before making a title commitment, a title company performs a _____ to discover any liens, encumbrances, restrictions, conditions, or easements attaching to the title.

   a. property investigation
   b. title search
   c. real estate deep dive
   d. commitment research

5. What is a loan with variable interest rate called?

   a. Fixed-rate loan
   b. Step-rate loan
   c. Customizable loan
   d. Adjustable rate loan

6. A final inspection before closing is called a(n) _____.

   a. buyer's walk-through.
   b. four-point inspection.
   c. appraisal.
   d. home tour.

7. Which of the following is credited to a seller at closing?

   a. Expenses
   b. Purchase price
   c. Loan balance
   d. Liens to be paid off

8. Gina applies for a mortgage loan and she gets a quote for a $250,000 loan, paid off in 10 years, with an interest rate of 3%. The quote is valid and in effect for 60 days after which the offer expires. What type of loan commitment is this?

   a. A "lock-in" commitment
   b. A conditional commitment
   c. A take-out commitment
   d. A firm commitment

9. Which statute was established to create a national standard for residential mortgage loan originators to be licensed and registered?

   a. RESPA
   b. Secure and Fair Enforcement for Mortgage Licensing Act
   c. SALE
   d. Professional Standards for Mortgagors Act

10. What is another name for housing expense ratio?

    a. Income ratio
    b. Gross income
    c. Cash flow ratio
    d. Payment obligation

11. Which fee is based on the price paid for the property?

    a. Doc stamps
    b. Closing tax
    c. Title fee
    d. Recordation tax

12. Which statute prohibits discrimination in extending credit based on race, color, and religion?

    a. TILA
    b. Fair Credit Reporting Act
    c. ECOA
    d. Consumer Financial Protection Act

13. A lender may require a _____ verifying that a newly built property complies with local building codes.

    a. closing statement
    b. final inspection
    c. building code authorization
    d. certificate of occupancy

14. The relationship between the loan amount to the property's value is called the _____ ratio.

   a. DTI
   b. CVT
   c. LTV
   d. LPI

15. Which statute granted the CFPB authority to enforce compliance with RESPA and its implementing regulations?

   a. Dodd-Frank Act of 2010
   b. TILA
   c. Fannie-Mae Act
   d. ECOA

16. In a _____ state, the mortgage is a lien held by the mortgagee against the property owned by the mortgagor.

   a. lender-friendly
   b. lien-theory
   c. consumer-friendly
   d. title-theory

17. Which rule integrates the disclosure requirements of RESPA and TILA?

   a. Good Faith Estimate
   b. Uniform Settlement Statement
   c. TRID
   d. Truth in Disclosures Act

18. The effective day of a real property conveyance in Tennessee is based on which of the following days/dates?

   a. Date of the instrument of conveyance
   b. The day the notary acknowledges the conveyance
   c. The date the title commitment is provided
   d. Date of final loan commitment

19. The financial components of a mortgage loan include principal, points, term, payments and _____.

   a. usury.
   b. interest rate.
   c. credit score.
   d. escrow.

20. Which of the following is the first step in the closing process?

    a. Paying expenses
    b. Recording the transaction
    c. Confirming performance of the sales contract.
    d. Closing the loan

21. Andrew's lender offers to make a loan if certain provisions are met. What type of loan commitment is this?

    a. Firm commitment
    b. Lock-in commitment
    c. Take-out commitment
    d. Conditional commitment

22. What is the name for the final expenses that a buyer or seller must pay at closing to complete the transaction?

    a. Closing costs
    b. Real estate taxes
    c. Purchase fees
    d. Contingency fees

23. If a closing occurs _____ rather than face-to-face, the principal parties deposit funds and documents with the appointed escrow agent.

    a. online
    b. in escrow
    c. overseas
    d. with a mobile notary

24. Which statute eliminates kickbacks and protects consumers?

    a. RESPA
    b. Fair housing law
    c. Fair Commissions Act
    d. Equal Opportunity Act

25. What is the final step in the settlement process?

    a. Identifying closing costs
    b. Completing the closing statement
    c. Disbursing funds
    d. Determining non-prorated credits

MODULE 9 – FINANCE & CLOSING

ANSWER KEY

1. d. hypothecation.
2. c. payoff statement.
3. a. Housing expense ratio
4. b. title search
5. d. Adjustable rate loan
6. a. buyer's walk-through.
7. b. Purchase price
8. a. A "lock-in" commitment
9. b. Secure and Fair Enforcement for Mortgage Licensing Act
10. a. Income ratio
11. d. Recordation tax
12. c. ECOA
13. d. certificate of occupancy
14. c. LTV
15. a. Dodd-Frank Act of 2010
16. b. lien-theory
17. c. TRID
18. a. Date of the instrument of conveyance
19. b. interest rate.
20. c. Confirming performance of the sales contract
21. d. Conditional commitment
22. a. Closing costs
23. b. in escrow
24. a. RESPA
25. c. Disbursing funds

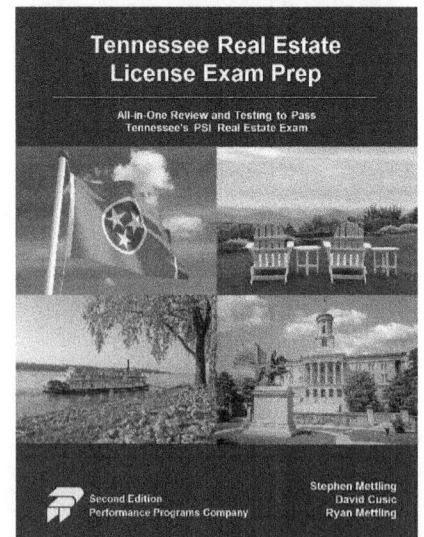

www.ingramcontent.com/pod-product-compliance
Lightning Source LLC
Chambersburg PA
CBHW080523220326
41599CB00032B/6184